DIALOGUES CONCERNING
NATURAL RELIGION

The Library of Liberal Arts
OSKAR PIEST, FOUNDER

DIALOGUES
CONCERNING
NATURAL
RELIGION

DAVID HUME

Edited, with an introduction, by
NORMAN KEMP SMITH

. . . .

The Library of Liberal Arts
published by
Bobbs-Merrill Educational Publishing
Indianapolis

David Hume: 1711-1776

DIALOGUES CONCERNING NATURAL RELIGION was
originally published in 1779

. . . .

The Bobbs-Merrill Company, Inc.
4300 West 62nd Street
Indianapolis, Indiana 46268

First Edition
Twelfth Printing — 1977

ISBN 0–672–60404–3 (pbk)
ISBN 0–672–51074–X

PREFACE

THE manuscript of Hume's *Dialogues* in the library of the Royal Society of Edinburgh is of great interest. It gives what we may believe to be the first version of the *Dialogues*, as completed in the period 1751-5. The revisions which it exhibits in every part and on almost every page also record the stages by which the *Dialogues* were later brought into their final form. As we know, the revisions were made by Hume in or prior to 1761, and again in the year of his death, in 1776.

It was from this manuscript that Hume's nephew obtained the text of the *Dialogues*. In accordance with Hume's instructions, he omitted whatever Hume had marked for omission, and incorporated the revisions and additions. Everything else in the manuscript he very rightly passed over without comment. His text is remarkably correct ; his intentional departures from the manuscript are few in number, and are justified by Hume's own preferences as shown in the works, the publication of which he had himself supervised. In all subsequent editions the nephew's text has been simply reprinted ; later editors have made no use of the manuscript, either to improve upon the text or to supplement it in any way.

Now, however, that the *Dialogues* are a recognized philosophical classic, and have themselves become a subject of discussion and of varying interpretation, we cannot any longer afford to neglect the light which the manuscript casts on Hume's own understanding of the course and outcome of his argument. This is the more necessary in that his intentions are by no means always evident on the surface, and have, indeed, as I have endeavoured to show, been very generally misunderstood. The revisions and additions recorded in the manuscript consist (1) in improvements of wording and phrasing, (2) in passages scored out but marked ' still to be printed ' (these being among the instructions which Hume's nephew has faithfully followed), (3) in passages scored out, and not hitherto printed, and (4) in additions, made on the margins, or when more lengthy on separate sheets, with marks to indicate where the additions belong in the manuscript as first composed. In re-editing the text I have transcribed the omitted passages, and taken note of all alterations in wording which have a bearing on the argument or are otherwise of special interest. My chief task, however, has been to distinguish between Hume's first version of the *Dialogues*, the additions made in or prior to 1761, and the additions made in 1776. As the circumstantial evidence seems sufficiently conclusive, I have felt justified in indicating in the text all major additions, and in distinguishing between those made in the earlier and those made in the later revisions. The additions referable to 1776 (notably in Part XII, which concludes the discussion) are, as we find, among the most definitely negative utterances in the *Dialogues*. This has a very important bearing on the issues that arise when we seek to determine how far, and in what precise respects, the spokesmen in the *Dialogues* express Hume's own personal views.

Such evidence as can be gathered from Hume's other writings, including his *Letters*, and not least from the treatise which he composed almost simultaneously with the *Dialogues*, his *Natural History of Religion*, corroborates the conclusion to which the clues in the manuscript would appear to point, namely, that the teaching of the *Dialogues* is much more sheerly negative than has generally been held. This may still allow of the *Dialogues* being spoken of as a contribution to the *via negativa*—the part of theology in which sceptics and believers may most easily come to some degree of mutual respect and understanding, to their common benefit. That, however, taken by itself, would be an extremely misleading description of Hume's intentions. He is nothing if not provocative, and certainly did not picture himself as preparing an eirenicon, and as recasting, or even merely delimiting, the essentials of religious belief. He is consciously, and deliberately, attacking "the religious hypothesis," and through it religion as such. None the less it remains true that in the century and a half since the publication of the *Dialogues*, their effects in determining the methods of argument favoured in theology have been at least equal to their effects in reinforcing sceptical and naturalistic ways of thinking. Their influence, that is to say, has been of the same wide-ranging character as, by universal consent, has been exercised by Hume's no less negatively inspired *Treatise of Human Nature* and by his *Enquiries*. Hume's philosophical gifts may be depreciated as being exclusively analytic and critical ; what cannot be challenged is that they are supreme in their own kind.

I am aware that some of my statements, in the Introduction, bearing on Hume's doctrine of ' detached ' impressions are insufficiently definite and are open to question. These and other connected matters I have had to reserve for fuller discussion elsewhere.

My grateful thanks are due to the Council of the Royal Society of Edinburgh for placing the manuscript unreservedly at my disposal. I am also indebted to Colonel Isham and to Mr. Harold K. Guinzburg for their generous permission to reprint Boswell's account of his last interview with Hume, as given in *The Private Papers of James Boswell* (vol. xii, 1931).

Professor R. D. Maclennan and Mr. William Menzies have very kindly read portions of my manuscript, and have made many helpful comments. Dr. R. A. Lillie and Mr. W. A. Sinclair have also assisted me in reading the proofs.

N. K. S.

EDINBURGH
June 1935

PREFACE TO SECOND EDITION

THE Supplement added in this Second Edition contains Hume's brief autobiographical *My Own Life*, together with Adam Smith's *Letter to William Strahan*. They have usually been printed together, and they can here be read along with Boswell's account of his interview with Hume.

As stated in my Preface to the first edition, I have left undiscussed certain questions bearing on Hume's general philosophy. These questions I have since dealt with in a volume published in 1941 : *The Philosophy of David Hume, A Critical Study of its Origins and Central Doctrines.* The chief relevant passages will be found on pp. 1–12 ; 43–7 ; 63–70, 73–6, 124–32, 154–5 ; 513–6 ; 543–6 ; 549–66.

N. K. S.

EDINBURGH
March 1946

CONTENTS

ix

EDITIONS, REPRINTS, AND TRANSLATIONS OF THE *DIALOGUES*

First edition, edited by Hume's nephew, [London], 1779, 8vo. Pp. 152

Reprinted in a larger type as ' second edition,' London, 1779, 8vo. Pp. 264

Reprinted as ' third edition,' London 1804. Pp. 264. The publisher of the first edition is known to have been Robinson. The third edition (save for the title-page, a reissue of the second edition) announces itself on the title-page as ' printed by and for Thomas Hughes.' As to the reasons for this change of printer and publisher in the very year of the appearance of the first edition, we have no information

Reprinted in *The Philosophical Works of David Hume*, edited by Hume's nephew, 4 vols., Edinburgh, 1826 ; and in *The Philosophical Works of David Hume*, edited by Green and Grose, 4 vols., London, 1874–5

Reprinted with a 6-page preface and notes, edited and published by Thomas Scott, London, 1875

Reprinted, with an Introduction, by Bruce M'Ewen, Edinburgh, 1907

Reprinted in *Hume Selections*, edited by C. W. Hendel, Chicago, 1927.

A French translation appeared in 1779. This translation has on its title-page ' à Edinbourg, 1779 ' ; and the anonymous translator states in his preface that he had received from a friend ' l'édition anglaise ' several months prior to its publication in Great Britain. The translation was probably printed in France or Holland, almost certainly not in Edinburgh. There is a copy in the Bibliothèque Nationale in Paris. There appears to be no copy extant in Britain. A new French translation was made by Charles Renouvier (Paris, 1887)

A German translation was made by J. G. Hamann in 1780. This translation was read by Kant in manuscript ; but was withheld from publication on the appearance of a translation by K. G. Schreiter (Leipzig, 1781). A new German translation was made by Friedrich Paulsen (Leipzig, 1877 ; 3rd edition, 1905)

TEXT OF THIS EDITION

THE manuscript of the *Dialogues* exhibits on almost every page a number of alterations and additions (*cf.* below, pp. 92 *sqq.*). Most of them are of a quite minor character. Those which bear on the argument or which are otherwise of sufficient interest are noted at the foot of the page. Major additions to the text are indicated by enclosure in square brackets, and when datable as belonging to the 1776 revision by enclosure in double brackets. Hume's punctuation and spelling are followed throughout, save in a few cases where they are not in conformity with his practice in the works which he has himself supervised for publication. This also justifies us—as it justified his nephew—in not following the manuscript in its use of a capital initial letter for all substantives. In deciding which substantives should retain their capitals, Hume's own very sparing use of capitals in the *Enquiries* has (with allowance for his variations in usage) been taken as the standard.

ABBREVIATIONS

Treatise, G. & G. = *A Treatise of Human Nature,* ed. by T. H. Green and T. H. Grose, 2 vols., London, 1874

Treatise, S.-B. = *Op. cit.,* ed. by L. A. Selby-Bigge, Oxford, 1896

Enquiry, S.-B. = *An Enquiry concerning Human Understanding, and an Enquiry concerning the Principles of Morals,* ed. by L. A. Selby-Bigge, Oxford, 1894

Essays, G. & G. = *Essays, Moral, Political and Literary,* 2 vols., ed. by T. H. Green and T. H. Grose, London, 1875

Letters = *Letters of David Hume,* ed. by J. Y. T. Greig, 2 vols., Oxford, 1932

INTRODUCTION

In short, there's so much probability, any Worship which subsists on a Falsehood, will one time or other degenerate, that we shou'd never give Quarter to Error, of what kind, or on what Pretences soever. I own the Scandal's less in encountring Errors before a long Possession has given them root in the Minds of Men, than when Antiquity has confer'd on them a kind of sacred Character. But as there's no prescribing against Truth, 'twere the highest Injustice to leave it continually bury'd in Obscurity, on pretence it never yet had seen the Light. BAYLE : *Pensées diverses* (eighteenth-century translation)

I HUME'S RELATIONS TO HIS CALVINIST ENVIRONMENT

HUME'S writings on religion are composed—this is at once their strength and their weakness—from the standpoint of the detached observer. The religious influences of his home environment he had very quickly shed ; and thereafter religion was brought to his attention not by anything in his own personal needs or convictions, but by the prominence—so surprising, as it seemed to him—with which it bulked in the lives of others, and by the strange vagaries of belief, observance, and conduct to which it gave rise. Both as a philosopher and as a historian he was constrained, ever and again, almost in spite of himself, to speculate anew upon it. It was so many-sided and so ambiguous in its manifestations, so puzzling in its lack of conformity to the other, more ordinary, aspects of human existence ! Hume had also to reckon with his own inborn temperament. It cut him off from what, in Calvinist teaching, was the sole gateway through which religion could be approached—the experience of that religious type of inner division and self-conflict which was entitled the consciousness of sin.

He was one of those who . . . are ' naturally good ' . . . Nature made him temperate, contented, kind, charitable, brave, and humorous—one who, as Montaigne advises, " never made a marvel of his own fortunes." His virtue, so far as can be learned, owed nothing to religion. He was ' born to be so,' as another man is born to be a poet. He had a native genius for excellence.

Though this was written not of Hume but of his friend and older contemporary, George Keith, the last Earl Marischal,[1]

[1] By Andrew Lang in *The Companions of Pickle* (1898), p. 4

it is no less true of Hume himself. The passage may be compared with Adam Smith's considered appreciation of Hume, in the letter which he made public a few months after Hume's death :

His temper . . . seemed to be more happily balanced, if I may be allowed such an expression, than that perhaps of any other man I have ever known. . . . The extreme gentleness of his nature never weakened either the firmness of his mind or the steadiness of his resolutions. His constant pleasantry was the genuine effusion of good-nature and good-humour, tempered with delicacy and modesty, and without even the slightest tincture of malignity, so frequently the disagreeable source of what is called wit in other men. . . . And that gaiety of temper, so agreeable in society, but which is so often accompanied with frivolous and superficial qualities, was in him certainly attended with the most severe application, the most extensive learning, the greatest depth of thought, and a capacity in every respect the most comprehensive. Upon the whole, I have always considered him, both in his lifetime and since his death, as approaching as nearly to the idea of a perfectly wise and virtuous man, as perhaps the nature of human frailty will permit.[1]

Adam Smith, quite evidently, is intentionally provocative. He is here—careful qualification of his terms would have been inappropriate—generously vindicating his friend's reputation, in face of the wellnigh universal prejudices of the uninformed, and misinformed, general public. The ' fanatical ' party was already making itself vocal in the pamphlets in which orthodoxy sought to wreak vengeance upon Hume's memory ; and it is in the light of this situation that Adam Smith's high-pitched estimate is to be understood. In substance, due allowances being made for the defects of Hume's qualities, characteristic of his time as well as of himself—his limitations of interest and of insight, his inability to have even the beginnings of any genuine understanding of the twice-born type, such as St. Paul or Calvin—the estimate is justified ; it is amply supported by the independent testimony of his clerical friends among the ' Moderates.'

In Hume's early years, the religion which prevailed in Scotland, with hardly even the suggestion of a serious rival, was of a highly specific type, extreme in its own kind, and quite the least suited, either by its doctrines or by its prescribed modes of life, to enlighten him regarding the limitations of his

---

[1] *Cf.* below, pp. 247–8

own contrary outlook. It was a popularized version of Calvin's teaching, retaining its darker features, and representing even these in a distorted and exaggerated form. With the ' Moderates ' Hume, probably, did not become intimate until after 1751,[1] the year of his settling in a house of his own in Edinburgh.

Hume is so happily in keeping with the spacious and forward-looking Edinburgh of the middle decades of the eighteenth century, that it comes upon us with a shock of surprise, in studying the period, to find how very different were the conditions prevailing throughout Scotland, and in Edinburgh, in the years when he was a boy at school and at the University. A harsh and unlovely type of poverty was the common fate ; even among the upper classes it was but little tempered by more gracious ways of life. Methods of agriculture were so primitive that even a single bad harvest brought famine and widespread mendicancy in its train. The effects also of the loss of the nation's savings through the bankruptcy of the Darien scheme were still felt in all sections of the community, and doubtless, in part, accounted for the delay in taking advantage of the wider markets for industry and commerce thrown open by the Union. (The Union of the Parliaments in 1707, it may be noted, came just four years prior to Hume's birth.) In the provincial towns such little trade as there had been was stagnant, and the population was declining. Edinburgh, the only town of any size, was losing its nobility and some of its most distinguished commoners to London. With so little to encourage the country to hopeful initiative, and so much to fill it with despair and gloom, it is not surprising that in the years preceding and following the Union the temper of the people should have reacted upon the life of the Church, and that its Calvinist teaching, always grimly austere, should have become even more bleak and gloomy, and that many old-time superstitions and fanaticisms should have gained a new lease of life. The tide was very soon to turn, but not until it had reached its lowest ebb.

During the seventeenth century Scottish religion had fallen greatly under the influence of English Puritanism ; and when to this we add the memory of the bitter strife of sixty years, and the economic misery of the moment, we can perhaps understand why at the

---

[1] *Cf.* J. Y. T. Greig, *David Hume* (1931), p. 163

Union, and for many years after, religion was seen in its grimmest form. . . . [It] depicted God as an implacable despot, swift to wrath. . . . It held by the doctrines of election and reprobation in all their severity. . . . Both in church and in home the most relentless discipline was maintained. . . . The observance of the Sabbath was enforced with penalties. All other sacred times and seasons were deliberately ignored.[1]

Dr. Greig in his life of Hume [2] has pictured ' David ' as sitting, Sunday after Sunday, through the three-hour-long morning service, which was then usual.[3] The service included a ' lecture ' as well as the sermon, each, it might be, an hour long. The preacher was required in each sermon to cover anew the essential points in the scheme of salvation—the Fall, man's present helpless and sinful condition, redemption through the Mediator, and the future life of the elect and of the reprobate, concluding with practical applications and reflections.[4] These themes were also the chief burden of the ' lecture.' Hume must therefore have been very thoroughly indoctrinated with the Calvinist creed, as it was then understood ; and there is evidence that for a time he struggled to conform his mind and temper to it.

The Chirnside Parish Church, at which the Ninewells household was in attendance, had as its Minister from 1688 to 1696 Henry Erskine, the father of Ralph and Ebenezer, the founders of the Secession Church. Chirnside had been a prominent centre of Covenanting activity ; and a body of Cameronians maintained a meeting-house in the village until well on in the nineteenth century. During Hume's childhood and youth the Minister of the Parish was George Home (ordained 1704, died 1755), whose father had suffered martyrdom for the Faith in the days of the Persecution. He was Hume's uncle by marriage. In view of the traditions of his family—we have no other data—George Home, we may presume, held to the letter of the Faith. But if there was anything wanting in the uncle's teaching, Hume would have ample opportunities of supplementing it, forced upon him if not self-sought, in the neighbourhood and in Edinburgh. At the

[1] The Rev. A. J. Campbell, *Two Centuries of the Church of Scotland 1707–1929* (1930), p. 28

[2] Pp. 43 *sqq.*

[3] Following upon morning household prayers, and itself followed by an afternoon service and by evening household prayers

[4] *Cf.* Alexander Carlyle, *Autobiography* (1910 edition), p. 106

annual Communions in which the parishes of the district joined forces, he may even have listened to Thomas Boston, the author of *The Fourfold State*. Boston was one of the most popular preachers in the Borders, and was much in demand at these services. His discovery, in a parishioner's house, of a copy of *The Marrow of Modern Divinity*, an English Calvinist treatise brought into the country by one of Cromwell's soldiers, and his own edition of it in 1726, determined much that happened in Church life in Scotland in the next half-century.

How far Hume's endeavours to adapt himself to this teaching may have carried him, we can only conjecture. The evidence is somewhat scanty. There are his statements to Boswell : " He said he never had entertained any belief in religion since he began to read Locke and Clarke. I asked him if he was not religious when he was young. He said he was, and used to read *The Whole Duty of Man* ; that he made an abstract from the catalogue of vices at the end of it, and examined himself by this ; leaving out murder and theft, and such vices as he had no chance of committing, having no inclination to commit them. This, he said, was strange work ; for instance, to try if, notwithstanding his excelling his schoolfellows, he had no pride or vanity." [1]

The Whole Duty of Man, an anonymous work which first appeared in 1658,[2] gives a somewhat tame version of Calvinist teaching, almost entirely omitting its sublimer features, and toning down the more difficult doctrines, yet without departing from them. The catalogue of vices to which Hume refers is entitled : " *Brief Heads of Self-Examination, especially before the Sacrament*, collected out of the foregoing Treatise, concerning the breaches of our Duty." The following are a few of the vices enumerated : not believing there is a God ; not believing his Word ; not desiring to draw near to him in his ordinances ; placing religion in hearing of sermons, without practice ; resorting to witches and conjurers, *i.e.* to the Devil ; not arranging any set or solemn times for humiliation and confession, or too seldom ; being puffed up with high conceits of ourselves, in respect of natural parts, as beauty, wit, &c., of worldly riches and honours, of Grace ; making pleasure,

---

[1] *Cf.* below, Appendix A, p. 76

[2] In this first edition it was entitled : *The Practice of Christian Grace, or the Whole Duty of Man*. It was probably composed by the Royalist divine, Richard Allestree (1619–81).

not health, the end of eating ; wasting the time or estate in good fellowship ; abusing our strength of brain to the making others drunk ; using unlawful recreations ; being too vehement upon lawful ones ; abstaining from such excesses not out of conscience but covetousness ; pinching our bodies to fill our purses.

The evidence of such early letters as have survived shows that in his teens Hume was shy and in love with solitude,[1] anxiously concerned in the confirming of his moral character, and absorbed in his studies—very different from the extro-verted, genial, somewhat pagan Hume of later years. His temper was then, indeed, so different, that he may, quite con-ceivably, have tasted of the experiences of conversion. Is it likely that a serious-minded, introspective youth, who sought to be religious and counted himself such, would altogether escape the more exciting and, as was then held, the indispens-able initial experiences of the avowed believer ? This, at least, would help us to understand the aversion with which, like so many of his contemporaries, he came to regard ' enthusiasm.' He speaks of it as almost inevitably generating an insincerity which is the more harmful in that its devotees are themselves unaware of its factitious character. " The religious hypocrisy, it may be remarked, is of a peculiar nature ; and being generally unknown to the person himself, though more dangerous, it implies less falsehood than any other species of insincerity." [2]

But, however this may be, there is no question that at an early age Hume shed the whole body of Calvinist teaching. It continued, however, to typify for him what he meant by religion ; and owing to the very strength of the aversion which he had come to feel towards it, it was an important factor in determining the *contrary* character of the beliefs to which, as his philosophy matured, he definitively committed himself.

A country may influence a generation of its children by reaction hardly less than by imitation ; in this dark period

---

[1] *Cf.* the character sketch in the Hume MSS., R.S.E. (Burton, *Life of David Hume*, vol. i, p. 226) : " Very bashful, somewhat modest, no way Humble . . . Sociable, though he lives in Solitude . . . An Enthusiast, without Religion, a Philosopher, who despairs to attain Truth." Among Hume's notes on his reading (R.S.E. MSS.) is the following from the Abbé de Bosse : " In a young Man, who applys himself to the Arts and Sciences, the Slowness with which he forms himself for the World is a good Sign."

[2] *History of England*, chap. lxii.

Calvinist Scotland gave birth to so many independent and critical spirits, that Hume had no difficulty in finding congenial friends and in making for himself an environment in which he could be quite happily at home. However intolerant the mass of the people might continue to be, there was fortunately, in the upper ranks, in the Government and even in the Church, so little of the ' Corporate State ' that he was free to have his say, even on the fundamentals of the Christian Faith. Writing (1747) to James Oswald of Dunnikier that he proposes to print his *Enquiry*, which included the essays *Of Miracles* and *Of a particular Providence and of a future State*, Hume says :

Our friend Harry [Home of Kames] is against this, as indiscreet. But in the first place, I think I am too deep engaged to think of a retreat. In the second place, I see not what bad consequences follow, in the present age, from the character of an infidel ; especially if a man's conduct be in other respects irreproachable. What is your opinion ? [1]

There is yet another piece of evidence bearing on Hume's early development : a passage written to Sir Gilbert Elliot in 1751.

Any Propensity you imagine I have to the other Side [*i.e.* in favour of the sceptical views of Philo in the *Dialogues concerning Natural Religion*] crept in upon me against my will : And tis not long ago that I burn'd an old Manuscript Book, wrote before I was twenty, which contained, Page after Page, the gradual Progress of my Thoughts on that head. It begun with an anxious Search after Arguments, to confirm the common Opinion : Doubts stole in, dissipated, return'd, were again dissipated, return'd again ; and it was a perpetual Struggle of a restless Imagination against Inclination, perhaps against Reason.[2]

The change in Hume's attitude must have come very early, probably, in its beginnings, in his sixteenth year. He had then completed his University courses, and was engaged in his own independent studies.

---

[1] *Letters*, vol. i, p. 106. *Cf.* Burton, *Life of David Hume*, vol. ii, p. 443. "[Hume] seemed to take a pride in contrasting his own personal reception by the world with that of his writings ; the one all courtesy, the other all prejudice and dislike. A late eminent judge remembered meeting him at dinner with Black, Smith, and others, a few months before his death. Smith was speaking on the ingratitude, perversity, and intolerance of human nature. Hume said he differed with him. There was he, who had written on history, on politics, and on morals—some said on divinity ; yet in discussing these exciting topics, he had not made a single enemy ; unless, indeed, all the Whigs, all the Tories, and all the Christians ! "

[2] *Letters*, vol. i, p. 154

As our College Education in Scotland, extending little further than the Languages, ends commonly when we are about 14 or 15 Years of age, I was after that left to my own Choice in my Reading, and found it encline me almost equally to Books of Reasoning & Philosophy, & to Poetry and the polite Authors. . . . I found a certain Boldness of Temper, growing in me, which was not enclin'd to submit to any Authority in these Subjects, but led me to seek out some new Medium, by which Truth might be establisht. After much Study, & Reflection . . . at last, when I was about 18 Years of Age, there seem'd to be open'd up to me a new Scene of Thought, which transported me beyond Measure, & made me, with an Ardor natural to young men, throw up every other Pleasure or Business to apply entirely to it.[1]

The outcome was *A Treatise of Human Nature*, completed when he was in his twenty-seventh year.

[1] In a letter (March or April 1734) to his physician, believed to be Dr. George Cheyne. *Letters*, vol. i, p. 13.

II HUME'S VIEWS REGARDING RELIGION IN GENERAL

THAT Hume was not without appreciation of the motives inspiring Calvinism in its higher forms is shown by his essay entitled *The Platonist*. It is a portrait in which it is easier to trace Calvinist than Platonic features.

The divinity is a boundless ocean of bliss and glory : Human minds are smaller streams, which, arising at first from this ocean, seek still, amid all their wanderings, to return to it, and to lose themselves in that immensity of perfection. When checked . . . they spread horror and devastation on the neighbouring plains.[1]

With the doctrine of original sin Hume has, needless to say, no sympathy ; but his views regarding it are expressed with moderation and with some degree of insight. " I am sensible that a delicate sense of morals, especially when attended with a splenetic temper, is apt to give a man a disgust of the world."[2] When comparison is made, as in St. Augustine and Calvin, between man and a Being of the uttermost perfection, all human distinctions are dwarfed and man's capacities cannot but appear ' very contemptible.' [3]

No teaching—it is probably correct to say—is so ill suited for popularization, and loses so much in the process, as the teaching of Calvin. This is especially evident in the type of preaching which prevailed so widely in Scotland in Hume's early years. It treated as central what Calvin had sought to keep in the background, as being a ' stone of stumbling ' and a ' mystery '—the Election of a few to glory, and of all others to reprobation. Hume is frank in the expression of his detestation of such doctrine :

Popular religions are really, in the conception of their more vulgar votaries, a species of daemonism ; and the higher the deity is exalted in power and knowledge, the lower of course is he depressed in goodness and benevolence ; whatever epithets of praise may be bestowed on him by his amazed adorers. Among idolaters, the words may be false, and belie the secret opinion : But among more exalted

---

[1] *Essays*, G. & G., vol. i, p. 211
[2] *Cf. Of the Dignity or Meanness of Human Nature. Essays*, G. & G., vol. i, p. 151
[3] *Ibid.*, p. 153

9

religionists, the opinion itself contracts a kind of falsehood, and belies the inward sentiment. The heart secretly detests such measures of cruel and implacable vengeance ; but the judgment dares not pronounce them perfect and adorable. And the additional misery of this inward struggle aggravates all the other terrors, by which these unhappy victims to superstition are for ever haunted.[1]

In a note to this passage Hume is even more explicit ; but in being more outspoken—attacking Calvinism directly, and not merely its popular forms—he feels constrained to resort to an indirect method of statement. He quotes a passage from the Chevalier Ramsay (at the time of writing, a convert to the Roman Catholic Church) which concludes as follows :

The grosser pagans contented themselves with divinising lust, incest, and adultery ; but the predestinarian doctors have divinised cruelty, wrath, fury, vengeance, and all the blackest vices.

Hume's references to the extremer consequences of Calvinist teaching are, however, merely incidental. His reasoned discussions are reserved for its central doctrines—its conception of all finite existence as *supernaturally* conditioned, its belief in a miraculously conferred enabling Grace, its belief in a miraculously directed special Providence, its belief in a supernaturally ordered after-life, and, as presupposed in all of these, its belief in an all-determining Divine Being. Even these doctrines, however, interest Hume chiefly as they cast light upon the nature of religion in general, as it has manifested itself in the beginnings of civilization, in Classical times, and in the Christian centuries. For Hume recognizes no uniqueness in Christianity such as would render it unseemly to place it, in discussion, on a level with the pagan religions of Greece and Rome. In one respect only does he recognize Christianity as standing by itself, namely, that for him and his contemporaries in Britain the Reformed Church teaching stood officially for religion, and that the good citizen was therefore in duty bound to pay it outward deference—the deference which Cicero, a member of the College of Augurs, paid to the state religion, while yet none the less reserving his right to criticize it freely in his own thoughts, and subject to certain recognized conventions also in his writings.

[1] *The Natural History of Religion. Essays*, G. & G., vol. ii, pp. 354-5. *Cf. Dialogues*, below, pp. 224-6

There is, indeed, little of the sceptical *inquirer* in Hume's writings on religion. Once he had succeeded in formulating the general lines of his own philosophy, he had quite definitely concluded that religion is not merely an ambiguous but in the main a *malign* influence. For Hume's own continuing personal difficulties were not in regard to this or that religious tenet, but in regard to religion itself : why, human life being what he took it to be, religion should exist at all ; why religion, being preposterous in any form, should yet be so universally influential in so many different forms ; and why in his own time it should be so widely prevalent in the grim and gloomy form of the Calvinist creed. The belief in omens, dreams, and oracles among the Greeks and Romans, the miracles of the Old and the New Testament among the Jews, in Roman Catholic teaching the doctrine of the Real Presence, in Calvinist teaching the doctrine of a predestined double Election—these, in Hume's view, stand all, more or less, on the same footing ; and, with the many other instances which he cites, illustrate the irrational, ineradicably superstitious character of religion as commonly understood—a character which, as he believed, it is likely, by all the signs, to continue to exhibit to the end of time.

To these doctrines we are so accustomed, that we never wonder at them : Though in a future age, it will probably become difficult to persuade some nations, that any human, two-legged creature could ever embrace such principles. And it is a thousand to one, but these nations themselves shall have something full as absurd in their own creed, to which they will give a most implicit and most religious assent.[1]

What a noble privilege is it of human reason to attain the knowledge of the supreme Being ; and, from the visible works of nature, be enabled to infer so sublime a principle as its supreme Creator. But turn the reverse of the medal. Survey most nations and most ages. Examine the religious principles, which have, in fact, prevailed in the world. You will scarcely be persuaded they are anything but sick men's dreams : Or perhaps will regard them more as the playsome whimsies of monkeys in human shape, than the serious, positive, dogmatical asseverations of a being, who dignifies himself with the name of rational.[2]

There are present-day thinkers who while writing in defence of religion yet describe it as ' titanism,' as " the place where not the health but the place where the disease of man becomes

---

[1] *Essays*, G. & G., vol. ii, p. 344   [2] *Ibid.*, p. 362

known, not where the harmony but where the disharmony of all things comes to expression," as often " the abyss and the horror," " the place where demons are seen." [1] Hume could have approved these statements, but in doing so would have interpreted them in a quite straightforward, non-dialectical fashion. Religion, especially in its theistic forms, suffers, he believed, from the same fundamental defect as Stoic ethics : it calls upon man to live an *artificial* life. The constitution of our human nature determines for us the objects of our happiness; and we should not entertain a lower opinion of nature's wisdom than of our own.

When by my will alone I can stop the blood, as it runs with impetuosity along its canals, then may I hope to change the course of my sentiments and passions. In vain should I strain my faculties, and endeavour to receive pleasure from an object, which is not fitted by nature to affect my organs with delight. [2]

An abstract, invisible object, like that which *natural* religion alone presents to us, cannot long actuate the mind, or be of any moment in life. [3]

Either, therefore, the senses and imagination are enlisted in support of religion, yielding entry to the superstitions and fanaticisms which characterize it in its *traditional* forms ; or it endeavours to restrain itself within the limits of a *philosophical* account of the Deity. The latter alternative is possible, Hume declares, only to the few. Calvin, and the Protestant Churches generally, had, as Hume recognized, sought a *via media* ; but without success. In opposing idolatry, they still were bent upon strengthening religion ; and in appealing to the more violent emotions, had reintroduced the old-time fanaticisms in new, and in some respects even darker forms.

Superstition and fanaticism (Hume also at times entitles the latter ' enthusiasm,' a term then still used in its etymological sense) [4] are in his view the twin diseases—from time to time

---

[1] *Cf.* McConnachie, quoting Karl Barth, *The Significance of Karl Barth* (1931), p. 148.

[2] *Essays*, G. & G., vol. i, p. 198

[3] *Ibid.*, p. 220. *Cf.* also *Letters*, vol. i, p. 51

[4] Hume's characteristic clarity is somewhat lacking in his modes of distinguishing between superstition and enthusiasm—a defect not surprising in view of the complicated nature of their interrelations in any given type of religion. In his essay *Of Superstition and Enthusiasm* (*Essays*, G. & G., vol. i, pp. 144 *sqq.*) he distinguishes them by reference to the differing emotions to which they are due. " Weakness, fear, melancholy, together with ignorance are . . . the true

taking epidemic form—in one or other of which, and generally
in both together, all ' popular ' religions betray their unnatural
character. Had Hume to choose between the two types of
religion, his choice would be for the superstitious type, not the
fanatical, and preferably in its pagan rather than in its Christian
variants. The pagan religions, as more purely ceremonial, and
therefore also more tolerant and sociable, " sit easy and light
on men's minds," and " make no such deep impression on the
affections and understanding." [1] These, in Hume's view—
religion being what it is—are positive merits.

In these and other similar utterances Hume might seem to
be speaking of the religion of the Greeks and Romans in a
nostalgic, almost sentimental manner, were it not so evident
that this is only his indirect method of expressing his distaste
for religion as he knew it in his own day. A paragraph from
his *History of England* may serve to show how completely he
had reacted against the Calvinist teaching of his early years.

Whatever ridicule, to a philosophical mind, may be thrown on
pious ceremonies, it must be confessed, that, during a very religious
age, no institutions can be more advantageous to the rude multitude,
and tend more to mollify that fierce and gloomy spirit of devotion,
to which they are subject. Even the English church, though it had
retained a share of popish ceremonies, may justly be thought too
naked and unadorned, and still to approach too near the abstract
and spiritual religion of the puritans. Laud and his associates, by
reviving a few primitive institutions of this nature, corrected the
error of the first reformers, and presented to the affrightened and
astonished mind, some sensible, exterior observances, which might
occupy it during its religious exercises, and abate the violence of its
disappointed efforts. The thought, no longer bent on that divine
and mysterious essence, so superior to the narrow capacities of mankind, was able, by means of the new model of devotion, to relax itself
in the contemplation of pictures, postures, vestments, buildings ;
and all the fine arts, which minister to religion, thereby received

sources of superstition. . . . Hope, pride, presumption, a warm imagination,
together with ignorance, are the true sources of enthusiasm." The former, he
adds, is favourable to priestly power, and therefore to the multiplication of rites
and ceremonies ; the latter, as demanding direct approach to the Divine Presence,
is not less but rather more contrary to priestly power than are sound reason and
philosophy. These last statements may fit in with Hume's account of certain
forms of the Christian religion—Romanism as priest-ridden and superstitious ;
Calvinism as enthusiastic and fanatical ; but in respect of their emotional accom-
paniments, their relations would seem in certain respects to be the reverse of those
here ascribed to them.

[1] *The Natural History of Religion. Essays*, G. & G., vol. ii, p. 352

additional encouragement. . . . His errors were the most excusable of all those which prevailed during that zealous period.[1]

In his *Natural History of Religion* Hume has dwelt at considerable length on the very different relations in which, as he holds, religion and philosophy stand to one another in the ancient as compared with the modern world. History, it is important to note, had not yet, in Hume's time, been divided in the threefold manner, ancient, medieval, and modern ; the current distinction was between the ancients and the moderns. As Mr. Christopher Dawson, writing on Gibbon,[2] has pointed out :

For three hundred years men had lived a double life. The classical world was the standard of their thought and conduct. In a sense, it was more real to them than their own world, for they had been taught to know the history of Rome better than that of England or modern Europe ; to judge their literature by the standard of Quintilian, and to model their thought on Cicero and Seneca. Ancient history was history in the absolute sense, and the ages that followed were a shadowy and unreal world which could only be rationalized by being related in some way to the past. . . . The first literary histories of medieval Europe were the works of humanists who wished to throw a bridge over the formless chaos of the Dark Ages. They were essentially histories of the Decline and Fall of the Roman Empire.

This was the tradition to which Hume (like Gibbon) became heir, and to which he adhered. The Christian centuries preceding the Renaissance were still for him ' the Dark Ages '—ages during which religion and reason did violence to one another, to their mutual detriment, in ways that, happily—so Hume likes to believe—have no parallels in the ancient world.

Religion, Hume teaches, originates independently of reason. Man is at first a barbarous, necessitous, unleisured animal, so pressed by numerous wants and passions that he starts no questions and engages in no inquiries. The traditional stories answer, in a manner suited to his intelligence, the only questions to which he is, of himself, inclined. The ' Divinities ' in which he believes are not really ' Gods ' in the genuine sense of the term. They are beings but little superior to human

---

[1] Chap. lvii, at the end
[2] *Edward Gibbon* (*Proceedings of the British Academy*, vol. xx, 1934)

creatures ; and there was no thought of ascribing to them the origin and fabric of the universe. These were questions first raised by philosophers.

It is precisely to this ' atheistic ' character of the first Gods that Hume would trace the origins of theism. The Gods being conceived as being influenced, like men, by gifts and flattery, each generation, under pressure of its fears and distresses, has outdone its predecessors, inventing new and more magnificent strains of adulation. " Thus they proceed : till at last they arrive at infinity itself, beyond which there is no further progress." And thus ' *by chance*,' in the notion of a perfect omnipotent Being, the Creator of the world, religion comes to coincide with the principles of true philosophy.

> They are guided to that notion, not by reason, of which they are in a great measure incapable, but by the adulation and fears of the most vulgar superstition.[1]

Thus the deity, who, from love, converted himself into a bull, in order to carry off *Europa* ; and who, from ambition, dethroned his father, *Saturn*, became the *Optimus Maximus* of the heathens. Thus the deity, whom the vulgar Jews conceived only as the God of *Abraham*, *Isaac*, and *Jacob*, became their *Jehovah* and Creator of the World.[2]

But while Christianity is thus even in its popular forms definitely theistic, this is not in Hume's view an unqualified advantage. So far from being so, it has, he declares, been the fateful source of three great evils. (1) When God is conceived as single and universal, unity of object calls for unity of faith and ceremonies, and so furnishes designing men with a pretence for discharging on each other " that sacred zeal and rancour, the most furious and implacable of all human passions." [3] Idolatry is sociable and tolerant ; all religions which maintain the unity of God are, he holds, as remarkable for the opposite principles.

The implacable narrow spirit of the Jews is well known. Mahometanism set out with still more bloody principles. . . . The human sacrifices of the Carthaginians, Mexicans, and many barbarous nations, scarcely exceed the inquisition and persecutions of Rome and Madrid.[4]

---

[1] *The Natural History of Religion. Essays*, G. & G., vol. ii, p. 330
[2] *Ibid.*, p. 331. The last sentence underwent changes in the successive editions.
[3] *Ibid.*, p. 337   [4] *Ibid.*, pp. 337-8

Nor are the victims any longer chosen merely by lot, or some external sign.

Virtue, knowledge, love of liberty, are the qualities which call down the fatal vengeance of inquisitors ; and when expelled, leave the society in the most shameful ignorance, corruption, and bondage.[1]

This thesis is developed more at length in Hume's early *Dialogue*, appended to the 1751 edition of the *Enquiry*. In the ancient world religion was limited to sacrifices in the temple ; outside the temple men were free to think as they pleased ; it was the business of philosophy alone to regulate men's ordinary behaviour. Philosophy now confines itself mostly to the closet.

Its place is now supplied by the modern religion, which inspects our whole conduct, and prescribes an universal rule to our actions, to our words, to our very thoughts and inclinations ; a rule so much the more austere, as it is guarded by infinite, though distant, rewards and punishments ; and no infraction of it can ever be concealed or disguised.[2]

(2) When the Gods are conceived to be only a little superior to mankind, and to have been, many of them, advanced from that inferior rank, men are more at their ease in addressing them, and aspire to emulation of them.

Hence activity, spirit, courage, magnanimity, love of liberty, and all the virtues which aggrandise a people.[3]

When, on the other hand, the Deity is represented as infinitely superior to mankind, this belief, however just, is apt, when joined with supernatural terrors, to sink the mind into such abasement that none save

the monkish virtues of mortification, penance, humanity, and passive suffering, are [represented as] acceptable to him.[4]

(3) Even more distinctive, Hume declares, is yet another difference between Christianity and pagan religions—it is also, he adds, another instance how the corruption of the best begets the worst [5]—the manner in which Christianity has perverted reason from its true and proper function. Since

---

[1] *The Natural History of Religion. Essays*, G. & G., vol. ii, p. 339
[2] *Essays*, G. & G., vol. ii, pp. 303-4
[3] *Ibid.*, p. 339
[4] *Loc. cit.*
[5] *Ibid.*, pp. 338n., 339

the heathen mythologies rested on traditional stories which varied from city to city—" numberless like the popish legends " [1] —and were all of equal authority, philosophical argument could play but little part in the pagan theologies. It was manifestly impossible to reduce them to a canon, or to any determinate articles of faith. Accordingly, religion and philosophy, in being thus so different, had each to be patient of the other. They made a ' fair partition ' of mankind between them. Philosophy catered for the needs of the learned and wise, religion for the no less rightful needs of the simple and illiterate.

How different, Hume exclaims, is the situation in the Christian centuries ! And at first sight, how much more in keeping with human reason ! In Christianity the authority is conveyed by a sacred book the comparatively consistent teaching of which has been so instilled into men by their earliest education that when they become speculative reasoners they continue in their assent to it, the more so as it is the professed support of the theism to which they are independently inclined. But how deceitful—Hume would have us observe—all these appearances turn out to be ! Philosophy soon finds that she is very unequally yoked with her new associate. Instead of regulating theology, as they advance together, she is at every turn perverted to serve the purposes of superstition. Reason aids in drawing the *logical* consequences of dogmas—consequences often so much more contrary to plain reason than the dogmas as first conceived. But over the dogmas reason has itself no control ; should it attempt to question them, and the reproach of heresy be bandied about among the disputants, the reproach always rests at last on the side of reason.

This pertinacious bigotry, of which you complain, as so fatal to philosophy, is really her offspring, who, after allying with superstition, separates himself entirely from the interest of his parent, and becomes her most inveterate enemy and persecutor. [2]
Amazement must of necessity be raised : Mystery affected : Darkness and obscurity sought after : And a foundation of merit afforded to the devout votaries, who desire an opportunity of subduing their rebellious reason, by the belief of the most unintelligible sophisms. [3]
It is thus a system becomes more absurd in the end, merely from

---

[1] *The Natural History of Religion.* *Essays*, G. & G.. vol. ii., p. 348
[2] *Enquiry*, S.-B., p. 133 ; *Essays*, G. & G., vol. ii, pp. 109–10
[3] *The Natural History of Religion.* *Essays*, G. & G., vol, ii, pp. 341–2

its being reasonable and philosophical in the beginning. . . . And the same fires, which were kindled for heretics, will also serve for the destruction of philosophers.[1]

' Modern religion,' this ' fanatical,' ' intolerant,' ' grotesque,' ' scholasticism '—these are Hume's terms—is thus, in Hume's view, due to a kind of miscegenation. It is the monstrous Caliban-like offspring of reason on superstition ; and as Hume also believed, is still active and influential, however modified by Protestant reforms.

But the tale of the sins which Hume would lay at the door of religion is not yet complete. More general and more immediately operative are, he declares, its baleful effects in the moral sphere. These effects, as he enumerates them are, in the main, twofold. First, there is the tendency, characteristic of the traditional religions, to multiply new and frivolous species of merit, in the observance of rites or in the holding of abstruse beliefs ; and to treat them as being of higher value than the duties of everyday life. These specifically religious duties, if otherwise harmless, still divide the attention, and so tend to weaken men's attachment to the natural motives of justice and humanity.[2]

The specifically religious duties are of two kinds. There are *outward* observances. These constitute what Hume regarded as the kindlier, less dangerous side of religion—the side in which it turns towards rites and ceremonies. But among the religious duties are also counted—this, Hume points out, is the very essence of religion in its modern as distinguished from its ancient forms—the cultivation of certain feelings and the holding of certain beliefs ; and it is to these inner obligations that he traces the further, yet greater, evils to which, as he contends, religion has given birth. These inner obligations, unlike outward acts, cannot be voluntarily fulfilled ; they depend on ' Grace.' The utmost the worshipper can at will command is a *profession* of belief—an insincerity which, as it becomes confirmed, affects the whole character and takes to itself permanent form in the darker vice of hypocrisy. Hume maintains, evidently with mischievous intent, that the ancients, no matter how wildly irrational their beliefs and practices, are as sincere in them as are the adherents of any of the Christian

[1] *The Natural History of Religion. Essays*, G. & G., vol. ii,p. 342
[2] *Cf. Dialogues*, pp. 222-3

creeds.[1]   This, again, is only his indirect way of declaring that religious belief is at best never more than half-belief—*make-belief treated as a religious duty.*

Men dare not avow, even to their own hearts, the doubts which they entertain on such subjects : They make a merit of implicit faith ; and disguise to themselves their real infidelity, by the strongest asseverations and most positive bigotry. But nature is too hard for all their endeavours, and suffers not the obscure, glimmering light, afforded in these shadowy regions, to equal the strong impressions, made by common sense and experience. The usual course of men's conduct belies their words, and shows, that their assent in these matters is some unaccountable operation of the mind between disbelief and conviction, but approaching much nearer to the former than to the latter.[2]

Owing to the religious and other conditions in Hume's time —as is shown by the literature of this period, and not least by the writings of those whose zeal for religion is not in question —hypocrisy was a much more common vice, at least in its religious forms, than it would now seem to be. Hume draws attention to it repeatedly and with unusual emphasis.

Many religious exercises are entered into with seeming fervour, where the heart, at the time, feels cold and languid : A habit of dissimulation is by degrees contracted : And fraud and falsehood become the predominant principle. Hence the reason of the vulgar observation, that the highest zeal in religion and the deepest hypocrisy, so far from being inconsistent, are often or commonly united in the same individual character.[3]
When we have to do with a man, who makes a great profession of religion and devotion, has this any other effect upon several, who pass for prudent, than to put them on their guard, lest they be cheated and deceived by him ? [4]

Hume, as the reader will have observed, has been careful to avoid attacking religion directly ; he professes to be attacking only what he describes as being its popular, superstitious, fanatical forms. But it is far from clear what it is that remains when these are discounted ; and the few, brief, passages in which he has expressed his mind on the subject are more bewildering than helpful. Thus in the *Enquiry* we are told that

---

[1] *The Natural History of Religion.*   *Essays,* G. &. G., vol. ii, pp. 342 *sqq.*
[2] *Essays,* G. & G., vol. ii, p. 348.   *Cf. Dialogues,* p. 225
[3] *Dialogues,* p. 222.   *Cf.* passage in *History of England* cited above, p. 8
[4] *Dialogues,* p. 221.   *Cf.* also *The Natural History of Religion.   Essays,* G. & G., vol. ii, pp. 359–60, and Boswell's interview with Hume, below, pp. 97–8.

true religion is " nothing but a species of philosophy " ; [1] and the only explanation which he has thought good to add is that this species of philosophy is sceptical, not in the extreme Pyrrhonian fashion, but in its more mitigated form " when its undistinguished doubts are, in some measure, corrected by common sense and reflection." [2]

On first reading Hume nothing, indeed, is more difficult to harmonize with his other doctrines than this repeated assertion that true religion is a species of philosophy. We are left asking how on his teaching religion can be true, or, even if true, how it can be a philosophy, least of all his own philosophy. The posthumously published *Dialogues* alone supply an answer to these questions ; and I shall now so far anticipate as to indicate in outline the character of the answer which he has there given.

In the *Dialogues* Hume makes much more explicit than in any of his other writings the quite negative character of his views regarding Divine Existence ; and he is equally frank in what amounts to a virtual denial of religion. A *virtual* denial ; for just as he continues to use the term ' God ' in expounding his scepticism, so he continues to use the term ' religion ' in a sense almost directly contrary to any in which it is ordinarily employed. He has himself no belief in miracles nor consequently in a special Revelation ; he has no belief in an afterlife or in any type of specifically religious duties ; he has no belief in a Divine Being to whom moral attributes can be ascribed and none therefore in ' God ' as religiously understood. What he calls ' true religion ' is, as we find, little more than a repudiation of all superstition, alike in belief and in practice.[3] " *To know God . . . is to worship him.* All other

---

[1] S.-B., p. 146 ; *Essays*, G. & G., vol. ii, p. 120. In Hume's vocabulary ' natural ' is a term of supreme approval, and ' true,' ' genuine ' religion is also so described. It is with ' natural religion ' that the *Dialogues* are concerned.

[2] *Enquiry*, S.-B., p. 161 ; *Essays*, G. & G., vol. ii, p. 132

[3] *Cf.* Francis Bacon's eulogy of atheism at the expense of superstition, in his essay (XVII) *Of Superstition*, with which Hume must have been familiar. It expresses precisely Hume's own sentiments. " It were better to have no opinion of God at all than such an opinion as is unworthy of him ; for the one is unbelief, the other is contumely : and certainly superstition is the reproach of the Deity . . . and, as the contumely is greater towards God, so the danger is greater towards men. Atheism leaves a man to sense, to philosophy, to natural piety, to laws, to reputation . . . but superstition dismounts all these, and erecteth an absolute monarchy in the minds of men : therefore atheism did never perturb states ; for it makes men wary of themselves, as looking no further ; . . . but superstition . . . bringeth in a new ' premium mobile,' that ravisheth all the spheres of government."

worship is indeed absurd, superstitious, and even impious." [1]
(This is what Hume has meant in saying, in the *Enquiry*, that
true religion is *nothing but* a species of philosophy.) These statements occur at the close of the final section of his *Dialogues*,
in a passage which he added in an early revision of them
(probably in or prior to 1761) ; and when he made a further
revision in 1776, the year of his death, he added yet other
passages,[2] which are significant as being the sole passages in
all his writings in which he is outspoken in acknowledging the
quite indefinite, and as he himself says ' somewhat ambiguous '
character of the only knowledge of God that he is prepared to
allow. Our knowledge of God exhausts itself, he declares, in

one simple, though somewhat ambiguous, at least undefined proposition, *that the cause or causes of order in the universe probably bear some
remote analogy to human intelligence :* If this proposition be not capable
of extension, variation, or more particular explication : If it afford
no inference that affects human life, or can be the source of any
action or forbearance : And if the analogy, imperfect as it is, can
be carried no farther than to the human intelligence ; and cannot
be transferred, with any appearance of probability, to the other
moral qualities of the mind : If this really be the case, what can
the most inquisitive, contemplative, and religious man do more
than give a plain, philosophical assent to the proposition, as often
as it occurs ; and believe that the arguments, on which it is established, exceed the objections, which lie against it ? Some astonishment indeed will naturally arise from the greatness of the object :
Some melancholy from its obscurity : Some contempt of human
reason, that it can give no solution more satisfactory with regard
to so extraordinary and magnificent a question.[3]

Were that divine Being disposed to be offended at the vices and
follies of silly mortals, who are his own workmanship ; ill would
it surely fare with the votaries of most popular superstitions. Nor
would any of the human race merit his *favour*, but a very few, the
philosophical theists [above described] . . . : As the only persons
entitled to his *compassion* and *indulgence* would be the philosophical
sceptics, a sect almost equally rare, who, from a natural diffidence
of their own capacity, suspend, or endeavour to suspend all judgement with regard to such sublime and such extraordinary subjects.[4]

Cleanthes, the advocate of theism in the *Dialogues*, is made
to declare that " the proper office of religion is to regulate the

---

[1] *Dialogues*, p. 226
[2] The evidence is given below, Appendix C, pp. 93–5
[3] *Dialogues*, p. 227   [4] *Ibid.*, pp. 226–7

heart of men, humanise their conduct, infuse the spirit of temperance, order, and obedience," and in general to " enforce the motives of morality and justice." [1] These are not, however, Hume's own views, which are those voiced by Philo [2] in the above passages—namely, that religion, when not infected by superstition and fanaticism, yields no inference that can be the source of any action or forbearance, and no motives superior to, or additional to, the motives proper to ordinary everyday morality.

Hume opens his *Natural History of Religion* with the assertion that the whole frame of nature bespeaks an intelligent Author, and that no rational inquirer can suspend his belief a moment in " the primary principles of genuine religion." T. H. Huxley's comment is not unjust : " But, if we turn from the *Natural History of Religion*, to the *Treatise*, the *Enquiry*, and the *Dialogues*, the story of what happened to the ass laden with salt, who took to the water, irresistibly suggests itself. Hume's theism, such as it is, dissolves away in the dialectic river, until nothing is left but the verbal sack in which it was contained." [3]

This is also evident in the use which Hume makes of the teaching of Plato,[4] as interpreted by Cicero,[5] that there are three kinds of atheists : those who deny a Deity, those who deny his Providence, and those who assert that he is influenced by prayers, devotions, and sacrifices. That Hume should find himself able to agree in classing the second type as atheistic is due to his manner of interpreting the doctrine of Providence. Divine Existence, he teaches, is the source or principle of *order*, *i.e.* the principle determining the regular course of nature—

---

[1] Below, p. 220

[2] *Ibid.*, pp. 226 *sqq.* Hume inserted in the second volume of his *History of England* (p. 494) a note apologetic of the attacks which he had made on religion in the first volume. In this note he speaks in the manner of Cleanthes. But he omitted the note in all later editions ; and doubtless did so, as Hurd suggests (*Supplement to the Life of David Hume Esq.* (1777), p. 20), as being inconsistent with his real convictions. Hume's friend, George Dempster, commenting on the note, writes (1756) to Sir Adam Fergusson : " Pray do you think this a sufficient justification for the liberties which Hume takes almost at every turn with the religion of the ages whose history he writes. It seems difficult for me (for me who dotes upon David) to believe that he can have a great regard for even the best mode of religion and the least extravagant, if we consider how destitute he is of that only support of it, Faith." (*Letters of George Dempster* (1934), p. 22.)

[3] *Hume* (English Men of Letters Series, 1887), p. 146

[4] *The Laws*, pp. 889 *ff.* *Cf.* A. E. Taylor's Introduction to his translation of *The Laws* (1934), p. lii. *Cf.* also Hume's *Letters*, vol. i, p. 50.

[5] *De Natura Deorum*, Bk. I, 1, 2, 43–4 ; Bk. II, 1, 29–30 ; Bk. III, 3

the order which by its fixed laws enables us to arrange our lives with prudence and foresight, and in so doing to benefit by the goods which 'Providence' has provided. Similarly, Hume's reason for classing as atheists the third type—those who believe that God is influenced by prayers and sacrifices, and that there are therefore *special* religious duties—is that they conceive God in unworthy anthropomorphic fashion as intervening, like man and the other animals, only by *special* acts in *special* circumstances—through auguries, dreams, and oracles, as the Greeks and Romans believed, through certain special happenings and revelations as the Jews and Christians teach.

Even at this day, and in Europe, ask any of the vulgar, why he believes in an omnipotent creator of the world ; he will never mention the beauty of final causes, of which he is wholly ignorant : He will not hold out his hand, and bid you contemplate the suppleness and variety of joints in his fingers, their bending all one way, the counterpoise which they receive from the thumb, the softness and fleshy parts of the inside of his hand, with all the other circumstances, which render that member fit for the use, to which it was destined. To these he has been long accustomed ; and he beholds them with listlessness and unconcern. He will tell you of the sudden and unexpected death of such a one : The fall and bruise of such another : The excessive drought of this season : The cold and rains of another. These he ascribes to the immediate operation of providence : *And such events, as, with good reasoners, are the chief difficulties in admitting a supreme intelligence, are with him the sole arguments for it.*[1]

And just as disorders, prodigies, miracles—the *departures* from the order of nature—are, Hume, contends, what chiefly impress the religious, so also

madness, fury, rage, and an inflamed imagination, though they sink men nearest to the level of beasts, are, for a like reason, often supposed to be the only dispositions, in which we can have any immediate communication with the Deity.

And it is, accordingly under such conditions which " disjoint the ordinary frame of the mind, and throw it into the utmost confusion," [2] (as the contexts show, Hume has in mind the requirements of conversion as Calvinistically conceived and as

---

[1] *The Natural History of Religion. Essays,* G. & G., vol. ii, pp. 328–9. Italics not in text.

[2] *Dialogues,* p. 226. *Cf.* pp. 225–6

he understood them) that the traditional religions most power-fully operate.

It is in face of such views that Hume formulates his own counter-positions.

All the philosophy, therefore, in the world, and all the religion, which is nothing but a species of philosophy, will never be able to carry us beyond the usual course of experience, or give us measures of conduct and behaviour different from those which are furnished by reflexions on common life. No new fact can ever be inferred from the religious hypothesis ; no event foreseen or foretold ; no reward or punishment expected or dreaded, beyond what is already known by practice and observation.[1]

Hume's attitude to true religion can therefore be summed up in the threefold thesis : (1) that it consists exclusively in *intellectual* assent to the " somewhat ambiguous, at least un-defined " proposition, ' God exists ' ; (2) that the ' God ' here affirmed is not God as ordinarily understood ; and (3) as a corollary from (1) and (2), that religion ought not to have, and when ' true ' and ' genuine ' does not have, any influence on human conduct—beyond, that is to say, its intellectual effects, as rendering the mind immune to superstition and fanaticism.

---

[1] This is the nearest Hume has come, in any of his other writings, to a state-ment of the views more explicitly formulated in the *Dialogues*. The passage is from Section XI of the *Enquiry concerning Human Understanding* (S.-B., p. 146. *Essays*, G. & G., vol. ii, pp. 120–1), which is also in dialogue form. How early in life Hume had come to hold such views appears from a letter written in 1743 to his friend William Mure (*Letters*, vol. i, p. 50), regarding W. Leechman's *Sermon on Prayer*, then just published : " As to the argument I could wish Leechman wou'd in the second Edition answer this Objection both to Devotion & to Prayer [*i.e.* that to conceive God as influenced by them is a kind of atheism], and indeed to everything we commonly call Religion, except the Practice of Morality, & the Assent of the Understanding to the Proposition *that God exists*."

III HUME'S REASONS FOR RETAINING THE TERMS 'GOD' AND 'RELIGION' IN DEFINING HIS OWN POSITIONS AS BEARING ON THE ARGUMENT OF THE *DIALOGUES*

HUME'S threefold thesis is so neutral and colourless, and borders so closely on sheer negation, that we cannot help asking why, having advanced so far, he has stopped so abruptly. He has reduced the content of the concepts ' God ' and ' religion ' to a beggarly minimum. Why has he thought good still to retain them ? Is he consistent with himself in so doing ? These are questions which obviously demand an answer ; and, as it happens, they also serve as a convenient line of approach to the many problems which arise in connexion with his *Dialogues concerning Natural Religion*. As I shall endeavour to show, the answer to the above questions is to be found in certain considerations peculiar to the period in which Hume lived, and which, just for that reason, are apt to be overlooked by present-day readers.

(1) The first set of considerations influencing Hume in his retention of orthodox language has a very direct bearing upon much of his argument in the *Dialogues*. Whether we take Cicero, Francis Bacon, Pierre Bayle, or Samuel Clarke—all of whom had some degree of influence on Hume's mental development—we find the argument for Divine Existence at its strongest when Epicurean, atomist, or materialist teaching is under discussion. Senseless bodies, moving fortuitously, could never, Cicero teaches, have given rise to the order of nature.

I do not understand why any one who thinks this possible, should not also think that if an infinite number of the one-and-twenty letters of the alphabet, whether composed of gold, or any substance whatever, were flung together somewhere, that from them so cast to the ground, the annals of Ennius could be produced in such a way that they might then be read. I doubt whether fortune could make a single verse of them. How therefore can the Epicureans assert the world to have been made from minute particles possessing neither colour, nor any kind of quality (what the Greeks call ποιότης) nor sensation, but coming together by chance and accident ? But if a concourse of atoms can make a world, why not a porch, a temple, a house, a city, which are works of less labour and difficulty ? [1]

---

[1] *De Natura Deorum*, Bk. II, 37

25

Bacon is no less emphatic :

That school which is most accused of atheism doth most demonstrate religion : that is the school of Leucippus, and Democritus, and Epicurus ; for it is a thousand times more credible that four mutable elements, and one immutable fifth essence, duly and eternally placed, need no God, than that an army of infinite small portions, or seeds unplaced, should have produced this order and beauty without a divine marshal.[1]

Clarke, in similar terms, speaks of the ' ridiculous ' character of the ' Epicurean hypothesis.' It has, he declares, been given up by all ' atheists '—meaning thereby, not any thinkers who have declared themselves to be atheists, but those who in his view *ought* to have so described themselves. And he points out that even apart from the objections referred to by Cicero and Bacon, namely the complexity of *arrangement* in nature, there is the further objection that the order of nature to the extent to which it is more than merely ' material ' is also *more than merely arrangement*.

All possible changes, compositions, or divisions of *figure*, are still nothing but *figure* : And all possible compositions or effects of *motion*, can eternally be nothing but mere *motion*. If therefore there ever was a time when there was nothing in the universe but matter and motion, there never could have been anything else therein, but matter and motion. And it would have been as impossible there should ever have existed any such thing as intelligence or consciousness ; or even any such thing as light, or heat, or sound, or colour, or any of these we call secondary qualities of matter ; as 'tis now impossible for motion to be blue or red, or for a triangle to be transformed into a sound.[2]

These, in general, are positions which Hume himself in the person of Philo adopts in the *Dialogues*. He is not concerned to put forward a ' system ' of his own. The *mysterious* character of reality he allows ; and upon it he rests his scepticism. There are a great number of different systems of cosmogony, each of which has " some faint appearance of truth " ; but " it is a thousand, a million to one " that any one of them is the true system. The ' Epicurean hypothesis ' (he uses

---

[1] *Essays*, XVI. *Of Atheism*. *Cf.* Bayle, *Dictionnaire*, art. ' Ovide' : " la folle et extravagante hypothèse des épicuriens."

[2] *Discourse concerning the Being and Attributes of God* (1704), 7th ed., p. 55. This, is the work (pp. 8 *sqq.*) from which the argument put into the mouth of Demea in the *Dialogues* (below, p. 188), is borrowed by Hume.

Clark's phrase) is, he agrees (and he is evidently referring to
Cicero and Clarke, among others), " commonly, and I believe,
justly esteemed the most absurd system, that has yet been
proposed." [1]

Commentators on Hume have, as a rule, shown themselves
very unwilling to take these statements of Hume at their face
value. Interpreting, as they do, all Hume's philosophy in the
light of his doctrine of *detached* impressions, and this doctrine
in the light of the very misleading account which he gives of
it in the opening of the first volume of his *Treatise*, they fail
to observe that the impressions upon which Hume mainly
relies at the chief turning points in the development of his
philosophy are the impressions not of sensation but of reflection,
and that these impressions are of a *biological* character—instincts
and passions, propensities and sentiments, by no means appropriately describable as detached—and rest, as Hume recognizes
that thought (or reason) itself rests, upon a complication of
secret causes.

Nothing seems more delicate with regard to its causes than thought.
. . . As far as we can judge, vegetables and animal bodies are not
more delicate in their motions, nor depend upon a greater variety
or more curious adjustment of springs and principles.[2]

Hume does indeed speak of the self as a " heap or collection "
of perceptions; but his purpose in thus overstating his position
is to contrast it with the equally one-sided view of Descartes
and his followers. The sentence in which the phrase first occurs[3]
makes this sufficiently clear.

We may observe, that what we call a *mind*, is nothing but a heap
or collection of different perceptions, united together by certain
relations, and suppos'd, though falsely, to be endow'd with a perfect
simplicity and identity.

As Hume emphasizes in his ethics, and insists in his general
philosophy, complexity and changeableness are fundamental
features of the self; ' complications of circumstances,' bodily

---

[1] *Dialogues*, p. 182
[2] Ibid., p. 161
[3] *Treatise*, Bk. I, Pt. IV, sect. ii, S.-B., p. 207 ; G. & G., vol. i, p. 495. Its
second occurrence (sect. vi, S.-B., p. 252 ; G. & G., p. 534) is in a section devoted
to the discussion of ' personal identity,' and there the counter considerations are
duly emphasized.

and mental, partly known but for the most part secret and ever-changing, determine its states and operations. In other words, it has only that *problematic* type of identity which we ascribe to vegetable and animal bodies, or to a commonwealth. As he states in the *Treatise* :

> Self or person is not any one impression, but that to which our several impressions and ideas are suppos'd to have a reference. . . . To explain it perfectly we must take the matter pretty deep, and account for that identity, which we attribute to plants or animals ; there being a great analogy betwixt it, and the identity of a self or person.[1]

These considerations, as already said, have an important bearing upon Hume's methods of argument in the *Dialogues*. The *Dialogues* are a criticism of the argument from design in the form in which that argument was current in Hume's time —a form in which it persisted into the nineteenth century in the writings of Paley [2] and so many others, and which survives in popular and semi-popular forms to the present day. This argument, it cannot be too emphatically insisted, is not a teleological argument of the Aristotelian type. It does not, that is to say, consist in the thesis that the natural order, with which man is so integrally bound up, fulfils an end of absolute and intrinsic worth. It is an essentially anthropomorphic type of argument, resting upon an alleged analogy between natural existences and the artificial products of man's handicraft. We can, it was maintained, gain a sufficient basis for the conception of God as an ordering intelligence in our knowledge of the self and of its relation to the products which it consciously designs.

---

[1] *Treatise*, Bk. I, Pt. IV, sect. vi, ' Of Personal Identity,' S.-B., pp. 251–3 ; G. & G., vol. i, pp. 533–5. *Cf.* S.-B, p. 261 ; G. & G., p. 542 : " In this respect, I cannot compare the soul more properly to any thing than to a republic or commonwealth, in which the several members are united by the reciprocal ties of government and subordination, and give rise to other persons, who propagate the same republic in the incessant changes of its parts." That the facts of experience were not altogether in keeping with his account of what he took to be its *components*, Hume was very well aware, as his candid avowal in the Appendix to the 3rd volume of the *Treatise* (S.-B., p. 633 ; G. & G., vol. i, p. 558) shows. " But upon a more strict review of the section concerning *personal identity*. I find myself involv'd in such a labyrinth, that, I must confess, I neither know how to correct my former opinions, nor how to render them consistent."

[2] *Cf.* Cardinal Manning writing, when he was over seventy, regarding his youthful study of Paley's *Evidences* : " I took in the whole argument, and I thank God that nothing has ever shaken it." (Quoted by Lytton Strachey, *Eminent Victorians*, p. 6.)

Before this argument could be taken as establishing the existence of the God of religion, it had of course to be supplemented by other types of argument. These, however, are supplementary to the argument from design ; and their introduction is a virtual admission of its limited scope.

Now those who hold to this analogy stand committed to the assumption that natural existences do not, any more than artificial products, contain an *inherent* principle of order, *i.e.* that they are not *self*-ordering ; and this was supposed to be especially evident in the case of vegetable and animal organisms. Atomism—in its metaphysical form, as the theory that nothing has existed or now exists save atoms in their groupings and the void—was viewed as hardly calling for serious refutation ; the very barrenness of its womb, short of miracle, was regarded as a sufficient argument for a theism such as that supposed to have been taught by Plato in his *Timaeus*. Also, those who adopted atomism (or some modified version of it, such as that advocated by Descartes) as a hypothesis to account for *physical* happenings, were precisely those who supplemented it—Voltaire is a notable instance—by a theistic superstructure. Indeed, it was probably the view of matter propounded by Descartes and his followers, as passive and inert, which gave the belief in God so tenacious a hold even over those who were most sceptically inclined, and who in all practical issues had detached themselves from the religious influences with which, in the general mind, it was inseparably bound up. In the absence of an alternative explanation of a more credible kind, the ' religious hypothesis ' (to use Hume's phrase) held the field. It was not, as a rule, that it was thought out, and quite deliberately adopted, still less that it was held as a belief which played a specifically religious role in their minds. No alternative being in sight, it was conceded, especially as regards living organisms ; and having been conceded, it came in only when quite ultimate issues were raised ; and even then it was little more than an admission of ignorance, expressed in the terms of the traditional creed. This attitude was the more practicable, in that the argument from design was, as already stated, formulated with only incidental reference to moral or specifically religious considerations.

This is also one main reason why Hume was so peculiarly fitted to act as critic of the presuppositions of the argument from design and of its methods of reasoning. The argument, resting on purely intellectualist grounds, not only did not carry him into any field in which his limitations of interest and of insight might place him at a disadvantage, it supplied him with precisely the task for which his own special gifts of critical analysis supremely equipped him. This happy conjuncture of circumstances is, indeed, what has given the *Dialogues* their unique place in philosophical literature. They are unique in two respects. As Leslie Stephen has pointed out,[1] they were the first work in our literature to subject the argument from design to a passionless and searching criticism. And secondly, Hume's destructive criticism of the argument—allowing for the limitations, just noted, under which it was formulated—was final and complete. For a couple of generations, theologians, especially in Britain, may have continued on the old lines, as if the *Dialogues* had never been written. But in the altered outlook of present-day theology, these older ways of argument have in large measure ceased to be approved, and Hume's indictment of them is now but seldom challenged.

Kant, in his immediate acceptance of the main argument of the *Dialogues*, as in his appreciation of Hume's argument in the *Treatise*, outstripped his contemporaries and nearly all his immediate successors.[2] The manuscript of Hamann's translation of the *Dialogues* brought them to Kant's notice in 1780 [3] (*i.e.* in the year following their first appearance), on the eve of the publication of his *Critique of Pure Reason*. Recognizing Hume's main criticisms as unanswerable, he at once incorporated them in his discussion of the teleological argument in his final revision of the *Critique*. They were also among the influences leading Kant to a reformulation of the problems of teleology in his *Critique of Judgment*.

We may, in passing, note why Hume could himself positively approve the virtual ignoring, or at least the quite external and casual treatment, of moral experience in the argument from design. His ethical teaching, as developed at length in the

---

[1] *English Thought in the Eighteenth Century* (3rd ed., 1902), vol. i, p. 311

[2] *Cf.* Leslie Stephen, *op. cit.*, vol. i, p. 315. " The hollowness in theory and the impotence in practice of English speculation in the last half of the century, is but the natural consequence of the faint-heartedness which prevented English thinkers from looking facts in the face. The huge development of hypocrisy, sham beliefs, and indolent scepticism, is the penalty which we have to pay for our not daring to meet the doubts openly expressed by Hume, and by Hume alone."

[3] *Cf.* Hamann's *Schriften* (1824), Bd. VI, pp. 154, 158, 167

Treatise and *Enquiry concerning the Principles of Morals*, rests on a naturalistic interpretation of human life and destiny. When he dwells—as in his essay *Of the Dignity or Meanness of Human Nature*—upon the superiority of man over other animals, it is in man's *cognitive* capacities that he finds the chief source of the superiority.

[In man] we see a creature, whose thoughts are not limited by any narrow bounds, either of place or time ; . . . a creature who traces causes and effects to a great length and intricacy ; extracts general principles from particular appearances ; improves upon his discoveries ; corrects his mistakes ; and makes his very errors profitable.[1]

But even these rational capacities do not, in Hume's view, suggest that man's destiny transcends this present life.

[They] find sufficient employment, in fencing against the miseries of his present condition. And frequently, nay almost always, are too slender for the business assigned them.[2]

This, in Hume's view, is still more evident as regards man's *moral* capacities and needs. Moral distinctions, in any experience we have of them, are, he maintains, of purely human significance. Like the aesthetic satisfactions, they are inseparably bound up with the animal and other special conditions of our creaturely existence ; in forced abstraction from these, they have neither meaning nor validity.

Why, Hume asks, has Euclid in explaining all the properties of the circle said not a word about its beauty? The reason, he declares, is evident. The beauty is not a quality of the circle ; and it is in vain to seek for it either by the senses or by reasoning.

Attend to Palladio and Perrault, while they explain all the parts and proportions of a pillar. They talk of the cornice, and frieze, and base, and entablature, and shaft and architrave. . . . But should you ask the description and position of its beauty, they would readily reply, that the beauty is not in any of the parts or members of a pillar. . . . Till . . . a spectator appear, there is nothing but a figure of such particular dimensions and proportions : from his sentiments alone arise its elegance and beauty.
Again ; attend to Cicero, while he paints the crimes of a Verres

---

[1] *Essays*, G. & G., vol. i, p. 152
[2] *Ibid.*, vol. ii, *Of the Immortality of the Soul*, p. 401

or a Cataline. You must acknowledge that the moral turpitude results, in the same manner, from the contemplation of the whole, when presented to a being whose organs have such a particular structure and formation. . . . The crime or immorality is no particular fact or relation, which can be the object of the understanding, but arises entirely from the sentiment of disapprobation, which, by the structure of human nature, we unavoidably feel on the apprehension of barbarity or treachery.[1]

Our aesthetic and moral sentiments thus stand, Hume holds, on a level with the so-called secondary qualities of matter ; like them they are conditioned by the ' complication of circumstances,' [2] partly bodily and partly mental, which determines our mode of existence as animal. This is an analogy upon which he lays great stress.

Vice and virtue, therefore, may be compar'd to sounds, colours, heat and cold, which, according to modern philosophy, are not qualities in objects, but perceptions in the mind.[3]

Our human nature here exhibits

a productive faculty, and gilding or staining all natural objects with the colours, borrowed from internal sentiment, raises in a manner a new creation.[4]

In how sheerly naturalistic a manner Hume interprets these value-judgements, and how convinced he was that our moral experiences yield no data upon which a theology can be reared, *and that they are indeed less, and not more, worthy of being used as a basis of analogy, than our intellectual capacities,*[5] is shown by the letter which he wrote to Francis Hutcheson in 1740, prior to the publication of the concluding volume of the *Treatise*, and which agrees with his views as expounded in all his later writings.

I wish from my Heart, I coud avoid concluding, that since Morality, according to your Opinion as well as mine, is determin'd merely by Sentiment, it regards only human Nature and human Life. This has been often urg'd against you, & the Consequences are

[1] *Enquiry*, S.-B., pp. 292–3 ; *Essays*, G. & G., vol. ii, pp. 263–4
[2] *Loc. cit.*
[3] *Treatise*, Bk. III, Pt. I, sect. i, S.-B., p. 469 ; G. & G., vol. ii, p. 245. *Cf. Letters*, vol. i, pp. 39–40.
[4] *Enquiry*, S.-B., p. 294 ; *Essays*, II, G. & G., vol. ii, p. 265
[5] *Cf. Dialogues*, p. 219. " We have reason to infer that the natural attributes of the Deity have a greater resemblance to those of man, than his moral have to human virtues . . . the moral qualities of man are more defective in their kind than his natural abilities."

very momentous. If you make any Alterations on your Perform-
ances, I can assure you, there are many who desire you woud
more fully consider this Point ; if you think that the Truth lyes
on the popular Side. Otherwise common Prudence, your Character
& Situation forbid you touch upon it.[1] *If Morality were determined
by Reason, that is the same to all rational Beings : But nothing
but Experience can assure us, that the Sentiments are the same.
What Experience have we with regard to superior Beings ? How can we
ascribe to them any Sentiments at all ? They have implanted those Sentiments
in us for the Conduct of Life like our bodily Sensations, which they possess
not themselves.*[2]

It was from this standpoint that Hume also rejected, as unsupported by the data either of general or of moral experience,
the belief in an after-life, and together with it the ' probation '
or ' porch ' view of human life, so central in the theistic religions.

But to return to our consideration of the argument from
design, and of the grounds of its practically universal acceptance
in Hume's day, even by the sceptically minded. Hume himself
proceeds to its acceptance, but by a path which sets it in so
neutral a light, that his conclusions are of an almost opposite
character to those which are ordinarily drawn. He refused to
accept the Cartesian dogma of a passive, inert matter.[3] He
also refused to accept the laws of motion as supplying the key
for an *ultimate* explanation even of physical happenings. All
natural happenings, in his view, are, as regards their *ultimate*
causes, outside the sphere of possible knowledge : all that we
can do is to discover some few of the derivative uniformities.[4]
There was no obstacle, therefore, in the way of his accepting
life, or as he preferred to entitle it ' generation and vegetation,'[5]
as being no less fundamental in reality than ' matter ' and
' intelligence.' And inasmuch as there are points of analogy
between life and intelligence—analogies which do not hold

---

[1] Already in 1737 the Glasgow Presbytery had prosecuted Hutcheson for
teaching the heresy that we can have knowledge of good and evil without, and
prior to, a knowledge of God. *Cf.* Rae, *Life of Adam Smith* (1895), pp. 12–13.

[2] *Letters*, vol. i, p. 40. Italics not in text

[3] *Cf. Dialogues*, pp. 174, 191

[4] *Cf.* Hume's eulogy of Newton (*History of England*, chap. lxxi) : " . . . the
greatest and rarest genius that ever rose for the ornament and instruction of the
species." " While Newton seemed to draw off the veil from some of the mysteries
of nature, he shewed at the same time the imperfections of the mechanical philosophy ; and thereby restored her ultimate secrets to that obscurity in which they
ever did and ever will remain."

[5] ' Organization ' is Hume's term for ' life ' : generation, in distinction from
vegetation, he uses in the narrower sense as meaning *animal* life.

between either of them and 'mere matter'—the way was opened for him to maintain that he was not questioning the existence of God but only our powers of determining his attributes.

Intelligence, in our human experience, appears, as Hume points out, always and only in connexion with 'generation,' that is, in animal life. None the less Hume is careful not to go the length of maintaining—to have done so would have been inconsistent with what he recognized to be the limits of our knowledge—that animal organization is the key (as its sufficient, originating source) to mind, reason, or intelligence. What Hume is here maintaining is only the *negative* thesis, that intelligence cannot be shown to be the key to organization.

Judging by our limited and imperfect experience, generation has some privileges above reason : For we see every day the latter arise from the former, never the former from the latter.[1]

What generation itself, or its origins, may be, Hume does not profess, and cannot rightly be required, to discuss. He nowhere claims to carry his inquiries beyond the secondary causes, into which alone experience gives us any degree of insight.

And if every attack, as is commonly observed, and no defence, among theologians, is successful ; how complete must be *his* victory, who remains always, with all mankind, on the offensive, and has himself no fixed station or abiding city, which he is ever, on any occasion, obliged to defend ? [2]

To repeat, the tendency among commentators on Hume to reduce his philosophy to his doctrine of *detached* impressions, and their consequent assumption that Hume's sympathies must therefore lie with an atomic theory, in psychology and physics, has made his discussion of the argument from design in the *Dialogues* seem more obscure and less conclusive than in actual fact it really is. Once we recognize that for Hume, as for those who favour the argument from design, the chief impression made upon the mind by nature arises in connexion with the phenomena of animal life, the main lines of Hume's criticism of the argument from design, and his own conclusions, quite appropriately follow.

[1] *Dialogues*, pp. 179–80   [2] *Dialogues*, p. 187

Look round this universe. What an immense profusion of beings, animated and organized, sensible and active ! You admire this prodigious variety and fecundity. But inspect a little more narrowly these living existences, the only beings worth regarding. How hostile and destructive to each other ! How insufficient all of them for their own happiness ! How contemptible or odious to the spectator ! The whole presents nothing but the idea of a blind nature, impregnated by a great vivifying principle, and pouring forth from her lap, without discernment or parental care, her maimed and abortive children.[1]

Since for Hume generation is itself as much or as little an ultimate as are any of the entities appealed to in a ' mechanistic ' philosophy, the grounds upon which the argument to and from design had been made to rest are entirely cut away.

In this little corner of the world alone, there are four principles, *reason, instinct, generation, vegetation*, which are similar to each other, and are the causes of similar effects. . . . Any one of these four principles . . . (and a hundred others which lie open to our conjecture) may afford us a theory, by which to judge of the origin of the world ; and it is a palpable and egregious partiality, to confine our view entirely to that principle, by which our own minds operate. Were this principle more intelligible on that account, such a partiality might be somewhat excusable : But reason, in its internal fabric and structure, is really as little known to us as instinct or vegetation ; and perhaps even that vague, undeterminate word, nature, to which the vulgar refer every thing, is not at the bottom more inexplicable. The effects of these principles are all known to us from experience : But the principles themselves, and their manner of operation, are totally unknown.[2]

Among the Hume manuscripts preserved by the Royal Society of Edinburgh are memoranda, consisting mainly of notes on reading, and probably written, as Burton conjectures, prior to 1741.[3] Three of the observations are as follows : they may be said to be the keynotes of the *Dialogues* :

Strato's Atheism the most dangerous of the Ancient, holding to the Origin of the World from Nature, or a Matter endued with Activity.

---

[1] *Dialogues*, p. 211. This passage is an addition inserted in an early revision in or prior to 1761. *Cf.* below, Appendix C, pp. 93–5.

[2] *Ibid.*, p. 178

[3] The watermarks (*cf.* below, p. 95) on the sheets of the memoranda occur also on paper used in the years 1734, 1739, and 1743, but not, so far as I have observed, on any later, definitely datable R.S.E. manuscripts. The contents of the memoranda, as Burton points out, suggest a date of origin *subsequent* to the completion of the *Treatise*. *Cf.* Burton, *Life of David Hume*, vol. i, pp. 124 *sqq.*

Baile [*sic*] thinks there are none but the Cartesians can refute this Atheism.

A Stratonician coud retort the Arguments of all the Sects of Philosophy. Of the Stoics, who maintained God to be fiery and compound and of the Platonicians, who asserted the Ideas to be distinct from the Deity. The same question [which Strato might propose to all of them], Why the Parts or Ideas of God had that particular Arrangement ? is as difficult [a question] as why the World had.[1]

It is from the standpoint of these citations that Hume's own position is expounded by Philo in the *Dialogues*.

Were I obliged to defend any particular system . . . I esteem none more plausible than that which ascribes an eternal, inherent principle of order in the world ; though attended with great and continual revolutions and alterations. This . . . is, at least, a theory, that we must, sooner or later, have recourse to, whatever system we embrace. How could things have been as they are, were there not an original, inherent principle of order somewhere, in thought or in matter ? And it is very indifferent to which of these we give the preference.[2]

To sum up : in the *Dialogues* Hume reaches, among other conclusions, the following : First, organization (Hume's term for ' life,' animal and vegetable) is, like all other natural processes, essentially mysterious. Secondly, in brutes and men it conditions, or at least is accompanied by, intelligence—an intelligence which in man no less than in the other animals, though with certain appropriate differences, is fundamentally instinctive in character.[3] Thirdly, there are, consequently, points of analogy between organization, instinct, and intelligence ; all three are agencies to which *order* is due. If, therefore, belief in God be taken as consisting in the assertion that something not altogether different from human intelligence is

---

[1] Burton, *Life of David Hume*, vol. i, pp. 344–5. Strato was Head of the Peripatetic School from 287 to 269 B.C., in succession to Theophrastus. Hume's notes are a summary of the lengthy passage in Bayle's *Continuation des pensées diverses* (1705), § cvi, of which I have given a translation in Appendix B (below, pp. 80–6).

[2] P. 174

[3] Unfortunately it is not possible, within the limits of this Introduction, to discuss Hume's view of reason. That would involve treating of his doctrine of natural belief, and of his whole theory of knowledge. Usually by ' reason ' Hume means what may be named *synthetic*, or as he himself entitles it, experimental reason (*i.e.* reason viewed as an ordering, designing, creative agency), to distinguish it from those discursive activities of the mind to which comparison and the other processes of analytic thinking are due. It is to synthetic reason that he is referring when he states in the *Treatise* (Bk. I, Pt. III, sect. xvi, S.-B., p. 179 ;

the ultimate determining source of order in the universe, Hume is not questioning this belief, but is merely insisting that it is a more ambiguous, less definite assertion than is commonly supposed.

If Hume, at the time when the *Dialogues* were first composed, conceived himself to be a theist, or rather, it would probably be more correct to say, as not being an atheist, this is only what we should reasonably expect. 'Atheism,' besides involving a much more positive view of reality than Hume himself claimed to possess, was a term of such general opprobrium that no-one was called upon needlessly to assume it. Had not the supporters of the 'religious hypothesis' themselves shown how easily this could be avoided, by applying it to opponents who in any way departed from their own favoured ways of conceiving Divine Existence; and had not Bayle very effectively turned the tables upon popular modes of belief by showing how easily they can be classed as superstition or idolatry, and by claiming, quite in accordance with the orthodox doctrine of a *Deus absconditus*, that only those who admit the unworthiness of *all* human conceptions have the right to lay claim to belief in a Being truly divine? This is the position adopted by Hume, in emulation of Bayle and his many imitators. Hume attacks not theism, but superstition and idolatry; he questions not the existence of God but only the mistaken arguments for such existence, and the unworthy modes of conception in which they result.

It is not unlikely that until the time of his second, longer visit to Paris in 1763-6 Hume had never found occasion seriously to ask himself whether he was really justified in disclaiming the title 'atheist.' There seems no reason to doubt the truth of the incident recorded by Sir Samuel Romilly in the words which he states were used to him by Diderot:

Je vous dirai un trait de lui [Hume], mais il vous sera un peu scandaleux peut-être, car vous Anglais vous croyez *un peu* en Dieu;

G. & G., vol i, p. 471) that reason is itself "nothing but a wonderful and unintelligible instinct in our souls"; and in the *Dialogues* (p. 178) that its "essence is incomprehensible," and again (*loc. cit.*) more explicitly that "in its internal fabric and structure [it] is really as little known to us as instinct or vegetation." These are the considerations which he has in mind when he concludes (*loc. cit.*) that it is not "less intelligible, or less conformable to experience to say, that the world arose by vegetation from a seed shed by another world, than to say that it arose from a divine reason or contrivance." *Cf.* Hume's summary of Strato's argument, above, pp. 35-6.

pour nous autres nous n'y croyons guère. Hume dîna avec une grande compagnie chez le Baron d'Holbach. Il était assis à côté du Baron ; on parla de la religion naturelle : " Pour les Athées," disait Hume, " je ne crois pas qu'il en existe ; je n'en ai jamais vu." " Vous avez été un peu malheureux," répondit l'autre, " vous voici à table avec dix-sept pour la première fois." [1]

The greater freedom of thought and expression in Paris can hardly have been without effect upon Hume ; and we are probably safe in concluding that though to the end he saw no reason for adopting ' theism ' as a satisfactory title for the teaching which he was advocating, he yet came to recognize that he was farther removed from anything properly describable as theism than he had previously realized. The new passages introduced in the final revision of the *Dialogues*, in 1776—if I am correct in so dating their new *third* ending [2]— are certainly much more explicit in their *negative* teaching than any of the passages of earlier date. What he continued to entitle his theism is little more than a recognition of the mysterious character of all ultimate modes of existence, and a refusal to allow as either possible or needful any asseverations of a more positive nature.

Such other evidence as has been cited [3] in support of the view that Hume in his own private thinking held to a theism of a less shadowy, more orthodox type, consists in reports, generally at second or third hand, of his conversation. They are not such as need call for any modification in the views to which we are led by his published correspondence and by his other writings. Even allowing that his words have been correctly reported, they indicate, at most, that like ordinary mortals he had moods in which he questioned both the doubts and the convictions to which he was yet prepared to give his considered assent.

We may now pass to a second, further set of conditions which influenced Hume in his retention of orthodox language. Toleration, as it arose in Protestant countries, was, as historians

---

[1] *Memoirs of Sir S. Romilly* (1840), vol. i, p. 179. Letter to the Rev. John Roget (November 16, 1781). Can this be what Hume had in mind when, speaking of the men of letters in Paris, he writes to the Rev. Hugh Blair : " It would give you & Jardine & Robertson great Satisfaction to find that there is not a single Deist among them "? (*Letters*, vol. i, p. 419.)

[2] *Cf.* below, pp. 70, 93–5

[3] *Cf.* Burton, *Life of David Hume*, vol. i, pp. 291–4, vol. ii, p. 451

are agreed in recognizing, a policy due to necessity and not to choice. Lutheran and Reformed Church teaching did not in this matter differ from that of the Roman Catholic Church. A questioning of the tenets of the Faith was regarded as impiety, and the State, a divinely sanctioned institution, as being in duty bound to use the weapon of the flesh in its repression. But owing to causes which neither Church nor State had been able to control, there had arisen in the Protestant countries a diversity of sects ; even within the State churches differences in doctrinal teaching had made their appearance ; and as a consequence there was a proportionately great extension of the field of free discussion. The relaxation tended steadily to increase, until, when Hume was writing his *Dialogues*, freedom of discussion in Britain was complete, subject only to certain agreed limitations—that there be no advocacy of atheism and no direct challenge to the supreme claims of the Christian Faith. Subject to these limitations, any and every form of theism, any and every interpretation of Christian teaching, could be freely avowed.

That even the most extreme ' free-thinkers ' could observe these limitations without violation of conscience and without any sense of cowardly shirking confession of the truth as they saw it, was due to yet another change which also arose by modification of the attitude inherited from pre-Reformation days. Within the Roman Church a distinction had been drawn between what was written by clerics for clerics and what was written for a wider public. Views which could rightly be canvassed in the schools, under the cover of a learned language, and in technical terms that could be understood only by the qualified few, might not be propounded in works likely to fall into the hands of the uninstructed. A writer ventured upon novelties at his own risk ; the Church was there to enter its interdict, should the permitted limits be transgressed. In the Protestant countries, even after the extension of education which followed upon the conviction that direct access to the Bible was the right of all, there still remained a great gulf between the educated few and those who had little else than the rudiments, if even these ; and accordingly, notwithstanding the adoption of the vernaculars in place of Latin and the growth of a considerable body of lay readers, the old-time principle continued to be observed—though with this significant difference, that sceptically minded writers tended to include the bulk of the clergy among those who must not be addressed save in the approved terms. In Hume we find this attitude well defined. He had no expectation that the truth, as he saw it, would be generally adopted. Was not his scepticism due to his aristocratically fastidious insistence on high and exacting standards of argument and evidence, suited, as he has himself so emphatically declared, only to the few ? In all matters which call for definiteness of decision, are not the working conventions of existing society our sole available guides ? And in recognizing them as conventions, not as dogmas, are we not the more likely to use them wisely, as appreciating their limitations and as not looking to them for any greater degree of rationality than conventions can allow ? This sceptically grounded conservatism was so entirely in keeping with all that is most characteristic in Hume's philosophical speculations, and so happily suited to his kindly, easy-going sociable temperament, that we need not be surprised to find him openly avowing it in the frankest terms.

Thus Hume writes (from Paris, 1764) to his friend Edmonstoune—supporting Edmonstoune's advice to a Mr. Vivian, that he adopt the ecclesiastical profession—as follows :

It is putting too great a respect on the vulgar, and on their superstitions, to pique oneself on sincerity with regard to them. Did ever one make it a point of honour to speak truth to children or madmen ? If the thing were worthy being treated gravely, I should tell him, that the Pythian oracle, with the approbation of Xenophon, advised every one to worship the gods—νόμῳ πόλεως. I wish it were still in my power to be a hypocrite in this particular. The common duties of society usually require it ; and the ecclesiastical profession only adds a little more to an innocent dissimulation, or rather simulation, without which it is impossible to pass through the world. Am I a liar, because I order my servant to say, I am not at home, when I do not desire to see company ? [1]

A characteristic passage of similar purport, in which Hume comments on the indiscretions of Frederick the Great in his published verse, occurs in a letter to Lord Minto, dated 1750 :

Throughout the whole, there are Insults on Religion, . . . he ridicules the Idea of a particular Providence, . . . explodes the Belief of a future State, and in plain Terms expresses great Contempt

[1] *Letters*, vol. i, pp. 439-40

of Christianity. . . . These Freedoms surely belong not to any body ; much less, to People that are in such a precarious & dependent Situation as Kings : They ought at least to leave them to their Betters.[1]

In this outward deference to current beliefs and practices Hume was conscious of taking the ancients, especially Cicero, as his model ; and it was a game into which he could zestfully enter. However conformist by temperament, the polite suppressions which the character of his times and the Edinburgh of his day imposed upon him must at times have irked him. He found a needed or at least a welcome relief in the playful sallies with which his writings abound.[2]

Hume's methods of meeting these conformist requirements vary with each of his chief works ; but in the main they are those of Pierre Bayle—namely, to maintain that there is no surer method of rendering religion doubtful than to subject it to the tests of reason and evidence, and at the same time to speak of it as resting solely on revelation. This way of speaking being so usual and so much a matter of agreed convention— and half measures being in this regard worse than useless— Hume had no hesitation in making Philo, the sceptical spokesman in his *Dialogues*, come forward with professions of belief in Revelation !

A person, seasoned with a just sense of the imperfections of natural reason, will fly to revealed truth with the greatest avidity : While the haughty dogmatist, persuaded that he can erect a complete system of theology by the mere help of philosophy, disdains any farther aid, and rejects this adventitious instructor. To be a philo-

---

[1] *Letters*, vol. i, pp. 326–7

[2] *Cf.* Hume's letter in 1761 to his friend, the Rev. Dr. Hugh Blair : " Permit me also the freedom of saying a word to yourself. Whenever I have had the pleasure to be in your company, if the discourse turned upon any common subject of literature or reasoning, I always parted from you both entertained and instructed. But when the conversation was diverted by you from this channel towards the subject of your profession ; tho I doubt not but your intentions were very friendly towards me, I own I never received the same satisfaction : I was apt to be tired, and you to be angry. I would therefore wish for the future, wherever my good fortune throws me in your way, that these topics should be forborne between us. I have, long since, done with all inquiries on such subjects, and am become incapable of instruction ; tho I own no one is more capable of conveying it than yourself." (*Letters*, vol. i, p. 351.) Hume himself seems to have found it difficult to keep to this contract. Writing to Blair from Paris, some four years later, he describes the English as " relapsing fast into the deepest Stupidity, Christianity & Ignorance." (*Letters*, vol. i, p. 498.)

sophical sceptic is, in a man of letters, the first and most essential step towards being a sound, believing Christian.[1]

This is also how Hume concludes his essay *Of Miracles* :

I am the better pleased with the method of reasoning here delivered, as I think it may serve to confound those dangerous friends or disguised enemies to the *Christian Religion*, who have undertaken to defend it by the principles of human reason. Our most holy religion is founded on *Faith*, not on reason ; and it is a sure method of exposing it to put it to such a trial as it is, by no means, fitted to endure.[2]

Similarly, his suppressed essay, *Of the Immortality of the Soul*— an essay quite definitely negative of any such belief—opens with the words :

By the mere light of reason it seems difficult to prove the immortality of the Soul. . . . But in reality, it is the gospel, and the gospel alone, that has brought life and immortality to light.[3]

Though in his *Natural History of Religion* Hume goes to even greater lengths in attacking the traditional religions, including the Calvinist version of Christian teaching, than in any other of his writings except only the *Dialogues*, he is yet careful in so doing to attack not religion but ' superstition ' ; and in order from the start to guard against the charge of seeming to teach sheer atheism, he opens with statements which may well seem to the reader to be so far reassuring :

The whole frame of nature bespeaks an intelligent author ; and no rational enquirer can, after serious reflection, suspend his belief a moment with regard to the primary principles of genuine Theism and Religion.[4]

[1] *Dialogues*, pp. 227–8
[2] *Enquiry*, S.-B., pp. 129–30 ; *Essays*, G. & G., vol. ii, p. 107. " To make this more evident," Hume proceeds to comment on the *Pentateuch*, considered not as the word or testimony of God himself, but as the production of a mere human writer and historian. " Upon reading this book, we find it full of prodigies and miracles . . . I desire any one to lay his hand upon his heart, and after a serious consideration declare whether he thinks that the falsehood of such a book, supported by such a testimony, would be more extraordinary and miraculous than all the miracles it relates ; which is, however, necessary to make it be received, according to the measures of probability above established." Hume then allows himself, with mischievous intent, to parody the Calvinist account of how Faith, a supernaturally conferred gift, must be taken as operating. *Cf.* below, p. 47.
[3] *Essays*, G. & G., vol. ii, p. 399
[4] *Essays*, G. & G., vol. ii, p. 309. *Cf. Treatise*, Appendix, S.-B., p. 633n. ; G. & G., vol. i, p. 456n. " The order of the universe proves an omnipotent mind. . . . Nothing more is requisite to give a foundation to all the articles of religion."

But it is in his *Dialogues concerning Natural Religion* that the problem of expressing his mind freely, while yet not too greatly violating the established code, meets Hume in its most difficult form. For in the *Dialogues* he is doing precisely what was above all else forbidden, namely, to make a direct attack upon the whole theistic position. Hume, in his *Enquiry concerning Human Understanding*,[1] has remarked that though there is no subject to which a greater number of philosophical works are devoted than the existence of God and the fallacious character of all atheistic teaching, their authors yet still dispute whether any man can be so blinded as to be a speculative atheist. Is not this, Hume asks, strange and contradictory?

The knights-errant, who wandered about to clear the world of dragons and giants, never entertained the least doubt with regard to the existence of these monsters.

Hume might have quoted, as typical, the remarks with which Clarke concludes his *Discourse concerning the Being and Attributes of God*. After declaring that the *a priori* argument in proof of God's existence which he has been engaged in expounding [2] is no less certain and undeniable than the proposition that the three angles of a triangle are equal to two right angles, Clarke does indeed add the qualification that those who have not turned their minds to these subjects may easily be ignorant of these infallible truths. But even this minor admission Clarke is careful to set in what he regards as being its proper light, and accordingly proceeds, in immediate sequence, to dwell upon the primacy and the no less coercive validity, of what he alleges to be the universally accepted argument from design. He does so in the following terms :

Yet the notices that God has been pleased to give us of himself, are so many and so obvious ; in the constitution, order, beauty, and harmony, of the several parts of the world ; in the form and structure of our own bodies, and the wonderful powers and faculties of our souls ; in the unavoidable apprehensions of our own minds, and the common consent of all other men ; in everything within us, and everything without us : that no man of the meanest capacity and greatest disadvantages whatsoever, with the slightest and most superficial observation of the works of God, and the lowest and

---

[1] S.-B., p. 149 ; *Essays*, G. & G., vol. ii, p. 122
[2] This is the argument stated and defended by Demea, and criticized by Cleanthes, in Part IX of the *Dialogues*. *Cf.* above, p. 26n.

most obvious attendance to the reason of things, can be ignorant of Him ; but he must be utterly without excuse.

This was the view almost universally held in Hume's day. Whatever supplementary arguments for God's existence might be put forward, the argument from design was regarded as the all-sufficient ground of belief. To attack it was to assault the very citadel of religion, and might not be excused even by the plea that reason and argument were here usurping the prerogatives of faith. The ' argument ' from design was really counted to be not argument, but a body of fact in which the interpretation so patently coincided with the facts as itself to share in their self-evidencing character. To question the argument was to uphold atheism in its most flagrant form, outdoing even the heathen in extremity of disbelief. This, however, was precisely what Hume had set himself to do in the *Dialogues*, to the consternation of his friends. How, while holding tenaciously to his main purpose, he none the less contrived to conform in outward seeming—and as the after-history of the *Dialogues* shows, almost too successfully—to the current conventions, I shall consider shortly.

IV HUME'S ARGUMENT AGAINST MIRACLES, AND HIS CRITICISM OF THE ARGUMENT FROM DESIGN, IN THE *ENQUIRY*

THE systematic argument of the *Dialogues* can best be approached by way of those sections in the *Enquiry concerning Human Understanding* in which Hume has raised theological issues—Section X entitled *Of Miracles*, and Section XI entitled *Of a Particular Providence and of a Future State*. The *Enquiry*, it must be borne in mind, is a rewriting of such parts of his youthful *Treatise of Human Nature* as he considered likely to be of general interest. He was anxious that it should appeal to a wide public, and not merely to students of technical philosophy ; and for this reason he also desired to include certain other sections which, on the eve of publication, he had omitted from the *Treatise*.

In December 1737 Hume—then in London making arrangements for the publication of the *Treatise*—wrote to Henry Home in the following terms :

Having a frankt letter, I was resolved to make use of it ; and accordingly inclose some *Reasonings concerning Miracles*, which I once thought of publishing with the rest, but which I am afraid will give too much offence, even as the world is disposed at present. . . . I am at present castrating my work, that is, cutting off its nobler parts ; that is, endeavouring it shall give as little offence as possible. . . . This is a piece of cowardice, for which I blame myself, though I believe none of my friends will blame me.[1]

The ' nobler parts,' evidently, were theological in character, and of the kind in which the reading public would be likely to be most interested. These he now resolved to include in the *Enquiry*.

Hume's argument against miracles is too closely bound up with the central doctrines of his general philosophy to allow of adequate treatment within the limits imposed by this Introduction. There are, however, some main points which we may note in passing.

1. The section *Of Miracles*, though the most famous, is by

---

[1] *Letters*, vol. i, pp. 24–5, *cf.* p. 361

no means one of the most lucid sections in the *Enquiry*. This
is largely due to its having been composed for insertion in
the *Treatise* and to Hume's retention of much of the original
wording, especially as regards the quite preposterous doctrine
of belief which had inspired it.

This doctrine of belief is modelled on analogies drawn from
the Newtonian physics.[1] (The youthful Hume, ' transported
beyond Measure' by the ' new Scene of Thought,'[2] that had
so suddenly opened to his view, in his ' Ardor ' was carried by
each new influence into some excess.) Gravity is inherent in
each particle of a body ; belief attaches to each observation.
Gravity varies only quantitatively, however different be the
bodies in which it inheres, so " every past experiment has the
same weight, and 'tis only a superior number of them which
can throw the balance on any side."[3] And just as, when
different forces act on a body, the effect is a compounded
effect, so the belief which attends probability is a compounded
belief, the negative beliefs cancelling out an equal number of
positive beliefs, and leaving a preponderant belief corresponding
in degree to the number of the positive units that are left.
Hence Hume's unfortunate emphasis upon mere number of
instances—the feature peculiarly unfavourable to miracles—
in the opening paragraphs of the section, and again towards
the close of the section.[4]

This view of belief is at variance with the distinction, so
much more fundamental in his philosophy, between the wise
and the vulgar. If the vulgar have any one distinctive characteristic, it is, Hume holds, their credulity ;[5] the wise preserve
always a measure of initial scepticism. To the vulgar any
uniformity, however accidental (*i.e.* complexly conditioned)
and temporary, is as good as any other. The wise have learned
that only *invariable* sequences can be regarded as causal and

---

[1] *Cf. Treatise*, Bk. I, Pt. III, sect. xii, S.-B., pp. 132*ff.* ; G. & G., vol. i, pp.
430*ff.*

[2] *Cf.* above, p. 8, and *Letters*, vol. i, p. 13

[3] *Treatise*, Bk. I, Pt. III, sect. xii, S.-B., p. 136 ; G. & G., vol. i, p. 433

[4] In substance, Hume's professedly ' decisive ' argument against miracles is
that a complete induction based on *all* previously experienced instances of the
kind can never be overturned by testimony (itself a mode of experience) to what,
as miraculous, is *ex hypothesi*, contrary to this induction—*i.e.* " a weaker evidence
[numerically considered] can never destroy a stronger."

[5] *Cf. Treatise*, Bk. I, Pt. III, sect. ix, S.-B., p. 112 ; G. & G., vol. i, p. 412 :
" No weakness of human nature is more universal and conspicuous than what
we call *Credulity*."

46

as reliable grounds of belief.[1] Once this all-important lesson has been learnt, a single instance properly determined—as a rule this can be done only experimentally [2]—may cancel out all previous instances of a seemingly contrary character, however numerous. For these seemingly contrary instances are then recognized as having been due, not to any variability in the causal relation, but to the manner in which, in ' the complication of circumstances,' laws, simultaneously operative, have neutralized one another's effects. In holding to his early doctrine of belief, and with it to his ' decisive ' argument against miracles, Hume has done less than justice to his own more considered positions.

2. No passage has been more frequently quoted—it is probably the most notorious passage in all Hume's writings—than the concluding paragraph of this section :

> So that, upon the whole, we may conclude that the *Christian Religion* not only was at first attended with miracles, but even at this day cannot be believed by any reasonable person without one. Mere reason is insufficient to convince us of its veracity : And whoever is moved by *Faith* to assent to it, is conscious of a continued miracle in his own person, which subverts all the principles of his understanding, and gives him a determination to believe what is most contrary to custom and experience.[3]

Unfriendly critics have cited this passage as a shameful example of the scoffing, irresponsible spirit in which Hume deals with sacred topics. In fairness to Hume, they ought, however, to have reminded their readers of what, in Hume's day, was the declared teaching of the Reformed Churches, that Faith (or even an understanding reading of the Scriptures) is impossible save with the aid of a divinely conferred Grace, and that Faith is then operated in a sheerly miraculous manner. This is the teaching upon which Hume has deliberately patterned these concluding sentences ; and in the circumstances his irony is surely not unpardonable. Is it not upon this dogma of a miraculously conferred Grace that the Calvinist doctrines of Predestination and of a double Election, to glory and to wrath, so logically follow ?

[1] *Cf. Treatise*, Bk. I, Pt. III, sects. xii, xiii, xv, S.-B., pp. 131, 149, 173–5 ; G. & G., vol. i, pp. 429, 445, 466–8 ; *Enquiry*, S.-B., pp. 58, 87 ; *Essays*, G. & G., vol. ii, pp. 48–9, 71.
[2] *Cf. Treatise*, S.-B., p. 175 ; G. & G., p. 468
[3] *Enquiry*, S.-B., p. 131 ; *Essays*, G. & G., vol. ii, p. 108

3. Hume lays himself open to misunderstanding by the careless and loose manner in which he speaks of miracles being ' a violation ' of the laws of nature. As Leslie Stephen has pointed out,[1] the very purpose of Hume's argument is to set aside as irrelevant the question as to the *a priori* possibility of miracles, and the endless discussions as to the meaning of natural laws, and the possibility of their being modified. The term ' law '—it should be noted—Hume uses in the plural, as part of the phrase " the laws of nature," [2] and by their violation he intends to signify solely what is contrary to " the common course of *nature*," *i.e.* in theological phraseology, the *supernatural*. " Nothing is esteemed a miracle, if it ever happen in the common course of nature," [3] No event, he adds, however unusual or wonderful, is, merely for that reason, rightly describable as miraculous. In giving a second ' accurate ' definition of miracle, as being what is due to the particular volition of a Divine Being, Hume is therefore only stating more explicitly what, from the start, he has been intending to convey, though certainly not very successfully.[4]

4. Hume never dreamt of denying that man and the other animals can actively intervene to alter the course which natural happenings would otherwise take, *e.g.* men in building a ship, birds in building a nest. As belonging to nature they have a share in determining the conditions under which the laws of nature are to be allowed to operate. The inviolability, *i.e.* invariablity, of the laws, as laws, is not thereby called in question. Nor would a Divine Being, *if operating in a similar manner*, in any way transgress them. If, however, God has to be conceived as non-animal, purely spiritual, then in Hume's view his existence will have to be regarded as non-natural, and his interventions as miraculously altering the course of nature.

---

[1] *English Thought in the Eighteenth Century*, vol. i, p. 339

[2] The only exception is in his use of ' law,' in the singular, in his second definition of miracle : there, however, the *supernatural* character of the transgression is what is emphasized, *i.e.* that it is the *course* of nature, not this or that law, which is being violated.

[3] *Enquiry*, S.-B., p. 115 ; *Essays*, G. & G., vol. ii, p. 93. *Cf.* Cicero, *De Divinatione*, xxviii.

[4] Samuel Clarke in his second *Discourse*, 1705 (7th ed. 1727, p. 382), combines the two methods of definition : " It is a work effected in a manner unusual, or different from the common and regular method of providence, by the intervention either of God himself, or of some intelligent agent superior to man, for the proof or evidence of some particular doctrine, or in attestation to the authority of some particular person."

5. Notwithstanding Hume's own contrary claims, the strength of his position lies not in the more formal features of the ' decisive ' and ' elegant ' argument to which he attaches such weight—though deluded by no sanguine hopes of converting the multitude to its acceptance [1]—but in the circumstantial evidence which he adduces as *corroborative* of it : (*a*) that it is among ignorant and barbarous nations that miracles most abound ; (*b*) that the passions of surprise and wonder to which they appeal are agreeable emotions, and when joined with a spirit of religion lead to all manner of excesses ; (*c*) that since the purpose of each miracle is to establish the particular system to which it is attributed, and since in matters of religion what is different is contrary, the miracles of any one religion have to be counted as evidence against the credibility of the miracles of all the others.

The balance of this evidence is, Hume claims, so over-whelming that the proper and legitimate attitude to adopt to any particular alleged miracle—if it be not merely the ' unusual,' and therefore such as calls for investigation in regard to its unknown *natural* causes—is as to why it should have come to be believed, not whether it has indeed happened. The credulity of men is so common a phenomenon, and is so forced upon our attention in the course of experience, that this *general* policy is, in actual fact, the policy followed even by those who are prepared to make an exception in favour of some one traditional system. It represents the attitude which they automatically adopt towards the alleged miracles of all the other competing systems.[2]

6. But that in coming to this conclusion Hume has been influenced by considerations additional to any which he has

---

[1] *Cf. Enquiry*, S.-B., p. 110 ; *Essays*, G. & G., vol. ii, p. 89. " I flatter myself, that I have discovered an argument . . . which, if just, will, with the wise and learned, be an everlasting check to all kinds of superstitious delusion, and con-sequently, will be useful so long as the world endures. For so long, I presume, will the accounts of miracles and prodigies be found in all history, sacred and profane."

[2] Hume, commenting on the manuscript of George Campbell's *Dissertation on Miracles*, writes to the Rev. Hugh Blair (1761) : " Does a man of sense run after every silly tale of witches or hobgoblins or fairies, and canvass particularly the evidence ? I never knew any one, that examined and deliberated about nonsense who did not believe it before the end of his inquiries." *Letters*, vol. i, p. 350. George Campbell (1719-96) was Professor of Divinity and Principal of Marischal College, Aberdeen. This *Dissertation on Miracles* was shown to Hume in manuscript by the Rev. Hugh Blair in 1761, the year prior to its publication. For Hume's comments *cf. Letters*, vol. i, pp. 348-51, 360-1.

cited in this section is clear in view of the yet stronger assertion
which he proceeds to make : namely, that the very circumstance that miracles originate in a ' system of religion ' is " full
proof of a cheat, and sufficient, with all men of sense, not only
to make them reject the fact, but even reject it without farther
examination." [1] " Violations of truth are more common in
the testimony concerning religious miracles, than in that
concerning any other matter of fact." [2] And he quotes Francis
Bacon as saying that : " Above all, every relation [regarding
extraordinary happenings in nature] must be considered as
suspicious, which depends in any degree on religion, as the
prodigies of Livy." Thus, evidently, Hume's treatment of
miracles has a premiss to which he has not in this section
referred—namely, *that we have, and can have, no grounds either in
reason or in experience for postulating the kind of God to whom alone
the Scriptural or other miracles can fittingly be ascribed.* This, and not
the sheerly logical considerations bearing on belief, testimony,
and evidence generally, is the context within which the issues
regarding miracles properly arise. To supply this context
would, however, have left his argument very much in the air.
Hume's problem, therefore, in the *Enquiry*, was to introduce it
without yet saying too much. How was this to be done ?

Section XI of the *Enquiry* gives Hume's answer to this
question. [3] When it is carefully studied, two points become
clear :

[1] *Enquiry*, S.-B., pp. 128–9 ; *Essays*, G. & G., vol. ii, pp. 106–7
[2] *Cf.* Hume's letter of June 7, 1762, to George Campbell (*Letters*, vol. i, p. 361) :
" It may perhaps amuse you to learn the first hint, which suggested to me that
argument which you have so strenuously attacked. I was walking in the cloisters
of the Jesuits' College of La Flèche . . . and engaged in a conversation with
a Jesuit of some parts and learning, who was relating to me, and urging some
nonsensical miracle performed in their convent, when I was tempted to dispute
against him ; and as my head was full of the topics of my *Treatise of Human Nature,*
which I was at that time composing, this argument immediately occurred to me,
and I thought it very much gravelled my companion ; but at last he observed
to me, that it was impossible for that argument to have any solidity, because
it operated equally against the Gospel as the Catholic miracles ; —*which observation
I thought proper to admit as a sufficient answer.*" (Italics not in text.)
[3] As Sir Leslie Stephen (*English Thought in the Eighteenth Century,* vol. i, p. 310)
has pointed out : " So exclusively has attention been fixed upon these particular
pages [or miracles], that few of [Hume's] assailants take any notice even of the
immediately succeeding essay, which forms with it a complete and connected
argument." This criticism would seem to apply even to Selby-Bigge. For
though he has noted the close connexion between Sections X and XI, he yet
suggests (*cf.* his Introduction to the *Enquiry*, pp. xviii–xix), surely on very insufficient grounds, that Hume has inserted these theological sections in the *Enquiry*

1. That the main argument of the section—occupying no less than 14 of its 17 pages—is not what its title [1] would lead us to expect, a discussion of the doctrines of a particular providence and of an after-life, but a discussion of " the chief or sole argument for a divine existence," the argument from design. What Hume seeks to show is that this argument, *even if its own explicit assumptions be not questioned*, fails to establish the kind of Deity that belief in a particular providence (or in miracles) must require us to suppose. But while this limited conclusion is set in the foreground of the argument, as in the title of the section, the argument itself has other, much more wide-reaching consequences—later faithfully dealt with in the *Dialogues*—and it is these that really form its main burden.

2. How conscious Hume is that he is attacking the very citadel of religion, and not merely certain of its outworks, is shown by the extreme circumspection with which he has found it advisable to proceed. Departing from the methods of direct exposition employed in the rest of the *Enquiry*, he resorts, in this one section, to dialogue form ; and, to secure a quite free hand, goes out of his way to disavow, at the start, all personal responsibility for the difficulties raised.

I was lately engaged in conversation with a friend who loves sceptical paradoxes ; where, though he advanced many principles, of which I can by no means approve, yet as they seem to be curious, and to bear some relation to the chain of reasoning carried on throughout this enquiry, I shall here copy them from my memory as accurately as I can, in order to submit them to the judgement of the reader.[2]

Since, then, Hume gives in this section his first treatment of the argument from design, and in doing so sets it in a perspective which shows his line of approach to the problems of the *Dialogues*, it is essential that we should consider it in some detail.

The sceptical friend is made to suppose himself for the

from irrelevant and unworthy motives, "to disturb 'the zealots' at all costs." *Cf.* A. E. Taylor, *Philosophical Essays* (1934), pp. 331–2. *Cf.* Hume's letters quoted above, pp. 8–9, 57.

[1] Hume had difficulty in finding a title for this section which would not inconveniently emphasize its real character. His first choice of title was : " Of the Practical Consequences of Natural Theology." This he changed to the present title, probably revising the section somewhat to suit. Even so, it is misleading : providence is barely referred to, and the after life is touched on only by implication.

[2] *Enquiry*, S.-B., p. 132 ; *Essays*, G. & G., vol. ii, p. 109

moment to be Epicurus, and to maintain that a wise magistrate can never justly be jealous of free philosophical discussion, not even when it goes the length of " denying a divine existence, and consequently a providence and a future state." [1] Hume, in turn, is supposed to stand for the Athenian people, or rather for " the more philosophical part of [it], such as might be supposed capable of understanding [Epicurus'] arguments." [2]

Hume's friend, thus speaking as Epicurus, starts from what he takes to be the point of view of his audience, namely, that the sole or chief argument for a divine existence is derived from the order, beauty, and wise arrangement of the universe, and that from such order we can argue to ' project and fore-thought ' in its Author.

How far, Epicurus asks, will this mode of argument take us ? The argument is from the existence of a particular effect to the existence of a cause sufficient to produce it. The cause is supposed to be known solely through the effect ; and we are not, therefore, justified in ascribing to it any qualities beyond what are requisite to produce the effect. A body of ten ounces raised in a balance may serve as proof that the counterbalancing weight exceeds ten ounces ; it can never afford a reason that it exceeds a hundred. The cause, being proportioned to the effect, cannot be inferred to be a cause capable of yet other and greater effects. This, however, is what is done in the ' religious hypothesis.' No sooner have the gods been inferred to possess the degree of power, intelligence, and benevolence which is exhibited in their workmanship, than ' exaggeration and flattery ' are called in to supply the defects of the argument. The ascent of reason is aided by the wings of imagination. We mount to Jupiter, and having done so we proceed to argue that the present effects are not entirely worthy of his glorious attributes, and that " he must produce something greater and more perfect than the present scene of things, which is so full of ill and disorder." We have reversed the order of the pro-fessed argument. What, at the start, is recognized as being the only evidence is now alleged to be but a minor part of a greater whole—" but a porch which leads to a great and vastly different building." Accordingly, we have still to ask why

---

[1] *Enquiry*, S.-B., p. 133 ; G. & G., p. 110
[2] *Ibid.*, S.-B., p. 134 ; G. & G., p. 110

we ascribe to the cause any qualities which do not appear in the effect. For unless we have added something to the attributes of the cause beyond what appears in the effect, how can we, with propriety, add something to the effect in order to render it more worthy of the cause ? To conceive this life as merely a passage to something farther, the present scene of things as merely a porch which leads to a vastly different building, is mere possibility and hypothesis ; no such conclusion has been or can be established. Even the conclusion which is established—*if the validity of the argument from design is granted*—namely, that there exists an Author of nature, is an entirely *useless* conclusion.[1]

[This religious hypothesis] is useless ; because our knowledge of this cause being derived entirely from the course of nature, we can never, according to the rules of just reasoning, return back from the cause with any new inference, or making additions to the common and experienced course of nature, establish any new principles of conduct and behaviour.[2]
Why torture your brain to justify the course of nature upon suppositions, which, for aught you know, may be entirely imaginary, and of which there are to be found no traces in the course of nature ? [3]
The experienced train of events is the great standard, by which we all regulate our conduct. Nothing else can be appealed to in the field, or in the senate. Nothing else ought ever to be heard of in the school, or in the closet. In vain would our limited understanding break through those boundaries, which are too narrow for our fond imagination.[4]

At this point Hume intervenes to raise an objection. Allowing that experience is indeed the only standard of our judgement in this, as in other questions of fact, why may we not argue as the religious hypothesis requires ? If we see a half-finished building, surrounded by heaps of stone, mortar, and all the instruments of masonry, may we not infer that in due course it will be finished and complete ? If we see a human footprint on the seashore, may we not conclude that a man has passed that way, and has also left the traces of the other

---

[1] *Enquiry*, S.-B., p. 142 ; G. & G., p. 117. It is elsewhere alleged to be an *uncertain* conclusion, but this is an anticipation of argument not yet given, and is unconnected with the premises thus far allowed.
[2] *Loc. cit.*
[3] *Ibid.*, S.-B., p. 139 ; G. & G., p. 114
[4] *Ibid.*, S.-B., p. 142 ; G. & G., p. 117

foot, though effaced by the winds and the waves ? [1]   Why may we not employ the same method of reasoning in regard to the order of nature ?   Why embrace the one inference and reject the other ?

To this Hume's friend makes reply :   the *infinite* difference in the two subjects.   In works of human art and contrivance, we can advance from the effect to the cause, and having done so return back from the cause to make new inferences concerning the effect.   For man is a being regarding whom we have other knowledge ;   we know his motives and designs, his projects and experiences, and that these have a certain coherence according to the laws which nature has established for the government of such a creature.

When, therefore, we find that any work has proceeded from the skill and industry of man ;   as we are otherwise acquainted with the nature of the animal, we can draw a hundred inferences concerning what may be expected from him ;   and these inferences will all be founded in experience and observation.[2]

Similarly, the print of a foot proves, from our other experiences concerning the *usual* figure and members of that species of animal, that there was probably another foot which also left its imprint, though effaced by time and other accidents.[3]

In respect to the works of nature, on the other hand, we are not in a position to reason in this manner.   The Deity is known only by his productions, and is a *single* being, *not comprehended under any species or genus.*   We are inferring a particular, unique cause, to account for a particular, unique effect ;   and without ' licence of conjecture '—there being no *previous* or *other* experience to fall back upon, as there is in the case of man and his handiwork—we have no basis for adding to nature, beyond what nature is found to be.

---

[1] Hume, we may presume, had read *Robinson Crusoe*, which had appeared in 1719.

[2] *Enquiry*, S.-B., p. 144 ; G. & G., p. 118

[3] *Cf.* J. S. Mill, *Three Essays on Religion* (1874), p. 168 : " A very little consideration, however, suffices to show that though [the argument from design] has some force, its force is very generally overrated.   Paley's illustration of a watch puts the case much too strongly.   If I found a watch on an apparently desolate island, I should indeed infer that it had been left there by a human being ; but the inference would not be from marks of design, but because I already knew from direct experience that watches are made by men.   I should draw the inference no less confidently from a footprint, or from any relic however insignificant which experience has taught me to attribute to man : as geologists infer the past existence of animals from coprolites, though no one sees marks of design in a coprolite."

What we really do, when we so argue, is tacitly to consider ourselves as in the place of the Supreme Being, and to conclude that he will, on every occasion, observe the conduct which we ourselves, in his situation, would regard as reasonable and eligible. But this is only possible so long as we refuse to recognize that in the ordinary course of nature almost everything is regulated by principles and maxims very different from ours, and that its Author discovers himself only by some faint traces or outlines beyond which we have no authority to ascribe to him any attribute or perfection.

Hume agrees that this is indeed a genuine ' difficulty ' ; and then, in the concluding paragraph of this section, speaking in his own person, he proposes, ' without insisting upon it,' yet another difficulty—a difficulty which is a direct and obvious corollary of the conclusions arrived at in the earlier sections of the *Enquiry*. Is it ever possible, he asks, to know a cause from inspection of an effect, taken merely in and by itself? Prior to experience, anything, conceivably, may be the cause of anything else. Is not constant conjunction of events, both of which have to be directly experienced, or at least to be analogous with experienced events, the only legitimate ground for inferring either from the presence of the other ? These conditions are absent when, in the manner of the antagonists of Epicurus (*i.e.* in the manner of the argument from design), we suppose the universe, an effect quite simple and unparalleled, to be proof of a Deity, a cause no less simple and unparalleled. In causal inference we are dealing with *species* of objects, *i.e.* with repeated conjunction of multiple instances which are either exactly similar or in some degree analogous to their attributes. When we are faced by something which *belongs to no species*, direct observation and experience do not by themselves suffice to carry us beyond it ; and, in view of its *uniqueness*, analogy is not available.

If experience and observation and analogy be, indeed, the only guides which we can reasonably follow in inferences of this nature ; both the effect and cause must bear a similarity and resemblance to other effects and causes, which we know, and which we have found, in many instances, to be conjoined with each other. I leave it to your own reflection to pursue the consequences of this principle.[1]

---

[1] *Enquiry*, S.-B., p. 148 ; *Essays*, G. & G., vol. ii, p. 122. *Cf.* J. S. Mill, *Three Essays on Religion*, pp. 168–9 (in direct continuation of the passage quoted above,

This difficulty, it may be noted, raises an issue much more fundamental than that of Hume's sceptical friend. For it does not merely concern certain of the consequences generally drawn from a conclusion which the argument from design is allowed to have established ; it offers challenge to the argument in any and every form. It raises the question whether the argument from design, as an argument from analogy, can allow of being formulated in a tenable manner. This, indeed, as we shall find, is the thesis with which the *Dialogues* are primarily concerned, and to which they give what amounts to a definitely negative answer. Notwithstanding the disavowal with which the section opens, this last difficulty represents for Hume the crux of the theological situation. The argument from design is, he suggests, the ' religious hypothesis ' *par excellence,* and yet is not defensible.

p. 54*n.*) : " The evidence of design in creation can never reach the height of direct induction ; it amounts only to the inferior kind of inductive evidence called analogy. Analogy agrees with induction in this, that they both argue that a thing known to resemble another in certain circumstances (call those circumstances A and B) will resemble it in another circumstance (call it C). But the difference is that in induction, A and B are known, by a previous comparison of many instances, to be the very circumstance on which C depends, or with which it is in some way connected. When this has not been ascertained, the argument amounts only to this, that since it is not known with which of the circumstances existing in the known case C is connected, they may as well be A and B as any others ; and therefore there is a greater probability of C in cases where we know that A and B exist, than in cases where we know nothing at all. The argument is of a weight very difficult to estimate at all, and impossible to estimate precisely."

WHEN Hume, in the *Dialogues*, set himself to substantiate this criticism, he was well aware how invidious a task it would prove to be. Nor were his friends backward in dissuading him from it. Adam Smith, the friend whose advice he most valued, was no less discouraging than the others.[1] Hume so far yielded to their remonstrances as to defer publication of the *Dialogues* in the years following upon their completion. (They were, it would seem, completed some time in the period 1751–7, *i.e.* in his great productive period, when he was between forty and fifty years of age.[2]) But we hear of Hume revising them in 1761 ; and on the sudden failure of his health in 1775 they became the chief preoccupation of his remaining energies. He decided upon immediate publication. His bodily weakness increased, however, too rapidly ; and instead he had to content himself with the very carefully conceived precautions by which he made quite certain that they would not be suppressed after his death. " The work penned in the full vigour of his faculties, comes to us with the sanction of his mature years, and his approval when he was within sight of the grave." [3]

Hume presents his argument through the mouths of three protagonists, Cleanthes, Philo, and Demea ; and the conversations are reported by Pamphilus, who, in introducing his report, remarks on " the accurate philosophical turn of Cleanthes," " the careless scepticism of Philo," and " the rigid orthodoxy of Demea." This already indicates that Cleanthes is intended to be ' the hero ' of the *Dialogues* ; and the problem of their interpretation is largely the question how this intention is to be understood. Is it to be counted among the devices whereby Hume masks his batteries, that they may be the more effectively brought into action in demolishing the positions which Cleanthes is defending ? Or are we to agree with Pamphilus' verdict at the close of the discussion ? :

So I confess, that, upon a serious review of the whole, I cannot but think that Philo's principles are more probable than Demea's ; but that those of Cleanthes approach still nearer to the truth.[1]

One fundamental point may be taken as agreed. Hume's own teaching is not presented through any one of the characters ; it is developed in and through the argument as a whole, something of his own beliefs being put into the mouths of all three. But this takes us only a very little way towards a solution of our problem. Each protagonist, though incidentally saying much that one or both of the other participants may approve, stands for positions which exclude one another. Such common ground as they may share is certainly Hume's own. But when they differ, and they do so very radically, where does Hume himself come in ? Does he then agree with Cleanthes against Philo, or with Philo against Cleanthes ?

Dugald Stewart, who, like so many of his contemporaries, refused to consider as even possible that Divine Existence could seriously be questioned, interpreted the *Dialogues* as a straightforward document in which every statement is to be accepted at its face value, and Pamphilus' crowning of Cleanthes as victor in the discussion as therefore representing Hume's own view. " It must always be remembered that Cleanthes is the hero of the Dialogue, and is to be considered as speaking Mr. Hume's real opinions. I think it fair to recall this to the reader's memory, as the reasonings of Philo have often been quoted, as parts of Hume's philosophical system, although the words of Shylock or Caliban might, with equal justice, be quoted as speaking the real sentiments of Shakespeare." [2] In recent years the tendency has very definitely been to take a somewhat similar view, though in more guarded terms. Bruce M'Ewen, for instance, speaks of Pamphilus' verdict as being

---

[1] *Dialogues*, p. 228

[2] *Collected Works* (1854), vol. i, p. 605. *Cf.* Burton, *Life of David Hume* (1846), vol. i, p. 329 : " It is with [Cleanthes] that the author shows most sympathy, very nearly professing that the doctrine announced by Cleanthes is his own." The reviewer of the *Dialogues*, in the year of their appearance, in the *Monthly Review* (London, December 1779, vol. lxi, p. 343), takes the directly opposite view : " Philo is the hero of the piece "—only, however, in order to support (p. 354) the accusations against Hume to which Beattie and others had already given general currency: " His love of paradox, his inordinate pursuit of literary fame continued, whilst life continued ; it is scarce possible, indeed, with the utmost stretch of candour and charity, to assign any other motives for publishing what must shock the sense and virtue of his fellow-mortals, or to reconcile it with the character of a good citizen, and a friend to mankind."

Hume's "last utterance in speculation."[1]   This in substance
is also the interpretation of the *Dialogues* adopted by Pringle-
Pattison,[2] A. E. Taylor,[3] C. W. Hendel,[4] Rudolf Metz,[5] Laing,[6]
and André Leroy.[7]   As already indicated, I am unable to agree
with this reading of the *Dialogues* ; and my reasons can best
be given through an analysis of the total argument, noting
what each of the protagonists contributes to the discussion,
and what happens to their several contributions in the final
section.   I give this critical analysis in an appendix ;[8] and
must refer my readers to it for the more complete evidence
supporting my conclusions.   These I shall now state in a somewhat summary fashion, with no more than a general indication
of their main grounds.   I shall contend that Philo, from start
to finish, represents Hume ; and that Cleanthes can be regarded as Hume's mouthpiece only in those passages in which
he is explicitly agreeing with Philo, or in those other passages
in which, while refuting Demea, he is also being used to
prepare the way for one or other of Philo's independent
conclusions.[9]

[1] In his edition of the *Dialogues* (1907), p. cviii
[2] *Cf. Idea of God* (1917), p. 15 : "The consensus of passages from [Hume's]
various writings puts beyond reasonable doubt his sincere adherence to what he
calls ' genuine Theism ' and his acceptance of the argument from design as its
rational basis." This, in essentials, is the view taken by Friedrich Jodl (*Leben und
Philosophie David Humes*, 1872, p. 175), and by W. Windelband (*A History of Philosophy*, Eng. trans., 1896, pp. 494, 498).
[3] *Cf.* article on ' Theism ' in *Hasting's Encyclopedia of Religion and Ethics* (1921),
vol. xii, p. 273 : "Hume abstains from indicating his own sympathies except
in the final sentence, where he suggests that the ' opinions ' (he is careful not to
say ' the arguments ') of the ' natural theologian ' Cleanthes probably come
nearer to the truth than those of Philo, and those of Philo than those of Demea."
Pamphilus, it is true, does not use the term ' arguments,' but he also does not
use the term ' opinions ' ; he speaks of ' principles ' and of "the reasonings
of that day."
[4] *Cf. Studies in the Philosophy of David Hume* (1925), pp. 306–7 : "We can
identify the author only with ' Pamphilus '. . . . It is this Pamphilus who passes
the final judgment, after making significant comments from time to time throughout the course of the discussion."
[5] Metz, in the main, here follows Hendel. *Cf. David Hume, Leben und Philosophie*
(1929), pp. 345*ff.* Laird, *Hume's Philosophy of Human Nature* (1932), p. 297, is
non-committal.
[6] *David Hume* (1932), p. 179 : "Cleanthes is Hume "
[7] *La Critique et la Religion chez David Hume* (1934), pp. 289–93, 369
[8] Appendix D below, pp. 97 *sqq.*
[9] Here I find myself in some measure of agreement with T. H. Huxley (*Hume*,
1887, chap. viii) and with Sir Leslie Stephen (*English Thought in the Eighteenth
Century*, 1876, 3rd ed., 1902, chap. vi—a work which, after half a century, is still
without a rival). Huxley is somewhat non-committal in his interpretation of the
Dialogues. Stephen gives an admirable general discussion of Hume's theological

Many of the main features in the outward structure of the *Dialogues* were suggested to Hume by Cicero's *De Natura Deorum*. He borrowed from it much more than merely the dialogue form.

1. The three protagonists in Cicero's dialogue are Cotta the Academic or Sceptic, Balbus the Stoic, representative of orthodoxy, and Velleius the Epicurean. Philo, in Hume's *Dialogues*, corresponds to Cotta, and Cleanthes to Balbus. Hume's choice of the names 'Philo' and 'Cleanthes' was probably determined by the circumstance that Philo was the name of Cotta's teacher, and that Cleanthes was one of Balbus' masters in philosophy.

2. Cicero prefaces his dialogue by an introduction in which, speaking in his own person, he anticipates objections to the free discussion of so sacred a subject. Though himself, like Cotta, an Academic—having " learnt from the same Philo to be certain of nothing "—he is, he states, present at the discussion only " as an auditor, with an impartial and unbiased mind." Also, at the close of the dialogue Cotta is made to say that there is nothing he desires more than to be confuted, that he has been giving only his private sentiments, and that he is very sensible of Balbus' great superiority in argument. But Cicero is not content with thus weighting the conclusion (though not the argument) in favour of orthodox teaching. He concludes the dialogue with these words : " The situation when we broke up was as follows. Velleius thought Cotta's views the truer ; while I, on the other hand, thought that Balbus' views came nearer to what looked like the truth." [1] In adopting these devices, Hume modifies them in a manner which enables him to preserve his anonymity. He invents a character, Pamphilus, specially for the purpose of reporting the discussion and of passing judgment upon the parts played by the three participants.

3. Cicero tempers the rigour and scope of his argument by suggesting that the subject of the discussion is not so much the *existence* of the Gods as " that most obscure and difficult

writings. Neither Huxley nor Stephen favours the identification of Hume's positions with those of Cleanthes. Friedrich Paulsen in the introduction to his translation of the *Dialogues* (Leipzig, 3rd ed., 1905, pp. 19–20) identifies Hume with Philo, but also without discussion of the detail of the argument.

[1] " Haec cum essent dicta, ita discessimus, ut Velleio Cottae disputatio verior, mihi Balbi ad veritatis similitudinem videretur esse propensior."

question concerning the *nature* of the Gods," [1] and especially whether they intervene in the government of the world and of human life. Hume employs this distinction in the same general manner as Cicero, as tempering for the ordinary reader the force and proper scope of the sceptical objections. But Hume is also—as befitted the more exacting character of the orthodoxies of his day—more explicit and emphatic in the terms which he uses in stating the distinction :

What truth so obvious, so certain, as the *being* of a God ? . . . What truth so important as this, which is the ground of all our hopes, the surest foundation of morality, the firmest support of society, and the only principle which ought never to be a moment absent from our thoughts and meditations ? But in treating of this obvious and important truth ; what obscure questions occur, concerning the *nature* of that divine Being ; his attributes, his decrees, his plan of providence ? [2]

These sentiments are appropriately placed in the mouth of Pamphilus.

By means, then, of these devices, and by others which I shall note as we proceed, the reader is left free to be his own judge of the total argument ; and every excuse is made ready for him, should he be unconvinced and desirous of continuing in his customary beliefs.

In adopting Cicero's device of introductory and concluding comment, Hume, as we have noted, modifies it in one important respect. He abstains from speaking in his own person. Pamphilus, who introduces and alone passes comment on the outcome of the discussion, is described as standing in such close personal relations to Cleanthes, as a ' pupil,' and ' almost as an adopted son,' that he can fittingly be represented as continuing, like his Master, to be unconvinced by Philo's arguments and as therefore judging Cleanthes to be victor in the discussion. Thus, at least for the *narrator* of the *Dialogues*, Cleanthes is ' the hero.' This, however, is quite in keeping with the view that it is through Philo, not through Cleanthes, that Hume's own personal views are being conveyed. For if Hume's purpose be to show the insufficiency of the argument from design, a chief danger against which he had to guard was lest his argument should become so one-sided that the dramatic interest

[1] Bk. I, 1   [2] *Dialogues*, p. 128

of the *Dialogues* would be destroyed.[1] To prevent this, Hume has accordingly given Demea and Cleanthes a larger share in the argument than in conformity with their ways of thinking they could rightly claim. But whereas he feels free to allow Demea to discredit his contentions by the extremes to which he carries them and through the obviousness of the difficulties in which he lands himself, the counter-policy is followed in the case of Cleanthes. Compliments, by no means deserved, are paid him from time to time, expectations being aroused in the reader that Cleanthes has stronger arguments in reserve than any which he has so far employed. And finally, when there is danger that the attentive reader may be coming to recognize that Cleanthes, like Demea, is really being played with or at least humoured by Philo, Hume goes out of his way to conceal the full force of Philo's attack. These points we may now consider in more detail.

We may first observe how greatly both Demea and Cleanthes are lacking in intellectual self-consistence. Demea appears in the first sections as joining with Philo in maintaining the incapacity of reason in questions of theology ; and yet later (in Part IX) he is introduced as professing to be able, out of the internal resources of reason, to define and establish at once the existence and the nature of God. Also, though lacking in subtlety of mind and standing for a reactionary theology, he is represented as a student of Malebranche—surely one of the least likely of philosophers to be congenial to his type of mind —and so is made to give Philo an opening by quoting from Malebranche with high approval a passage which is in line with Philo's own ways of thinking, though in a different terminology.[2] No less inconsistent with Demea's philosophical limitations, and with his general outlook, is the exposition which he is made to give of Hume's view of the self : " What is the soul

---

[1] Hume, in his essay, " Of the Rise and Progress of the Arts and Sciences " (*Essays*, G. & G., vol. i, pp. 188–9), maintains that ' a spirit of dialogue ' requires that there be a tolerable equality maintained among the speakers, a " polite deference and respect, which civility obliges us to express or counterfeit towards the persons with whom we converse." He criticizes Cicero for failing to do this ; and suggests that the moderns have here advanced upon the ancients. Hume had already experimented with this literary form, not only in Section XI of the *Enquiry concerning Human Understanding*, but also in *A Dialogue* which he had attached to the first edition (1751) of his *Enquiry concerning the Principles of Morals*. *Cf. Letters*, vol. i, p. 68.

[2] *Dialogues*, pp. 141–2

of man ? A composition of various faculties, passions, sentiments, ideas ; united, indeed, into one self or person, but still
distinct from each other." [1]

Similarly in the case of Cleanthes. Though Hume has
made every effort to dignify the part assigned to him, there
are somewhat narrow limits to what can be done in this regard,
Cleanthes has so little aptitude for philosophical analysis that
he is unable to appreciate, much less to meet, Philo's criticisms.
This is shown, in particular, by the illustrations which he
employs in Part III of the *Dialogues*,[2] in his reply to Philo's
comments upon his assertion that the similarity of the works
of nature to those of human art are " self-evident and undeniable." These illustrations are indeed illustrative ; but
mainly of the difficulties which stand in the way of Cleanthes'
thesis ; and so far from helping to obviate Philo's objections,
they serve only to reinforce them. Yet, on the other hand, it
is the same Cleanthes who in Part IX is made to expound, in
criticism of Demea, Hume's teaching (so fundamental in Hume's
philosophy) in regard to matters of fact and existence, and to
do so with a force and a clarity quite out of keeping with the
general incapacity which he exhibits in the defence of his own
more distinctive doctrines.[3] This lack of psychological and
intellectual self-consistence in Demea and Cleanthes stands in
marked contrast with the very consistent part played by Philo,
from start to finish of the *Dialogues*—allowing, of course, for
the conventionally required concessions in regard to faith and
revelation, at the close of the *Dialogues*.

This contrast is confirmed on study of the dramatic interrelations of the three protagonists. Demea is, in general, used
as a foil to Philo, exhibiting Philo's arguments in their many
points of agreement with orthodox teaching and yet at the
same time serving to show how biased and inconsistent orthodox
teaching has been in the use which it has made of them. When
Demea has been employed to do this so often that the device
is at last becoming obvious to the reader, Cleanthes is allowed
to draw attention to the manner in which Philo has been
amusing himself, and to suggest that

[1] *Dialogues*, p. 159
[2] I have given a statement and criticism of these illustrations below, pp.
101–4.
[3] For another similar instance, *cf. Dialogues*, pp. 199–200, and below, pp.
115, 117.

the injudicious reasoning of our vulgar theology has given him [Philo] but too just a handle of ridicule. The total infirmity of human reason, the absolute incomprehensibility of the divine nature, the great and universal misery and still greater wickedness of men ; these are strange topics surely to be so fondly cherished by orthodox divines and doctors.[1]

Demea makes no reply, and soon " took occasion, on some pretence or other, to leave the company." [2] Meantime, however, Philo, thanks to Demea's simple-minded co-operation, has without undue self-prominence got the preliminaries and some of the essentials of his argument before the reader.

But while there is no concealment of the uses to which Demea has been put—and there is accordingly no important difference of view possible in regard to him—the relations between Philo and Cleanthes are much more complex, and not always easy of interpretation. The two are represented as standing on a footing of mutual respect and indeed affection —very much the relation in which Hume and Gilbert Elliot stood to one another. There is, however, the same disparity of intellect in both cases ; [3] and Philo practises a carefully observed respect and forbearance towards Cleanthes which would have been condescending and inappropriate had he been dealing with an intellectual equal. Thus while Cleanthes is really *managed* by Philo almost as much as Demea is, the differences in the two cases are due mainly to the fact that since Cleanthes is the advocate of the argument from design —the argument with which the discussion as a whole is concerned—the reader's respect for Cleanthes must be maintained to the very close of the *Dialogues*, otherwise their dramatic balance would be upset.

To achieve this purpose two requirements had to be satisfied. In the first place, Cleanthes must never be represented as having been definitely and finally refuted. Philo is permitted to make his points ; but however cogent and conclusive they may be, something must always be done to preserve Cleanthes' dignity and to cover over his failure to make any effective reply.

[1] *Dialogues*, p. 213   [2] *Ibid., loc. cit.*
[3] Elliot's reply to Hume's appeal for help in strengthening Cleanthes' argument is given in Dugald Stewart's *Collected Works* (vol. i, pp. 605–7). It shows sufficiently clearly that Elliot had no such philosophical aptitudes as would justify Hume's expectation of help in the matter. Notoriously Hume had the kindly failing of over-estimating the abilities of his friends.

To this end Hume employs two special devices. Through the intervention of Demea [1]—aided in some degree by the division of the *Dialogues* into ' Parts '—the discussion is suddenly shifted to some other topic. The other device is that of making Philo speak on the necessary occasions [2] somewhat irresponsibly, and so making it appropriate that Cleanthes should excuse himself from replying, on the plea that Philo is talking " between jest and earnest," propounding " such whimsies as . . . may puzzle, but can never convince us." [3] Hume could play this game with zest ; it afforded him opportunities for those playful sallies, partly ironical, partly mischievous, generally more than half in earnest, with which he was wont to rally his orthodox friends.

To consider now the chief instances of these devices. As Hume has suggested in his letter to Gilbert Elliot,[4] Cleanthes has shot his bolt by the close of Part III, and nothing which he advances later in any way substantially increases the force of his main contentions. It was necessary, therefore, if the dramatic interest of the remaining nine Parts was to be maintained, that Cleanthes' arguments should make as strong and favourable an impression upon the reader as possible ; and even that it be suggested that they are little likely to be overthrown. Accordingly at this point (the close of Part III) Pamphilus, the narrator of the *Dialogues,* is permitted one of his few interventions.

Here I could observe . . . that Philo was a little embarrassed and confounded. But while he hesitated in delivering an answer, luckily for him, Demea broke in upon the discourse, and saved his countenance.[5]

The careful reader can hardly, however, fail to note that in the immediately preceding passages, Cleanthes, so far from replying to the very damaging criticisms that Philo has already made, has by his mode of restating his positions presented them anew in a form to which these criticisms even more forcibly apply. This restatement of Cleanthes' positions has, indeed, been determined throughout, not by any expectation, on Hume's part, of *strengthening* them—as Hume has come to recognize, that is not indeed possible—but for the quite con-

---

[1] *Cf. Dialogues,* pp. 155, 188, 212 [2] *Ibid.,* pp. 169, 180
[3] *Ibid.,* p. 181 [4] *Letters,* vol. i, p. 157 [5] *Dialogues,* p. 155

trary purpose of leading on to the even more damaging criticisms which Philo still has in reserve. Philo has the situation very well in hand, and can afford to stand back, while Demea entangles Cleanthes in yet further admissions.

Hume's comment on this passage in his letter to Elliot suggests that he was himself somewhat uneasy, lest he had here, perhaps, been too obviously 'artful' in his management of the argument :

> The Instances I have chosen for Cleanthes are, I hope, tolerably happy, and the Confusion in which I represent the Sceptic seems natural. But si quid novisti rectius, &c.[1]

Another instance of this careful and considerate handling of 'the hero' of the *Dialogues* comes in Part VII. As Philo has there pointed out, to maintain that all order in animals proceeds ultimately from design is to beg the question, and moreover to beg it in a manner directly contrary to the evidence of experience. In all cases which we have experienced reason rests on animal conditions, not animal conditions on reason.

> Judging by our limited and imperfect experience, generation has some privileges above reason : For we see every day the latter arise from the former, never the former from the latter. . . . And if he [Cleanthes] pretends to carry on *my* hypothesis a step farther, and to infer design or reason from the great principle of generation, on which I insist ; I may, with better authority, use the same freedom to push farther *his* hypothesis, and infer a divine generation or theogony from his principle of reason. I have at least some faint shadow of experience, which is the utmost that can ever be attained in the present subject. Reason, in innumerable instances, is observed to arise from the principle of generation, and never to arise from any other principle.[2]

Cleanthes is not in a position to answer this argument consistently with his avowed principles (especially with his main principle that " no question of fact can be proved otherwise than by experience," [3]) and nowhere in the subsequent sections of the *Dialogues* does he even attempt to do so. Philo, however, proceeds to provide the necessary excuse by talking in a less responsible manner as follows :

> The Brahmins assert, that the world arose from an infinite spider, who spun this whole complicated mass from his bowels. . . . And were there a planet wholly inhabited by spiders (which is very

possible), this inference would there appear as natural and irrefragable as that which in our planet ascribes the origin of all things to design and intelligence, as explained by Cleanthes. Why an orderly system may not be spun from the belly as well as from the brain, it will be difficult for him to give a satisfactory reason.[1]

This gives Cleanthes the needed excuse for ignoring Philo's preceding argument, and for commenting only on his irresponsibility.

I am not ashamed to acknowledge myself unable, on a sudden, to solve regularly such out-of-the-way difficulties. . . . though I clearly see, in general, their fallacy and error. . . . You must be sensible, that common sense and reason is entirely against you, and that such whimsies as you have delivered, may puzzle, but never can convince us.[2]

Philo's main argument is repeated in Part VIII :

Let us once more put it [the argument from design] to trial. In all instances which we have ever seen, ideas are copied from real objects, and are ectypal, not archetypal, to express myself in learned terms : You reverse this order, and give thought the precedence. In all instances which we have ever seen, thought has no influence upon matter, except where that matter is so conjoined with it, as to have an equal reciprocal influence upon it.[3]

Again Cleanthes makes no attempt to reply ; and this time his failure is covered over partly by Philo's speaking on to the close of the section, and partly by Demea's intervention at the opening of the next section (Part IX). Demea diverts the argument on to a quite new line, by coming forward as a defender of the *a priori* method of reasoning. When Cleanthes next speaks, it is to criticize Demea's argument in collaboration with Philo.

Another crisis in the controversy between Cleanthes and Philo comes at the close of Part X. It is treated, however, in a very different manner. Demea has brought into view yet another set of facts with which the argument from design has to be reconciled : the unhappiness of man and the corruptions of his nature. " The whole earth, believe me, Philo, is cursed and polluted." [4] Philo then joins with Demea in enumerating the evils of animal and human life ; and having done so he turns upon Cleanthes with the question how, in face of all

---

[1] *Dialogues*, pp. 180–1   [2] *Loc. cit.*   [3] *Ibid.*, p. 186   [4] *Ibid.*, p. 194

these facts, he " can assert the *moral* attributes of the Deity, his justice, benevolence, mercy, and rectitude, to be of the same nature with these virtues in human creatures ? " [1] " Here, Cleanthes . . . I triumph." [2]

This is the first time that Philo has come out into the open as victor, and that he should be allowed to do so marks a main turning-point in the discussion. Philo's claim to triumph comes, it may be noted, at the close of Part X ; and in the two remaining Parts he takes complete charge of the argument. Parts XI and XII are practically monologues placed in the mouth of Philo. Demea speaks only a few more sentences, and soon takes occasion to leave. Even Cleanthes ceases to share in the argument. For, though Parts XI and XII are among the longest in the *Dialogues*, and Part XII actually the longest, Cleanthes occupies less than one and a half pages out of the 11 pages in Part XI, and less than 3 pages out of the 14 pages in Part XII ; and these he uses solely for repeating his previous assertions, not for rebutting Philo's objections to them.

Further, Hume's method of maintaining the dramatic interest is, from this point on, the direct opposite of that which he has so far been employing. Hitherto Philo has been the critic of the argument from design, but is represented as failing to convince Cleanthes of the relevance and cogency of his objections. Also, the suggestion has been that Cleanthes will in the end be found to have been holding in reserve a sufficient defence. But now that the discussion is drawing to a close, quite other tactics are called for ; and those adopted by Hume have all the necessary features of surprise and suspense. For it is Philo, *not* Cleanthes, that is made to come forward as the champion of the case for design, rehabilitating it, in a manner not open to the preceding criticisms. A highly ambiguous champion it is true ! But this the reader is not to know until Philo (in Part XII), under cover of these professions, has completed his argument.

The passage in which this sudden change of tactics occurs is as follows :

Here, Cleanthes, I find myself at ease in my argument. Here I triumph. Formerly, when we argued concerning the natural attributes of intelligence and design, I needed all my sceptical and metaphysical subtilty to elude your grasp. In many views of the

---

[1] *Dialogues*, p. 198   [2] *Ibid.*, p. 201

universe, and of its parts, particularly the latter, the beauty and fitness of final causes strike us with such irresistible force, that all objections appear (what I believe they really are) mere cavils and sophisms ; nor can we then imagine how it was ever possible for us to repose any weight on them. But there is no view of human life or of the condition of mankind, from which, without the greatest violence, we can infer the moral attributes, or learn that infinite benevolence, conjoined with infinite power and infinite wisdom, which we must discover by the eyes of faith alone. It is your turn now to tug the labouring oar, and to support your philosophical subtilties against the dictates of plain reason and experience.[1]

Cleanthes does *not* proceed ' to tug the labouring oar.' As we have already noted, he retires into the background ; and while still protesting, allows the case, by default, to go against him.

Obviously the argument has here taken a very strange and indeed bewildering turn. Philo claiming to believe in final causes ! Philo declaring all his arguments to have been mere cavils and sophisms ! If so, must not those commentators be in the right who find that Cleanthes, much more truly than Philo, is the mouthpiece of Hume, and that Cleanthes is justly crowned by Pamphilus as victor in the discussion ?

This view may seem to be confirmed by Philo's further statements, in the opening of the next and concluding section (Part XII) :

Notwithstanding the freedom of my conversation and my love of singular arguments, no one . . . pays more profound adoration to the divine Being, as he discovers himself to reason, in the inexplicable contrivance and artifice of nature. A purpose, an intention, a design strikes everywhere the most careless, the most stupid thinker ; and no man can be so hardened in absurd systems, as at all times to reject it.[2]

These, indeed, are the passages which afford whatever justification there may be for holding that when Philo and Cleanthes differ, it is to Cleanthes much more truly than to Philo that we must look for the expression of Hume's personal beliefs, and for Hume's own estimate of the final outcome of the argument. Clearly, our interpretation of these passages must be decisive of our interpretation of the *Dialogues* as a whole ; and I need therefore offer no apology for dealing with them in some detail.

---

[1] *Dialogues*, pp. 201–2   [2] *Ibid.*, below, p. 214

Aha!

Philo's terms, in the second of the above confessions of faith, are more ' artfully ' chosen than at first sight appears.[1] The God here avowed is an object of adoration *transcending* our powers of comprehension ; the ' contrivance and artifice of nature ' is *inexplicable*. Philo adds, indeed, the phrase ' *as he discovers himself to reason* ' ; but only, as the sequel shows, in order to point out that the Deity thus revealed is not to be equated with the God of religion ; and so to withdraw nearly all that he has seemed to allow. For as he proceeds to argue, though with considerable indirectness, and with avoidance of any quite direct challenge of Cleanthes' conclusions, the impression which nature makes upon the mind is not due to nature acting alone ; the influence of custom, and of the traditional beliefs to which nurture and education give the force of custom, has intervened, infusing into the impression a definiteness of meaning which it does not rightfully possess. Accordingly, there falls to reason the important negative function of distinguishing this impression from the more specific beliefs which have thus come to be identified with it.[2]

This second confession of faith is, indeed, no sooner made than Philo, with mischievous intent, describes ' the contrivance and artifice of nature ' in a manner which, while in the spirit of Cleanthes' teaching, parodies his own. There are, Galen has demonstrated, 600 muscles in the human body, each of them adjusted to at least 10 distinct circumstances. " So that in the muscles alone, above 6000 several views and intentions must have been formed and executed." [3] Similarly, there are 284 bones, each adjusted to about 40 distinct purposes, *i.e.* in this regard, a further 11,360 intentions.

What a prodigious display of artifice, even in these simple and homogeneous parts ! . . . If the infidelity of Galen, even when these natural sciences were still imperfect, could not withstand such striking appearances ; to what pitch of pertinacious obstinacy must

---

[1] *Cf.* the letter to Adam Smith (August 15, 1776) in which Hume is urging him to stand surety for the publication of the *Dialogues* : " On revising them (which I have not done these 15 Years) I find that nothing can be more cautiously and more artfully written. You had certainly forgotten them." (*Letters*, vol. ii, p. 334.) *Cf.* below, p. 91.

[2] As already noted (p. 38), it was in the final revision in 1776 that Hume appears to have added the passages on pp. 217, 227, in which the negative and quite general character of Philo's conclusions is thus emphasized. *Cf.* below, Appendix C, pp. 87 *sqq.*

[3] *Dialogues*, p. 215

a philosopher in this age have attained, who can now doubt of a supreme intelligence.[1]

This betrays Cleanthes (as it was evidently intended to do) into a complacent renewal—all Philo's criticisms having passed harmlessly over his head—of his original thesis :

The comparison of the universe to a machine of human contrivance is so obvious and natural, and is justified by so many instances of order and design in nature, that it must immediately strike all unprejudiced apprehensions, and procure universal approbation.[2]

The most that can be done, in opposition to this theory, Cleanthes declares, is ' to start doubts and difficulties ' ; and so, at most, to cause ' suspense of judgment.'

Suspense of judgment, Philo agrees, is not possible. But what this leads him to suspect—and here, at last, he proceeds to expound in less ambiguous terms 'his unfeigned sentiments'[3] —is that " there enters somewhat of a dispute of words into this controversy, *more than is usually imagined.*"[4] This, he points out, is particularly apt to happen in controversies regarding the degrees of any quality or circumstance—the degree of greatness in Hannibal or of beauty in Cleopatra.

Degrees of these qualities are not, like quantity or number, susceptible of any exact mensuration, which may be the standard in the controversy. That the dispute concerning theism is of this nature . . . will appear upon the slightest enquiry. I ask the theist, if he does not allow, that there is a great and immeasurable, *because incomprehensible*, difference between the *human*, and the *divine* mind. The more pious he is . . . the more will he be disposed to magnify the difference. . . . I next turn to the atheist, who, I assert, is only nominally so, and can never possibly be in earnest ; and *I ask him whether . . . there be not a certain degree of analogy among all operations of nature, . . . whether the rotting of a turnip, the generation of an animal, and the structure of human thought be not energies that probably bear some remote analogy to each other : It is impossible he can deny it.* . . . Where then, cry I to both these antagonists, is the subject of your dispute ? The theist allows, that the original intelligence is very different from human reason : The atheist allows, that the original principle of order bears remote analogy to it. Will you quarrel, Gentlemen, about the degrees, and enter into a controversy, which admits not of any precise meaning, nor consequently of any determination ?[5]

---

[1] *Dialogues*, p. 215   [2] *Ibid.*, p. 216   [3] *Ibid.*, p. 219
[4] *Ibid.*, p. 216. Italics not in text
[5] *Ibid.*, p. 218. Italics not in text

It was not in Hume's programme to *force* these very negative conclusions upon unwilling readers ; otherwise he might
have illustrated his thesis—that the differences, *and the agree-
ments*, between the disputants are at bottom more verbal than
real—by also dwelling upon the ambiguity of such terms as
' design,' ' final cause,' ' contrivance,' ' adjustment,' ' order.' [1]
Unless, as he has indirectly shown in the earlier sections, these
terms are sharply discriminated and precisely defined, they
encourage the very usual confusion—Hume has himself taken
advantage of it in the above confessions of faith—between an
argument *from* design and an argument *to* design. In the argument *from* design, design is taken in the neutral sense merely
of order and of the ' adjustments ' which order involves,[2] *i.e.*
as an undeniable datum. In the argument *to* design, the identification of order with the designed is recognized as the main
point requiring to be established.

One further step completes Philo's formulation of the
positions in which he so greatly differs from the teaching of
Cleanthes.

As the works of nature have a much greater analogy to the effects
of *our* art and contrivance, than to those of *our* benevolence and
justice ; we have reason to infer that the natural attributes of the
Deity have a greater resemblance to those of man, than his moral
have to human virtues.[3]

In other words, admittedly wide as the disparity is between
the natural attributes of God and of man, the ' remoteness of
the analogy ' is even greater in the case of the moral attributes.
And had Hume desired to underline, instead of toning down,
the agnostic character of his conclusions, he might have introduced here, instead of placing it earlier, in the mouth of
Cleanthes, the statement :

For to what purpose establish the natural attributes of the Deity,
while the moral are still doubtful and uncertain ? [4]

Save for Cleanthes' advocacy, in two brief passages, of the
' probation ' or ' porch ' view of human destiny, the next 14
pages are occupied by Philo's exposition of Hume's counter-
views. Religion, he declares, ought to have no practical con-

---

[1] *Cf.* below, pp. 98–9, 102–3, 106
[2] *Ibid.*, p. 185. *Cf.* pp. 174–5, 183, 191
[3] *Ibid.*, p. 219
[4] *Ibid.*, p. 199

sequences. It " affords no inference that affects human life, or can be the source of any action or forbearance." [1] And Philo dwells on the manifold evils which follow when it takes the form either of ' superstition ' or of ' enthusiasm,' enumerating these evils in the manner which we have already considered. [2]

What, Philo finally asks—repeating and reinforcing this teaching—is the conclusion to which we are brought ? The whole of natural theology, he declares, " resolves itself into one simple, though somewhat ambiguous, at least undefined proposition, *that the cause or causes of order in the universe probably bear some remote analogy to human intelligence.*" [3] This proposition, he adds, is " not capable of extension, variation, or more particular explication," and " affords no inference that affects human life or can be the source of any action or forbearance." And lastly, " the analogy, imperfect as it is, . . . cannot be transferred, with any appearance of probability, to the other [*i.e.* moral] qualities of the mind." [4]

Hume, in keeping with his general policy of stating his sceptical positions with the least possible emphasis compatible with definiteness, abstains from further underlining the quite negative character of this conclusion ; and accordingly does not repeat his previous contention, which he has not withdrawn, that the analogy in its ' remoteness ' applies to *all* the operations of nature, to the rotting of a turnip and the generation of an animal, no less than to the structure of human thought.

In these passages Hume has given his answer to the difficulty which in 1751 he had invited Elliot to assist him in solving,[5] why the dissimilitudes of the works of nature to the products of art do not weaken the belief in design so much as we might naturally expect. The manner in which Hume has worded the passage in Part III in which Cleanthes draws attention to the verdict of feeling in this matter is significant of his ultimate intentions.

Consider, anatomize the eye : Survey its structure and contrivance ; and tell me, from your own feeling, if the idea of a contriver does not immediately flow in upon you with a force like that of sensation. The most obvious conclusion surely is in favour of design ; and it *requires time, reflection and study, to summon up those* frivolous, though abstruse, *objections, which can support infidelity.*[6]

[1] *Cf.* below, p. 227   [2] Above, pp. 11 *sqq.*   [3] *Dialogues,* below, p. 227
[4] *Loc. cit.*   [5] *Letters,* vol. i, pp. 155, 157   *Cf.* below, Appendix C., p. 87
[6] *Dialogues,* p. 154

The words which I have italicized in this passage already indicate what is to be Philo's reply to these contentions. Nature, he allows, does actually produce on the mind an overwhelming impression ; but the impression, he maintains, is less definite, more ambiguous, than is here assumed. Accordingly time is needed ; until reason has had its say, and the effects of acquired beliefs have been discounted, feeling, however seemingly immediate and pure, is an untrustworthy guide. When the feeling is carefully scrutinized, and reflectively weighed, Cleanthes' interpretation of it cannot, Philo, contends, be upheld.

Hume closes the discussion with the conventionally required proviso, placed in the mouth of Philo, that in a well disposed mind this profound ignorance will arouse

a longing desire and expectation, that Heaven would be pleased to dissipate, at least alleviate, [it] by affording some more particular revelation to mankind.[1]

To be a philosophical sceptic is, in a man of letters, the first and most essential step towards being a sound, believing Christian ; a proposition which I would willingly recommend to the attention of Pamphilus : And I hope Cleanthes will forgive me for interposing so far in the education and instruction of his pupil.[2]

The ' pupil ' then passes his verdict in the manner appropriate to his relationship to Cleanthes.

Thus the conclusions voiced by Philo in the *Dialogues* are no other than those which Hume expounds in the closing paragraph of his *Natural History of Religion* :

The whole is a riddle, an aenigma, an inexplicable mystery. Doubt, uncertainty, suspense of judgment appear the only result of our most accurate scrutiny, concerning this subject. But such is the frailty of human reason, and such the irresistible contagion of opinion, that even this deliberate doubt could scarcely be upheld ; did we not enlarge our view, and opposing one species of superstition to another, set them a quarrelling ; while we ourselves, during their fury and contention, happily make our escape into the calm, though obscure regions of philosophy.

These conclusions are, however, more far-reaching, and more positive in their negations, than the argument of the *Dialogues* can by itself justify. Hume is here drawing on his general philosophy, on his theory of knowledge no less than

[1] *Dialogues*, p. 227   [2] *Ibid.*, p. 228

on his theory of morals ; and to discuss his contentions in these wider bearings would carry us beyond the limits proper to this Introduction. What Hume has achieved in the *Dialogues,* considered by themselves, is, at most, to show that the traditional arguments which he has been considering have in fact the defects which he asserts. The reader, should he approve Hume's criticisms, has still the alternatives before him, either to follow Hume in his thorough-going scepticism, or, should he so choose, to look to the *Dialogues* for instruction only in the *via negativa*—a discipline upon which theology, thanks to the mystics no less than to the sceptics, has itself found reason to insist.

If the problems of Divine Existence are now seldom approached in the manner favoured in the eighteenth century, and so conservatively held to also in the nineteenth century, this is traceable in no small degree to the influence of Hume, as conveyed through many channels, most notably through Kant.

AN ACCOUNT OF MY LAST INTERVIEW WITH
DAVID HUME, ESQ.[1]

Partly recorded in my Journal, partly enlarged from my memory,
3 March 1777

On Sunday forenoon the 7 of July 1776, being too late for Church,
I went to see Mr. David Hume, who was returned from London
and Bath, just a dying. I found him alone, in a reclining posture
in his drawing-room. He was lean, ghastly, and quite of an earthy
appearance. He was drest in a suit of grey cloth with white metal
buttons, and a kind of scratch wig. He was quite different from
the plump figure which he used to present. He had before him
Dr. Campbell's *Philosophy of Rhetorick*.[2] He seemed to be placid
and even cheerful. He said he was just approaching to his end.
I think these were his words. I know not how I contrived to get
the subject of Immortality introduced. He said he never had entertained any belief in Religion since he began to read Locke and
Clarke. I asked him if he was not religious when he was young.
He said he was, and he used to read the *Whole Duty of Man* ;[3] that
he made an abstract from the Catalogue of vices at the end of it,
and examined himself by this, leaving out Murder and Theft and
such vices as he had no chance of committing, having no inclination
to commit them. This, he said, was strange Work ; for instance,
to try if, notwithstanding his excelling his school-fellows, he had
no pride or vanity. He smiled in ridicule of this as absurd and
contrary to fixed principles and necessary consequences, not advert-
ing that Religious discipline does not mean to extinguish, but to
moderate, the passions ; and certainly an excess of pride or vanity
is dangerous and generally hurtful. He then said flatly that the
Morality of every Religion was bad, and, I really thought, was not
jocular when he said " that when he heard a man was religious, he
concluded he was a rascal, though he had known some instances
of very good men being religious." This was just an extravagant
reverse of the common remark as to Infidels. I had a strong curiosity to be satisfied if he persisted in disbeleiving a future state even
when he had death before his eyes. I was persuaded from what he
now said, and from his manner of saying it, that he did persist. I

---

[1] [From the *Private Papers of James Boswell*, edited by Geoffrey Scott and
Frederick A. Pottle, vol. xii (1931), pp. 227–32.]

[2] [*Cf.* above, p. 49n. The *Philosophy of Rhetoric* was published in 1776]

[3] [*Cf.* above, pp. 5–6]

asked him if it was not possible that there might be a future state. He answered It was possible that a piece of coal put upon the fire would not burn ; and he added that it was a most unreasonable fancy that he should exist for ever. That immortality, if it were at all, must be general ; that a great proportion of the human race has hardly any intellectual qualities ; that a great proportion dies in infancy before being possessed of reason ; yet all these must be immortal ; that a Porter who gets drunk by ten o'clock with gin must be immortal ; that the trash of every age must be preserved, and that new Universes must be created to contain such infinite numbers. This appeared to me an unphilosophical objection, and I said, " Mr. Hume, you know Spirit does not take up space." I may illustrate what he last said by mentioning that in a former conversation with me on this subject he used pretty much the same mode of reasoning, and urged that Wilkes and his Mob must be immortal. One night last May as I was coming up Kingstreet, Westminster, I met Wilkes, who carried me into Parliament street to see a curious procession pass : the funeral of a lamplighter attended by some hundreds of his fraternity with torches. Wilkes, who either is, or affects to be, an infidel, was rattling away, " I think there's an end of that fellow. I think he won't rise again." I very calmly said to him, " You bring into my mind the strongest argument that ever I heard against a future state " ; and then told him David Hume's Objection that Wilkes and his Mob must be immortal. It seemed to make a proper impression, for he grinned abashment, as a Negro grows whiter when he blushes. But to return to my last Interview with Mr. Hume. I asked him if the thought of Annihilation never gave him any uneasiness. He said not the least ; no more than the thought that he had not been, as Lucretius observes. " Well," said I, " Mr. Hume, I hope to triumph over you when I meet you in a future state ; and remember you are not to pretend that you was joking with all this Infidelity." " No, No," said he, " But I shall have been so long there before you come that it will be nothing new." In this style of goodhumour and levity did I conduct the conversation. Perhaps it was wrong on so aweful a subject. But as nobody was present, I thought it could have no bad effect. I however felt a degree of horrour, mixed with a sort of wild, strange, hurrying recollection of My excellent Mother's pious instructions, of Dr. Johnson's noble lessons, and of my religious sentiments and affections during the course of my life. I was like a man in sudden danger eagerly seeking his defensive arms ; and I could not but be assailed by momentary doubts while I had actually before me a man of such strong abilities and extensive inquiry dying in the persuasion of being annihilated. But I maintained my Faith. I told him that I beleived the Christian Religion as I beleived History. Said he : " You do not beleive it as you beleive the Revolution." " Yes," said I, " but the difference is that I am not so much interested in the truth of the Revolution ; otherwise I should have anxious doubts concerning it. A man who is in love has doubts of the affection of his Mistress, without cause." I mentioned Soame Jennyns's little book[1] in defence of Christianity, which was just published but which I had not yet read. Mr. Hume said, " I am told there is nothing of his usual spirit in it." He had once said to me on a forenoon, while the sun was shining bright, that he did not wish to be immortal. This was a most wonderful thought. The reason he gave was that he was very well in this state of being, and that the chances were very much against his being so well in another state ; and he would rather not be more than be worse. I answered that it was reasonable to hope he would be better ; that there would be a progressive improvement. I tried him at this Inverview with that topick, saying that a future state was surely a pleasing idea. He said No, for that it was allways seen through a gloomy medium ; there was allways a Phlegethon or a Hell. " But," said I, " would it not be agreable to have hopes of seeing our friends again ? " and I mentioned three Men lately deceased, for whom I knew he had a high value : Ambassadour Keith, Lord Alemoor, and Baron Muir. He owned it would be agreable, but added that none of them entertained such a notion. I believe he said, such a foolish, or such an absurd, notion ; for he was indecently and impolitely positive in incredulity. " Yes," said I, " Lord Alemoor was a beleiver." David acknowledged that *he* had *some* beleif. I some how or other brought Dr. Johnson's name into our conversation. I had often heard him speak of that great Man in a very illiberal manner. He said upon this occasion, " Johnson should be pleased with my *History*," Nettled by Hume's frequent attacks upon my revered friend in former conversations, I told him now that Dr. Johnson did not allow him much credit ; for he said, " Sir, the fellow is a Tory by chance." I am sorry that I mentioned this at such a time. I was off my guard ; for the truth is that Mr. Hume's pleasantry was such that there was no solemnity in the scene ; and Death for the time did not seem dismal. It surprised me to find him talking of different matters with a tranquillity of mind and a clearness of head which few men possess at any time. Two particulars I remember : Smith's *Wealth of Nations*, which he recommended much, and Monboddo's *Origin of Language*, which he treated contemptously. I said, " If I were you, I should regret Annihilation. Had I written such an admirable History, I should be sorry to leave it." He said, " I shall leave that history, of which you are pleased to speak so favourably, as perfect as I can." He

---

[1] [*A View of the Internal Evidence of the Christian Religion* (1776)—an argument that the divine origin of Christianity is shown by the purity and originality of its ethics. Jenyns is now chiefly remembered by Johnson's review of his *Free Inquiry into the Nature and Origin of Evil*. *Cf.* Boswell's *Life of Johnson* (Oxford, 1904), vol. i, p. 210.]

said, too, that all the great abilities with which Men had ever been endowed were Relative to this World. He said he became a greater friend to the Stuart Family as he advanced in studying for his History ; and he hoped he had vindicated the two first of them so effectually that they would never again be attacked. Mr. Lauder, his Surgeon, came in for a little, and Mr. Mure, the Baron's son, for another small interval. He was, as far as I could judge, quite easy with both. He said he had no pain, but was wasting away. I left him with impressions which disturbed me for some time.

Appendix B [1]

BAYLE ON STRATO'S 'ATHEISM'

ONE of the chief themes in Bayle's *Pensées diverses* (1682), and even more prominently in the sequel which he entitles *Continuation des pensées diverses* (1705), is that idolatry is a greater evil than atheism ; and in treating of atheism he maintains that in addition to so-called practical atheists (*i.e.* those who act as if there were no God, and who would therefore gladly be delivered from a belief which still continues to disturb them) there are also atheists by conviction. Strato, he holds, is the most important representative of the latter. It is, Bayle urges, Strato's teaching, and not that of Democritus and the Epicureans, which it most behoves the theist to refute—only those who like the Christians in religion and Descartes in philosophy believe in pure immaterial spirit can, Bayle claims, hope to do so —just as it is also the criticisms which Strato retorts upon the theists that are the most difficult of all to meet. Bayle further explains that while Strato is not concerned to deny that there is " a first being, a supreme God, a first principle," he identifies it with inanimate nature. [*Cf.* Leon Robin, *Greek Thought* (Eng. trans. 1928), p. 310 : " Because Strato follows the demands of Aristotle's naturalism to the end, and places the supernatural back in nature, he was regarded as a heterodox Peripatetic." *Cf.* also Zeller : *Aristotle* (Engl. trans. 1897), vol. ii, p. 455. " Strato re-nounced the idea of God as a Being separate and distinct from the world as a whole, and contented himself with ' nature.' "] This is why Bayle feels free to describe Strato's teaching (as he also described Spinoza's) in terms which Strato would not himself have used, namely, as atheistic. The section to which Hume's memoranda (above, p. 35) refer is § CVI of Bayle's *Continuation des pensées diverses*, which, like the work to which it is a sequel, is addressed to a Doctor of the Sorbonne. Bayle has asked his readers to suppose that Athenians are the protagonists of Strato's teaching, and that they are not merely defending their positions but are actively attacking the main argument ordinarily given in proof of theism, the argu-ment to design. As the reader will observe, many of Hume's chief devices, even to his turns of expression, are here already full-blown.

[1] To above, pp. 35-6

§ CVI. *Whether the Stratonician atheists in retorting the argument which has been drawn from the order and symmetry of the world would not have embarrassed the pagan philosophers.*

" To save you useless labour I call your attention to a thing which is absolutely necessary if you wish to employ the proof which first offers itself and which is really excellent. I mean that which is founded on the beauty and the regularity of the heavens and the ingenuity apparent everywhere in the animal mechanism, the various parts of which are manifestly directed to definite ends and made for one another. The Athenians who figure in our argument as followers of Strato were obliged to say that a nature without life and sense had produced all these fine works and that without knowing what she did she had bestowed on them a degree of symmetry and mutual adjustment which could not but be ascribed to a highly enlightened intelligence, choosing both its ends and its means. Here, you will say, is an objection, a difficulty which would have cured the atheism of these people had the depravity of their wills allowed them to seek the cure of their diseased understandings. Here you will have a splendid field before you, where you can run up and down and walk about as much as you please. But if such exercises are to bring you any return you will have to add to your plan of action the article I am now going to show you, for it is possible you might not think of it yourself.

" The proposition you have to prove must be this and no other : *the order apparent in nature is a consideration so convincing, that had not the Stratonicians perversely insisted on shunning the light the objection to their views resulting from this order would infallibly have converted them* EVEN THOUGH THEY COULD RETORT IT AGAINST THEIR OPPONENTS WITH STILL GREATER FORCE. Pray attend carefully to the last words of this sentence which I have intentionally marked with capitals ; for on them depends entirely the success of your undertaking.

" In the human mind there is a peculiarity which you cannot have failed to notice and which is this. The difficulties which men encounter on adopting an hypothesis do not cause them to abandon it if they see either that these difficulties are no more their own than their antagonist's or again that they are no greater than those that would be met with elsewhere. It would be unreasonable to censure men for not yielding to an argument which is as much their own as their adversary's, for every argument which makes as much impression on the assailant's position as on the defender's proves too much and so far proves nothing. It would therefore be but idle rhetoric to stigmatize as mere obstinacy and wilful blindness the case of a reasoner who refuses to change his views so long as his opponent's difficulties are the same or much the same as his own. His refusal is quite reasonable. Let us see then, and here

Sir, *your* part begins, if your young Athenians could resort the difficulty in question. Should they be able to do so I do not see how it is possible for you to furnish the proof of the thesis I set you, and you will agree perhaps that it is better to attribute to the delusions of the intellect what you attributed to the perversity of the heart. Nothing, I should think, could be more crushing for a Stratonician philosopher than to say to him that it was impossible for a cause destitute of knowledge to make our world with its beautiful order, its exact mechanism and its just and constant laws of motion. For since the humblest house was never built without a cause which had the idea of the house and which directed its labours by that idea, how should it be possible that the human body should have been organized by a cause destitute of sense and that the world, a product infinitely more difficult than the animal body, should have been produced by an inanimate nature which, so far from being capable of directing its own forces, does not so much as know that it possesses any ? The question once put, nothing else was needed to make the Stratonicians feel the unintelligible nature of their hypothesis and bring them to the straits of a *reductio ad absurdum*. Their only possible consolation after that would be to bring their opponents into the same state.

" The Stratonicians would not have made their case by arguing that no intelligent cause produces the human body ; for if the point had been conceded that the organization of the foetus does not come from the soul of the father or of the mother or even of the infant, the reply would still have been possible that the organization is due to God himself or to some genius on whom he devolves the task. This reply alone would stop the Stratonicians ; every other would have been in their favour. They would have asked for nothing better than to refer their opponents to seminal virtues, plastic powers, and other similar causes which know nothing of what they execute. But if the assumption of a genius put in charge of the formation of animals should dispose in a satisfactory manner of the first assault, this could only serve to precipitate the main engagement, since the Stratonicians would not have failed to show that it was necessary to go straight to the first being, the first principle of the other sects. Let us match them for a bit with the Stoics and assume that they talk to them as follows.

" ' You admit two principles of all things, God and matter ; God as active principle, matter as passive. God according to you is an eternal ever living fire, and is therefore an assemblage of restlessly moving particles, this being the essence of fire. It is impossible that a whole composed of various corporeal moving particles should exist without a certain arrangement and a certain degree of movement among the particles. A thing considered in general and without any individualizing limitation can indeed exist as an object in our minds but it cannot exist as a real thing outside our minds.

That which is real and exists outside our minds must be precisely this or that, and if it is a body in motion it must have each of its parts shaped and located in a certain way with a determined degree of motion, such or such rather than any other. You must therefore say that from all eternity there has been in the fiery particles which compose the nature of God a certain arrangement and a certain quantity of motion different from every other possible arrangement and from every other possible quantity of motion. Pray tell us on what depended this precise arrangement, this particular degree of motion ? Were they chosen by an intelligent cause and preferred to every other possible arrangement and to every other possible quantity of motion by a nature which knew what it was doing and why it did it ? You cannot say this ; for to do so would be to say that God has been produced by an antecedent cause, that he is not a being uncreated, that he is not the first efficient principle of all things, and we shall have to mount up to this antecedent cause, explain to ourselves its essence, and say whether it is a fire, etc. The same question would thus return upon us, and so on *ad infinitum*. You must therefore stop at this fiery being which you call God, and agree that the arrangement of its parts and their degree of motion have not been regulated by a cause which knew what it ordered and what it moved. Now since this arrangement and this degree of motion, which did not depend on any intelligent directing cause, have none the less, on your view, sufficed to constitute the most perfect of all beings, and a nature infinitely more complete than the world, why do you not let the world be the work of a cause which acts without knowing itself ? By what right do you reject our principle of all things on the pretext that it is an inanimate principle ? If it is not possible that the world should be the work of such a principle, it will still less be possible that your Jupiter, a God who makes all things, who provides for all things, who disposes all things with sovereign goodness and with infinite wisdom, should have acquired so many perfections without any intelligent cause presiding over the arrangement and movement of the particles of which he is composed. He has certainly not done so himself in so far as endowed with intelligence and will ; for his intelligence and his will are not antecedent to his complete existence. He has been a fire as soon as [he has been] a God : the arrangement and the determinate motion of the parts of this fire have neither preceded nor followed the intellectual perfections of Jupiter. They have not therefore any other cause than the very necessity of nature which is the reason of the existence of the active principle which in your Stoic teaching you distinguish as we do not from matter. Finally, if you would have us explain to you how there is order in nature without the directing control of any intelligent being, we would have you explain to us how there is order in the fiery corpuscles of God without the government of any intelligent cause. Your task is greater than ours, since you have to account for an effect infinitely more perfect than nature or the world.'

" That is what Strato's disciples might say to the Stoics. I shall be glad if you will send me a really good reply.

" The other philosophical sects were hardly less exposed than the Stoics to a similar retort. Only the Christian philosophers, and especially the Cartesians, are in a position to overthrow this Stratonician teaching, without fear that their own arguments will be retorted upon them. It is easy to understand that all those who attributed to God a corporeal nature should expose themselves to this *argumentum ad hominem* which I have put forward against the Stoics. And as regards those who believed that God was the soul or the understanding of matter, they also could not escape this retort. For that soul was in fact composed of parts, each of which has its own particular virtues and faculties, which God had not given it by a free act of his will. The necessary and eternal being has not a will antecedent to his other attributes ; he has power, understanding and wisdom just as soon as acts of will. If, then, the soul of the world were God, it would have from all eternity all the virtues of which it is capable, and these virtues would not have been regulated and distributed by any other antecedent cause, ordering and choosing, any more than they would have been so disposed by the soul itself as intelligence.

" You will perhaps consider that a Platonist who ascribed to God an incorporeal nature would easily have silenced the Stratonician sectaries. But do not be too confident of this. For, firstly, the Platonic doctrine regarding deity is not the same in all Plato's works. They contain so many things at variance with one another, that we do not know what to hold to. Secondly, his teaching in this matter is a mere tissue of arbitrary assumptions which he delivers magisterially one after the other, none of them with any proof. Thirdly, he is so obscure that he repels all those who are in search of light and light alone. Cicero, who admires him so greatly on other topics would not pay his hypothesis regarding the divine nature the bare compliment of examining it. Fourthly, Strato could have asked the Platonists this question : Is it true that you allow eternal ideas separate from the substance of God ? If so, you must say either that they exist of themselves, or that God has produced them as a copy of the original ideas which are not separate from his substance. If they exist of themselves, then you have things which without depending on any cause are endowed with directive control and with life, and have each their proper qualities, this one representative of ' man,' this other of ' horse,' etc. Whence could come to them any one determinate quality rather than another, whence could come their differences, their relations and their subordinations, if it were true as you pretend that no insensible cause is capable of effecting anything in which there is proportion and the tendency towards a certain end ? If they are only the copies of original ideas intimately united to the substance of God, the difficulty is thrown back on the original ideas. Each of these latter will have its properties ; they will stand to one another in relations and subordinations. Where is the determining principle of all this ? It is not in the will of God, since God does not know things by free choice but by the necessity of his nature ; nor in God's understanding, which likewise has no freedom of indifference to know this or that, or to know it in some one fashion rather than in another.

"The doctrine of Aristotle in regard to the nature of God is so perplexed by variations and obscurities that it is still a matter of dispute whether it is impious or not. There are competent judges who think that it opened the way for the atheism of Strato. It was therefore hardly fitted to convert the Stratonicians, and you will oblige me greatly by showing me that it had nothing to fear from the conversion against it of its own arguments.

"The Stratonicians had the deadly advantage of being able to confront their opponents with the agreed assumption, *ex nihilo nihil fit*, that nothing is made from nothing, and that matter is consequently uncreated. [*Cf.* Hume on "the impious maxim of the ancient philosophy, *Ex nihilo nihil fit*, by which the creation of matter was excluded." *Enquiry*, S.-B., p. 164*n.*; *Essays*, G. & G., vol. ii, p. 135*n.*] It is not less strange to suppose that it exists of itself without any quality than with an active principle ; and this is why Cicero's Cotta reasoned that if matter were not the work of God's Providence, earth, air, fire and water were not so either, but must be the work of nature. This passage from Cicero formed part of the lost portion of the third book on the nature of the Gods. Lactantius has said some very good things against this speech of Cotta's, but most of them would have been feeble in the mouth of a Stoic. I shall not dwell on anything but this : ' What power could nature have,' asked Lactantius, ' nothing having given it any ? If it has power, it received it from some one who cannot be other than God. If it has no knowledge, it cannot produce anything ; if it can produce something, it has knowledge ; it is therefore God : one cannot otherwise name the power which conceives a plan and executes it. The capacity to make a thing can be found only in a being with thought and skill, nothing can be begun or finished unless an intelligent cause directs its execution and has the power and the will to work at it. That which is without sense remains ever inactive, nothing can issue from that from which voluntary movement is excluded. . . .' A Stoic reasoning on these principles would have been obliged to deny that matter existed independently of God, for otherwise he would have been asked in regard to its existence the very question that he had propounded in regard to its activity. If nothing exists without having been produced by an intelligent cause, then whence, a Stratonician would have asked, come the active virtues of the fire which compose your Jupiter ? Have they been given according to a cause which preceded Jupiter ? This would involve a progress *ad infinitum*, and we should never arrive at a first cause. If you would avoid this great abyss, you must allow that no idea, that no voluntary movement contributed to the existence of the eternal fire which you name ' God.' Your objections therefore prove too much. You recognize ordered forces in nature which are neither the sequel to nor the result of any knowledge, although they are accompanied by knowledge. What is wrong with our admitting an order and a determinate virtue in a nature which knows nothing ? Once this order exists without knowledge, it will go on so for ever : the hardest thing to do is done.

" You may recall some words of Euripides [*Troades*, ll. 884–8 : ' *Hecuba*. " Oh ! firm stay of earth and on the earth abiding who-ever thou art, hard to know by speculation, Zeus, whether necessity of nature or mind of mortals, to thee I offer my prayer ; for as thou goest on thy path thou governest justly all mortal things." *Menelaos*. " What means it ? What novel forms of prayer to heaven are these ! " '] and will note in them three remarkable observations. (1) Jupiter is there recognized as being for our minds incompre-hensible. (2) We invoke him whatever he might be, whether necessity of nature or human understanding. (3) We avow that he guides all things justly by a path that is hidden from us. It is Hecuba who speaks, and all this is too philosophical for a woman. But we may be sure that Euripides gives us in this portrait the character of certain people who in their anxiety to risk no chances would recommend themselves to God, although they were still uncertain whether he was an intelligence or only the blind and necessary force of nature. Such men would have invoked God with still more zeal, and with more pleasure if they had been certain of his intelligent nature. It was therefore the difficulty of the subject, and not wilful badness of heart which kept them in uncertainty.

" I may add that while assuming that the Stoics recognized matter as a passive principle distinct from God, I was quite aware of the words which Plutarch addresses to them : ' Your Jupiter, as you depict and imagine him, is he not, when he is most himself, a great continual fire ? But at the moment he gives way, he con-forms and transforms himself in all things by diverse mutations.' This is very clearly to declare that the God of the Stoics was him-self the material of all bodies, which can also be inferred from another passage containing the definition of God according to the Stoics. But since it appears from other authorities that the Stoics admitted a distinction between God and matter, I thought I was bound in considering their doctrine to be governed by the passage showing it in the least disadvantageous light."

Appendix C

EVIDENCE BEARING ON THE TIMES OF COMPOSITION AND REVISION OF THE *DIALOGUES*, AND ON HUME'S ARRANGEMENTS FOR THEIR POSTHUMOUS PUBLICATION

THE first notice we have of the *Dialogues* is in a letter written by Hume (March 10, 1751) to his friend Sir Gilbert Elliot (*Letters*, vol. i, p. 153). It opens with the words :

You wou'd perceive by the Sample I have given you, that I make Cleanthes the Hero of the Dialogue. Whatever you can think of, to strengthen that Side of the Argument, will be most acceptable to me.

Then follow the passages quoted above, p. 7. (*Cf.* also, above, p. 66.) Hume adds a very significant postscript :

If you'll be persuaded to assist me in supporting Cleanthes, I fancy you need not take Matters any higher than Part 3. He allows, indeed, in Part 2, that all our Inference is founded on the Similitude of the Works of Nature to the usual Effects of Mind. Otherwise they must appear a mere Chaos. The only Difficulty is, why the other Dissimilitudes do not weaken the Argument. And indeed it woud seem from Experience & Feeling, that they do not weaken it so much as we might naturally expect. A Theory to solve this woud be very acceptable. (*Cf.* above, p. 73.)

Apparently Hume's reason for calling his manuscript (already divided into Parts) a ' sample ' is that it did not contain the concluding Parts, and possibly stopped at the end of Part IV. Elliot's reply survives in the form of a draft, which has been printed in full by Dugald Stewart (*Collected Works*, vol. i, pp. 605–7). It contains no recognizable reference to anything beyond Part III. The references of Hume and Elliot to points in the sample show that the first three Parts were already written substantially, possibly entirely, in the form in which we now have them. Part XII was almost certainly not in the sample. Elliot urges Hume to reckon with

the dictates of feeling [*i.e.* with the immediate impression made upon the mind by the contemplation of Nature] as well as with the conclusions of reason and the reports of experience, and possibly to reckon with all these together.

This is precisely what Hume has set himself to do in Part XII ; and he may perhaps, in this respect, have been influenced by Elliot's advice. Hume's request for assistance in strengthening Cleanthes' argument proved, however, unavailing. In this, as in other respects, Elliot has kinship with Cleanthes.

" Had it been my good Fortune," Hume writes, " to live near you, I shou'd have taken on me the Character of Philo, in the Dialogue, which you'll own I coud have supported naturally enough : And you woud not have been averse to that of Cleanthes." (*Letters*, vol. i, p. 154.)

Hume appears to have completed the *Dialogues* either in 1751 or in the immediately following years. His *Natural History of Religion* was published in 1757, but was written some years earlier. Probably the two works were being composed more or less simultaneously. We know that Hume showed the *Dialogues* to friends ; and since we also know that he was ' revising ' them in or prior to 1761—in a letter of August 1776 to Adam Smith (*cf.* below, p. 91) he states that he had not revised them " these 15 Years "—they must have been completed some time prior to that date, and were therefore composed in his great productive period, when he was between forty and fifty years of age, and when his powers were in their prime. We can be almost equally certain that the final revisions in 1776, in the last months of his fatal illness, could not have been of any very extensive character.

Elliot, so far from approving the *Dialogues*, had persistently urged him not to publish them.

" Is it not hard and tyrannical in you," we find Hume writing to him in 1673, twelve years after the letter above quoted, " more tyrannical than any Act of the Stuarts, not to allow me to publish my Dialogues ? Pray, do you not think that a proper Dedication may atone for what is exceptionable in them ? " (*Letters*, vol. i, p. 380.)

During the years 1751–63 Hume had been showing his manuscript also to other friends, among whom was Adam Smith. One and all of them, it would seem, deprecated publication ; and with such effect that Hume took no further steps in the matter until 1776. Then, however, foreseeing an early end to the illness which had begun in the spring of 1775, he made elaborate, carefully conceived arrangements which show how greatly he valued the *Dialogues*, and how determined he was that they should not be destroyed or suppressed after his death.

His Will, made in January 1776, contains the following clause :

To my friend Dr. Adam Smith, late Professor of Moral Philosophy in Glasgow, I leave all my manuscripts without exception, desiring him to publish my Dialogues concerning Natural Religion, which are comprehended in this present bequest ; but to publish no other papers which he suspects not to have been written within these five years, but to destroy them all at his leisure. And I even leave him full power over all my papers, except the Dialogues above mentioned ; and though I can trust to that intimate and sincere friendship, which has ever subsisted between us, for his faithful execution of this part of my will, yet, as a small recompense of his pains in correcting and publishing this work, I leave him two hundred pounds, to be paid immediately after the publication of it. (*Cf.* Burton, *Life of David Hume*, vol. ii, p. 490 ; *Letters*, vol. ii, p. 317.)

Adam Smith, however, still persisted in his view that the *Dialogues* should not be published. When travelling north from London in April, he had by happy accident come upon Hume at the Inn in Morpeth—Hume being then on his way south to consult his physician, Dr. John Pringle, in London—and at this meeting had persuaded Hume to allow him discretionary power either to publish or not to publish, as he might finally decide. In confirming this agreement by letter Hume writes from London (May 3, 1776) :

I think, however, your Scruples groundless. Was Mallet any wise hurt by his Publication of Lord Bolinbroke ? He received an Office afterwards from the present King and Lord Bute, the most prudish Men in the World ; and he always justify'd himself by his sacred Regard to the Will of a dead Friend. At the same time, I own, that your Scruples have a specious Appearance. But my Opinion is, that, if, upon my Death, you determine never to publish these papers, you should leave them, seal'd up with my Brother and Family, with some Inscription, that you reserve to Yourself the Power of reclaiming them, whenever you think proper. If I live a few Years longer, I shall publish them myself. I consider an Observation of Rochefoucault, that a Wind, though it extinguishes a Candle, blows up a fire. (*Letters*, vol. ii, p. 316.)

With the letter from which the above passage is taken Hume enclosed an ' ostensible ' letter, of the same date, making the required changes of arrangement.

After reflecting more maturely on that Article of my Will by which I left you the Disposal of all my Papers, with a Request that you shou'd publish my *Dialogues concerning Natural Religion*, I have become sensible, that, both on account of the Nature of the Work, and of your Situation, it may be improper to hurry on that Publication. I therefore take the present Opportunity of qualifying that friendly Request : I am content, to leave it entirely to your Discretion at what time you will publish that Piece, or whether you will publish it at all. (*Letters*, vol. ii, pp. 317–18.)

But the compromise to which Hume was thus unwillingly brought proved too grievous to him ; and a few weeks later we find him decided upon immediate publication. Writing (June 8, 1776) to

William Strahan about the new edition of his *History* and of his *Essays*, he states that he has prepared a brief *History of my own Life* which he desired to have prefixed to it. He then adds :

I am also to speak to you of another Work more important : Some Years ago, I composed a piece, which woud make a small Volume in Twelves. I call it *Dialogues on Natural Religion :* Some of my Friends flatter me, that it is the best thing I ever wrote. I have hitherto forborne to publish it, because I was of late desirous to live quietly and keep remote from all Clamour : For though it be not more exceptionable than some things I had formerly published ; yet you know some of these were thought very exceptionable ; and in prudence, perhaps, I ought to have suppressed them. I there introduce a Sceptic, who is indeed refuted, and at last gives up the Argument, nay confesses that he was only amusing himself by all his Cavils ; yet before he is silenced, he advances several Topics, which will give Umbrage, and will be deemed very bold and free, as well as much out of the Common Road. As soon as I arrive at Edinburgh [Hume is writing from Bath whither he had gone for his health] I intend to print a small Edition of 500, of which I may give away about 100 in Presents ; and shall make you a Present of the Remainder, together with the literary Property of the whole, provided you have no Scruple, in your present Situation, of being the Editor : It is not necessary you shoud prefix your Name to the Title Page. I seriously declare, that after Mr. Millar and You and Mr. Cadell have publickly avowed your Publication of the *Enquiry concerning human Understanding*, I know no Reason why you should have the least Scruple with regard to these Dialogues. They will be much less obnoxious to the Law, and not more exposed to popular Clamour. What ever your Resolution be, I beg you wou'd keep an entire Silence on the Subject. If I leave them to you by Will, your executing the Desire of a dead Friend, will render the publication the more excusable. Mallet never suffered any thing by being the Editor of Bolinbroke's Works. (*Letters*, vol. ii, pp. 323–4.)

Increasing disabilities, however, very soon made it clear to Hume that he would not survive to see the *Dialogues* in print. Accordingly, in a codicil dated 7th August he cancelled in his Will the clause above quoted ; and in leaving his manuscript to Strahan, added :

I desire, that my Dialogues concerning Natural Religion, may be printed and published any time within two Years after my Death. . . . I also ordain, that if my Dialogues, from whatever Cause, be not published within two Years and a half of my Death, as also the Account of my Life, the Property shall return to my Nephew, David, whose Duty, in publishing them as the last Request of his Uncle, must be approved of by all the World. (*Letters*, vol. ii, p. 453.)

But this record of Hume's anxious and elaborate precautions to ensure publication of the *Dialogues* is still even yet not complete. Ten days prior to his death he wrote Adam Smith the letter here given in full (*Letters*, vol. ii, p. 334) :

Edinburgh 15 of Augt 1776.

My dear Smith,
    I have ordered a new Copy of my Dialogues to be made besides that which will be sent to Mr. Strahan, and to be kept by my Nephew. If you will permit me, I shall order a third Copy to be made, and consignd to you. It will bind you to nothing, but will serve as a Security. On revising them (which I have not done these 15 Years) I find that nothing can be more cautiously and more artfully written. You had certainly forgotten them. Will you permit me to leave you the Property of the Copy, in case they shoud not be published in five Years after my Decease ? Be so good as to write me an answer soon. My State of Health does not permit me to wait Months for it.

Yours affectionately,

DAVID HUME.

To Adam Smith Esqr. at Kirkaldy.

As already noted, this letter reveals the important fact that the *Dialogues*, after being completed and revised, had not been worked on in the years 1761–76. Hume also here avows that he had very deliberately composed the *Dialogues* in a cautious and ' artful ' manner.
    Replying from Kirkcaldy on 22nd August—Hume's letter, delayed in transit, had lain at the carrier's quarters " these eight days "—Smith states that he will be happy to receive a copy of the *Dialogues*, but adds :

With regard to leaving me the property in case they are not published within five years after your decease, you may do as you think proper. I think, however, you should not menace Strahan with the loss of anything in case he does not publish your work within a certain time. There is no probability of his delaying it, and if any thing should make him delay it, it would be a clause of this kind, which will give him an honourable pretence for doing so. It would then be said that I had published, for the sake of an Emolument, not from respect to the memory of my friend, what even a printer for the sake of the same emolument had not published, That Strahan is sufficiently zealous you will see by the enclosed letter, which I will beg the favour of you to return to me, but by the Post and not by the carrier. If you will give me leave I will add a few lines to your account of your own life, giving some account in my own name of your behaviour in this illness, if, contrary to my own hopes, it should prove your last. (*Letters*, vol. ii, pp. 334–5. *Cf.* the complete letter, as given from the R.S.E. Manuscripts, by Rae, *Life of Adam Smith*, 1895, pp. 300–1. *cf.* also below, p. 243.)

Then, finally, on 23rd August, just two days prior to his death, Hume dictated the last of his extant letters (*Letters*, vol. ii, pp. 335-6); it is addressed to Adam Smith :

Ednr. 23 August 1776.

My Dearest Friend,

I am obliged to make use of my Nephews hand in writing to you as I do not rise to-day.

There is No Man in whom I have a greater Confidence than Mr. Strahan, yet have I left the property of that Manuscript to my Nephew David in case by any accident it should not be published within three years after my decease. The only accident I could forsee, was one to Mr. Strahan's Life, and without this clause My Nephew would have had no right to publish it. Be so good as to inform Mr. Strahan of this Circumstance.

You are too good in thinking any trifles that concern me are so much worth your attention, but I give you entire liberty to make what Additions you please to the account of my Life.

I go very fast to decline, & last night had a small fever, which I hoped might put a quicker period to this tedious Illness, but unluckily it has in a great measure gone of. I cannot submit to your coming over here on my account as it is possible for me to see you so small a Part of the day but Dr. Black can better inform you concerning the degree of strength which may from time to time remain with Me.

Adieu My dearest Friend

DAVID HUME.

P.S. It was a strange blunder to send your Letter by the Carrier.

Adam Smith Esqr. Kirkaldy.

Such is the *external* evidence bearing on the times of composition and revision of the *Dialogues*. The conclusions which can be drawn may be tabulated as follows :

I. *Certainties.*

1. Portions of the *Dialogues*, possibly the whole, existed in draft in 1751 ; and these were then already divided into Parts.
2. Already in 1751 Parts I, II, and III existed substantially in their present form.
3. The manuscript was circulated (in sample or as a whole) among friends during the period 1751-63.
4. Hume speaks of having ' revised ' the *Dialogues* in (or prior to) 1761 ; and they must, by 1781, have existed in some completed form.
5. The manuscript was left untouched throughout the period 1761-76.
6. Hume, in the months immediately preceding his death, ordered two copies (he also speaks of a further third copy) to be made

of his manuscript, and uses terms which lead us to understand that he was himself then engaged in a further revision of the manuscript.

II. *Reasonably probable conclusions.*

1. The sample submitted to Elliot in 1751 included Part IV, and possibly other Parts, but not Part XII.

2. In writing Part XII, which deals with the difficulty that he had invited Elliot to assist him in solving, Hume has been influenced by Elliot's suggestion that the verdicts of feeling and of reason be treated together.

3. The *Dialogues* were completed in 1751-2 or in the immediately following years.

We may now pass to the *internal* evidence, supplied by the manuscript itself. The manuscript now in possession of the Royal Society of Edinburgh—the manuscript which Hume's nephew has meticulously followed in the printing of the *Dialogues*—contains revisions quite evidently made by Hume at different dates, and to judge by the variations in the handwriting, at widely separate dates. This manuscript, we therefore seem justified in concluding, must be the manuscript to which he refers as having been first revised in (or prior to) 1761. On the opening page of Part XI there is written on the margin, presumably by Hume's nephew : " I have sent two Leaves of the original Manuscript, as I have not been able to get the Copy compared with it." This shows that only a copy of the manuscript was sent to the printer, with the exception of this and the next leaf, which must have been returned, to preserve the manuscript intact. Dr. Greig (*David Hume*, p. 230) has concluded that the two leaves in the extant manuscript containing the nephew's inscription must be from a *copy* made by Hume himself. This assumption is, however, unnecessary, and is unsupported by any evidence in the leaves themselves. They are not written any more neatly than many others ; and they have themselves been revised in the manner of the other leaves. Also any evidence we have goes to show that the three copies to which Hume refers were made for, not by, him (*cf.* above, p. 91).

There are two sets of clues of which we can make use in attempting to distinguish between the revisions made in the earlier period and those made in the final revision in 1776. First, there are the modes in which the alterations are inserted. Small verbal changes are, as a rule, written in above the words scored out. Changes of some length, such as the rewording of whole sentences, or the addition of short passages, are entered on the margin. Additions which consist of still longer passages are given on separate sheets appended at the end of the Part concerned, with marks to indicate where the new passages belong. Secondly, there are, as we should naturally have expected in so long an interval as that between 1751 and

1776, changes in the handwriting. When these changes are collated with the corresponding changes in Hume's handwriting as shown in his letters and other writings of different dates, in the R.S.E. manuscripts (*e.g.* with the holograph codicil to his Will, of the date August 7, 1776) conjectures can be made as to whether the writing (in the case of the more lengthy additions) is of the earlier or the later period.[1]

These conjectures, based on the handwriting, are at once more important, and as it happens, owing to the corroborative character of the clues derived from mode of insertion, more reliable in the case of Part XII than in regard to the revisions in any earlier Part. (In the text of the *Dialogues* I have enclosed all *additions* made in revision in heavy square brackets, and when the evidence points to their belonging to the 1776 revision have added a second bracket. The passages which can be thus dated as belonging to the 1776 revision are all in Part XII. *Cf.* pp. 217, 227.) The manuscript shows no alteration of any kind in the concluding paragraph of the *Dialogues*. The mode of leading up to it has, however, been a matter of anxious concern to Hume. The stages in his revisions are as follows : (*a*) as originally written, the concluding paragraph was immediately preceded by what, in the final text, is now the *fourth* last paragraph. Hume made what may be described as a new, *second* ending, by inserting on the margin a new additional paragraph—the *third* last paragraph of the final text (" To know God," &c., p. 226) ; (*b*) Hume added yet another paragraph (" It seems evident," &c., p. 219) as a note to be inserted earlier—writing it on the concluding page of the original Part XII, below the word ' Finis.' The (*a*) and (*b*) additions were apparently made in (or prior to) 1761. (*c*) Hume scored out this note and the entire second ending, and on a new sheet rewrote the second ending without change, but with the addition of a new lengthy paragraph (" If the whole of natural theology," &c., p. 227, the *second* last paragraph of the final text), thus providing what may be described as a new, *third* ending. (*d*) On a further sheet (the concluding sheet of the manuscript) he rewrote, again without change, the note, and on the remainder of the sheet he added a new, very important, and lengthy paragraph (" All men of sound reason," &c., p. 217) in connexion with the new, *third* ending, with marks to indicate where the note and the paragraph belong in the main text (*i.e.* as below, pp. 219, 217). The (*c*) and (*d*) changes would seem to have been made in the 1776 revision. It also seems likely that the introductory pages of the *Dialogues* (pp. 127–9, prior to Part I), which are almost clear of corrections, are a clean copy made, to judge by the handwriting, at a later date than the main body of the manuscript, and

[1] I am indebted to Dr. Meikle, Keeper of the National Library of Scotland, and to Mr. Angus, Curator of Historical Records, Register House, Edinburgh, for assisting me in the examination of the variations in handwriting.

possibly likewise in the 1776 revision. There must from the start have been an introduction of some kind, but we have no direct evidence as to the nature of the changes made in its revision.

These changes, in Part XII, as above noted (pp. 38, 70) are mainly in the direction of making more explicit the quite negative character of Philo's teaching. But in being thus more outspoken Philo has endangered the balance of argument for and against ' the religious hypothesis,' which it has been the professed policy of the *Dialogues* to maintain. Accordingly, in conformity with the required conventions, Philo is made to declare more emphatically than he had previously done, that in limiting reason he has no intention of denying the need of revelation and faith. This, doubtless, is also why Hume has changed (p. 202) ' perhaps ' to the stronger ' I believe.' In rewriting the introductory pages he may have similarly strengthened the statements made by Pamphilus (*cf.* above, p. 61).

I had reached the above conclusions before it occurred to me to examine the watermarks on the sheets of Hume's manuscript. They form, as I then found, a third set of clues which yield important confirmatory evidence. The sheets used are double sheets, the first half having a quite simple watermark (the initials of the manufacturer), and the other half a watermark of more elaborate design. But while the form of paper used is uniform throughout, the watermarks vary in a very significant manner. (*a*) The sheets from the beginning of Part I up to, and including, the sheet containing the *original* ending of the *Dialogues* have all without exception watermarks of a uniform type. (*b*) The double sheet used in the Introduction to the *Dialogues*, and the single sheet on which the *third* ending is given, have another, quite different, and very distinctive type of watermark. (*c*) While this type of watermark, like that of the central sheets, exhibits minor variations (due presumably to differences in successive issues) the elaborate watermark in the introductory sheet is identical even in quite minor respects with the watermark of the sheet on which Hume wrote in the month of his death (on August 7, 1776) a holograph codicil to his Will. (*d*) The concluding single sheet of the manuscript (the sheet on which Hume has rewritten the note and also has added the lengthy paragraph introduced in support of the new third ending, as on pp. 219, 217–9) again has a quite distinctive watermark, entirely different from that of any earlier sheet. There is, as it happens, the same watermark on Edmonstoune's farewell letter to Hume, likewise of August 7, 1776.

On examining the other Hume manuscripts in the R.S.E. Collection I have found the watermark on the central sheets on letters dated 1752, 1757, and (from Paris) 1765. This clue is not, therefore, available for any more exact dating of the body of the manuscript, but is consistent with the dating above suggested.

William Strahan decided that publication of the *Dialogues* would come with more propriety from Hume's nephew, " as done in Obedience to the last Request of his Uncle " (*cf.* the letter from Strahan of February 13, 1777, and the correspondence between Strahan and Hume's brother in the R.S.E. manuscripts). The nephew was Hume's favourite nephew and namesake, David Hume the younger, the third son of John Home. Destined to have a distinguished career—as Sheriff, Professor of Scots Law in the University of Edinburgh, a principal clerk of Session, and Baron of the Scottish Exchequer—he was at the time of Hume's death only nineteen years of age. His uncle's trust he very loyally executed, following in the most careful manner the instructions given on the manuscript. The *Dialogues* appeared in 1779, published by Robinson (as appears from the notices in the *Weekly Magazine*, Edinburgh, October 1779, and the *Monthly Review*, London, December 1779), but with no publisher's name given, and without editorial preface or comment of any kind.

Appendix D

A CRITICAL ANALYSIS OF THE MAIN ARGUMENT OF THE *DIALOGUES*, WITH SOME EXPLANATORY NOTES [1]

PAMPHILUS, in forwarding the twelve parts of the *Dialogues* to Hermippus, dwells on the suitability of the subject to dialogue form. Natural theology deals with a point of doctrine which is so *obvious* as scarcely to admit of dispute and so *important* that it cannot be too often inculcated ; and yet at the same time it leads into philosophical questions which are so *obscure* and *uncertain* that no one can reasonably be positive in regard to them. The point of doctrine which is so obvious and so important is the *being* of God. The obscure and uncertain philosophical questions to which the discussion leads are the *nature* of this divine Being, his attributes, his decrees, his plan of providence.

PARTS I AND II

After some further considerations, also of an introductory character, the argument opens (p. 134) with the question how far reason is a possible and reliable guide in matters of theology, and in what respects, if any, the methods of reasoning proper to theology differ from those which we employ in common life and in science. According to Cleanthes there is no difference. Wherever evidence discovers itself, we adhere to it, no matter what *general* scepticism we may profess. " There is indeed," he points out, " a kind of brutish and ignorant scepticism, as you [Philo] well observed, which gives the vulgar a general prejudice against what they do not easily understand." This species of scepticism, however, " is fatal to knowledge, not to religion " (p. 136). Nor are the philosophical sceptics in a better position. They are obliged to acknowledge that in science the most abstruse and remote objects are those which are best explained. Light is successfully ' anatomized,' and yet the coherence of the parts of bodies and the nourishment of our bodies by food is still an inexplicable mystery. In every question, therefore, they " are obliged to consider each particular evidence apart, and proportion their assent to the precise degree of evidence, which occurs " (p. 137). But if this be their practice in all mathematical, natural and political science, why not also in theology ? " In vain would the sceptic make a distinction between science and common life, or between one science and another "

---

[1] The notes are given in square brackets

97

(p. 137). The differences are differences in the evidence, not in the reasoning processes involved.

Thus far Cleanthes is propounding what in substance are also the views of Philo. Both are agreed that experience, and reasoning in the light of experience, are the sole sources of knowledge, and that wherever such knowledge is possible, the quite general objections of the sceptic may safely be left out of account. To make clear the point of divergence between Cleanthes and Philo, Cleanthes is represented as making the further assertion that if there be any difference between common sense and science, or between one science and another, the advantage lies entirely on the side of theology and natural religion (p. 137) ; while Philo comes forward to maintain that " our ideas reach no farther than our experience : we have no experience of divine attributes and operations : I need not conclude my syllogism : You can draw the inference yourself " (p. 143).

Having thus come to an understanding of the issue between them, Cleanthes proceeds to state the *a posteriori* argument which he represents as incontrovertible—the argument from design. Evidentially, it is securely anchored in experience ; logically, it is reasoning by analogy of the most cogent type. " Look round the world : Contemplate the whole and every part of it : You will find it to be nothing but one great machine, subdivided into an infinite number of lesser machines. . . . The curious adapting of means to ends, throughout all nature, resembles exactly, though it much exceeds, the productions of human contrivance. . . . Since therefore the effects resemble each other, we are led to infer, by all the rules of analogy, that the causes also resemble ; and that the Author of nature is somewhat similar to the mind of man ; though possessed of much larger faculties, proportioned to the grandeur of the work which he has executed " (p. 143).

Philo, with equal directness, states his first criticism. So far from being the most conclusive of empirical inferences, the argument from design is an inferior instance of the type. " That a stone will fall, that fire will burn, that the earth has solidity, we have observed a thousand and a thousand times ; and when any new instance of this nature is presented, we draw without hesitation the *accustomed* inference " (p. 144). Similarly, " if we see a house, we conclude with the greatest certainty, that it had an architect or builder ; because this is precisely that *species of effect* which we have experienced to proceed from that *species of cause* " (p. 144). Stronger evidence is never desired or sought after ; the analogy relied on is a complete analogy. But when Cleanthes proceeds to allege that *the universe is of the same species with a house and therefore has the same species of cause,* he is appealing to an analogy which is by no means entire and perfect. The dissimilitude is so striking that the utmost we can pretend is to " a guess, a conjecture, a presumption concerning a similar cause " (p. 144).

To enforce this objection, and to prepare the way for his further criticisms, Philo gives a restatement of Cleanthes' argument. This restatement he prefaces by a brief formulation of the presuppositions, and of the consequent type of empiricism in which he and Cleanthes are so far in agreement (p. 145). Man cannot, in the absence of experience, merely from his own ideas, determine what in actual fact is and is not possible ; all possibilities are then on an equal footing. Again, even after he opens his eyes, and contemplates the world, as it really is, it is still impossible for him, from direct observation, to assign the cause of any one event. Only repeated experience can reveal the actual cause of any phenomenon ; and until experience has thus given its verdict, we are not in a position to make any valid assertion. This Cleanthes has tacitly allowed. What then follows ? An all-important conclusion, namely, " that order, arrangement, or the adjustment of final causes is not, of itself, any proof of design ; but only so far as it has been *experienced* to proceed from that principle " (p. 146).

[The reader may note how ' order,' ' arrangement,' and ' adjustment of final causes ' are here treated as if they were equivalent expressions. *Cf.* above, p. 72, and below, pp. 102–3.]

" For aught we can know *a priori*, matter may contain the source or spring of order originally, within itself, as well as mind does " (p. 146).

These, then, are presuppositions common to Cleanthes and to Philo ; and in terms of them Philo restates Cleanthes' argument as follows. By *experience* we learn that there is an original principle of order in mind, not in matter. " Throw several pieces of steel together, without shape or form ; they will never arrange themselves so as to compose a watch : Stone and mortar, and wood, without an architect, never erect a house. But the ideas in a human mind, we see, by an unknown, inexplicable œconomy, arrange themselves so as to form the plan of a watch or house. Experience, therefore, proves that there is an original principle of order in mind, not in matter. From similar effects we infer [by analogy] similar causes. The adjustment of means to ends is alike in the universe, as in a machine of human contrivance. The causes, therefore, must be resembling " (p. 146).

Philo asks Cleanthes whether he allows this to be a fair representation of his argument, and Cleanthes having assented, he proceeds to enforce the criticisms already made, and to add yet another. The two criticisms already made are now restated in more explicit terms. They are : (1) that Cleanthes is assuming that the universe may be taken as *of the same species* with houses, ships, furniture, machines ; (2) that he is assuming that the thought, design, reason, or intelligence in men and other *animals*, which we experience as operative *within* nature as an active cause by which one part of nature produces alterations in other previously and independently existing parts—can be used to account for the *origin* and very *existence* of nature *as a whole*.

[Though Hume, in keeping with his scepticism, is usually careful to qualify his assertions, he occasionally allows himself expressions which are more forcible than legitimate, and which in effect beg the issue by the very terms employed. An instance occurs on p. 148, when Philo very inconsistently speaks of " this little agitation of the brain which we call thought " (*cf.* Doughty, *Arabia Deserta* (1888), vol i, p. 405 : " That short motion and parasitical usurpation which is the weak accident of life in matter ") ; and again on pp. 180–1, where, speaking of the Brahmin theory that the world arose from an infinite spider, he asks, " why an orderly system may not be spun from the belly as well as from the brain." Philo is here arguing as Hume, speaking in his own person, has done in his essay *Of Suicide* : " It would be no crime in me to divert the *Nile* or *Danube* from its course, were I able to effect such purposes. Where then is the crime of turning a few ounces of blood from their natural channels ? " (*Essays*, G. & G., vol. ii, p. 410.)

Hume now adds (3) the further criticism, namely, that Cleanthes is also tacitly assuming that thought in the sense of design is the *only* principle of order disclosed in experience, ignoring the infinite number of springs and principles which even our limited experience of nature shows her to possess, such as heat and cold, attraction and repulsion, vegetable and animal organization.

Taking the first two points together, Philo returns to enforce his previous objection (given on p. 144). " When two *species* of objects have always been observed to be conjoined together, I can *infer*, by custom, the existence of one wherever I *see* the existence of the other : And this I call an argument from experience. But how this argument can have place, where the objects, as in the present case [nature as a whole and its Author], are single, individual, without parallel . . . may be difficult to explain " (p. 149). To justify such an inference, should we not require to have had experience of the origin of worlds, such experience as we have of the origin of houses and machines ?

Cleanthes replies that reason, properly analysed, is nothing but a species of experience, and that to prove the origin of the universe it is no more necessary to have *observed* its origin than in proof of the motion of the earth it is necessary that we should be in position to *see* it *move*. Or have we, he asks, other earths which we have seen to move ?

This gives Philo his opportunity. " Yes ! we have other earths. Is not the moon another earth, which we see to turn round its centre ? . . . All the planets, are they not earths, which revolve about the sun ? " (p. 150). By these analogies and resemblances, with others—*supported by proof that there is no ground for a distinction between terrestrial and celestial substances*—the Copernican theory is brought into line with our general experience, and receives detailed confirmation. Are there any such analogies to which the argument from design can appeal?

PART III

Cleanthes replies to Philo's question. In theology no such elaboration of detailed proof is, he claims, necessary. The similarity of terrestrial and celestial matter had been denied, and therefore had to be proved. Proof is not, however, required to establish the similarity of the works of nature to those of art ; their similarity is *self-evident and undeniable* (p. 152). " The same matter, a like form : What more is requisite to show an analogy between their causes ? "

Cleanthes, that is to say, makes no kind of reply to Philo's criticisms, beyond dogmatically reaffirming his original assertions. A reply, he contends, is unnecessary. The self-evident, if mistakenly challenged, can be reinforced only by illustrations, not by arguments.

The illustrations employed for this purpose by Cleanthes are two in number. (1) Were an articulate voice heard in the clouds, speaking to each nation in its own language and dialect, and conveying some instruction worthy of a being superior to mankind, could we hesitate a moment concerning the cause of the voice, and must we not instantly ascribe it to some design or purpose ?

[This example, it may be noted, chiefly serves to illustrate Cleanthes' entire failure to recognize the point and force of Philo's criticisms. He is taking advantage of the fact that human experience repeatedly and universally testifies that articulate speech has one and only one *species* of origin, and that we experience in ourselves what this mode of origin is. Did a voice speak to us from the clouds, then however it might differ from the human in its melodiousness and in its greater command of languages and dialects, these differences would not, it may be agreed, so weaken the analogy as to render it invalid. The effect appealed to is an instance of a *species* familiar in experience, and as described maintains the degree of analogy required for concluding that it has the same *species* of previously experienced cause. Philo is not, therefore, concerned to challenge the force of the illustration as an illustration of what, under the supposed circumstances, would be a legitimate inference by analogy. But it does not even *attempt* to meet Philo's criticisms, and is therefore both irrelevant and misleading.]

(2) In his second illustration, Cleanthes' general thesis is that " the anatomy of an animal affords many stronger instances of

design than the perusal of Livy or Tacitus " (p. 154). It is to illustrate this thesis that he makes the curiously artificial supposition of an animal or vegetable library. He supposes " that there is a natural, universal, invariable language, common to every individual of the human race ; and that books are natural productions, which perpetuate themselves in the same manner with animals and vegetables, by descent and propagation " (p. 153). Inasmuch as an *Iliad* or *Aeneid* contains infinitely fewer parts and less contrivance in its composition than the coarsest organized body, the propagation of these works is, he declares, an easier supposition than that of any plant or animal.

[How, we may ask, is that which, to judge by our experience of the actual, is utterly impossible, the self-propagation of books describable as ' easier ' ? Of course if the books are to be conceived not as books, but as animals, the impossibility then vanishes, but so also does the illustration.]

Could we, then, on entering a library thus peopled by natural volumes, and on finding that they contained the most refined reasoning and exquisite beauty, doubt that their originating cause bore the strongest analogy to mind and intelligence ?

[This illustration is a very bewildering one ; and that it should be found so is probably part at least of Hume's intention in introducing it here. Such, he is virtually saying, is the best that can be done in support of Cleanthes' assertion that " the similarity of the works of nature and those of art . . . is self-evident and undeniable." It is indeed *illustrative* ; but mainly of the difficulties that stand in the way. For what is peculiarly characteristic of the argument from design—at once its strength and its greatest weakness—is that it has always professed to find its chief and most convincing evidence precisely in the field where the analogy to which it appeals is *least* applicable, namely, in the field of animal and vegetable life. The organic is not only organized ; it is self-organizing. Organisms are self-developing, self-maintaining, self-regulating, self-propagating. Their ' form,' that is to say, is as native and natural to them as is the ' matter ' of which they are composed. In an artificial product, on the other hand, the form, so far from being native to it, depends for its existence on an external artificer. This difference may not be so striking when the objects are simple and made out of one single material ; it is ' self-evident and undeniable ' in proportion as the objects are complexly articulated. The adult organism—to employ terms not used by Hume—comes into being through the *differentiation* of the previously homogeneous ; artificial objects come into being through the *external fitting together* of bodies antecedently shaped and formed.

Any examples, therefore, which are designed to 'illustrate' the 'self-evident' similarity of organisms to artificial products must either ignore these differences, by viewing organisms as if they had a machine-like origin, or else suggest that machines, all appearances to the contrary notwithstanding, are precisely what organisms present themselves as being. Cleanthes, however, in his supposition of a vegetating library does neither the one nor the other, to the bewilderment of the attentive reader. In so doing—as I have already suggested this was probably Hume's intention in employing it here—it helps to prepare the way for an appreciation of Philo's counter-argument, that it is in organization, whether vegetable or animal, that the *disparity* between the artificial and the native is most evident. Organization, he points out, is a principle of order additional to, and alternative to, conscious purpose ; and supplies, therefore, a competing method of accounting for ' order and final causes '—the more so in that, if we may trust experience, mind is conditioned by organization, not organization by mind. Consequently, it is precisely the differences between ' project and forethought' as revealed in articulate speech, in a book, or in a machine, and ' order and final causes' as exhibited in plants and animals, that have to be reckoned with. In Cleanthes' illustration they are confounded together, not distinguished. If a book is really a book it is due to ' project and forethought,' *not* to propagation ; if, on the other hand, it is due to propagation it must be a vegetable or animal, and to term it a book is to insist on a resemblance while refusing the conditions which can alone make it relevant.

Cleanthes is also unfairly taking advantage of the fact that works such as the *Aeneid* are the outcome of *creative* art. The type of activity to which they are due cannot be identified either with Divine activity (presumed to be creative in the absolute theological sense) or with our merely *repetitive* activities. Through repetitive activities, in the light of *previous* experience, by way of project and foresight, we are able to advance to an antecedently defined goal. Creative art (*e.g.* the creative activities of the architect, in distinction from the activities of the contractor, whose activities are governed, from start to finish, by the architect's plans (raises the wider issues dwelt upon by Philo in Parts VI, VII, and VIII. In his *Essays* Hume has drawn attention to the *conditioned* character of creative art. " Art may make a suit of clothes : But nature must produce a man. Even in those productions, commonly denominated works of art, we find the noblest of the kind are beholden for their chief beauty to the force and happy influence of nature. . . . How poor are those songs, when a happy flow of fancy has not furnished materials for art to embellish and refine ! " (*Essays*, G. & G., vol. i, p. 197 ; *cf.* p. 177.) As Hume here suggests, even our ' creative ' activities afford no analogy that can supply the key to, *i.e.* render comprehensible to us, the nature of creation in the strict theological sense. *Our creative activities are more, not less, complexly conditioned than our repetitive activities. Cf.* below, p. 106.

In these two illustrations, with their preceding arguments, Cleanthes has shot his bolt. It is, however, too early in the *Dialogues* for this to be allowed to become apparent ; and the criticisms which I have outlined are reserved for later statement, in other contexts.]

Cleanthes, continuing his argument uninterrupted, is made to draw attention to what, as we know (*cf.* above, pp. 87-8), had impressed Hume as being a chief, outstanding difficulty—the fact, namely, that " the dissimilitudes " between the works of nature and of human art do not weaken the inference to design as much as we might properly expect ; or more correctly stated, that the verdict of feeling seems here to stand out in opposition to the verdict of reason. The issues thus raised are so different from those involved in the argument from design, in its intellectualist form, and are so much more complex, that Philo is careful not to attempt any kind of reply at this stage. He prepares the way by much preliminary discussion ; and it is not until the very close of the *Dialogues*, in Part XII, that he proceeds to answer the question which Cleanthes propounds here in the following terms :

" Consider, anatomize the eye : Survey its structure and contrivance ; and tell me, *from your own feeling*, if the idea of a contriver does not immediately flow in upon you *with a force like that of sensation*. The most obvious conclusion surely is in favour of design ; and it requires time, reflection and study, to summon up those frivolous, though abstruse, objections, which can support infidelity " (p. 154). Cleanthes concludes his argument by further comments, all of which are directed to enforcing the thesis, that the argument from design, however irregular as regards logical forms, is irresistible in its actual influence on the mind, and is universally recognized.

At this juncture (p. 155) Pamphilus is brought forward to suggest that Cleanthes' argument left Philo " a little embarrassed and confounded," and that he was hesitating in his reply when Demea " broke in upon the discourse and saved his countenance."

The burden of Demea's comments, sufficient to give the discussion a new turn, is that the volume of nature " contains a great and inexplicable riddle, more than any intelligible discourse or reasoning " (p. 156). We can make no such approach to the Deity as we can to the mind of the author of a book. The sentiments and ideas which " compose the whole furniture of human understanding " are " fluctuating, uncertain, fleeting, successive, and compounded ; and were we to remove these circumstances, we absolutely annihilate its essence " (pp. 156-7). So little do the infirmities of our nature " permit us to reach any ideas which in the least correspond to the ineffable sublimity of the divine attributes " (p. 157).

PART IV

Demea continues this line of thought ; and in preparation for Philo's argument he expounds Hume's view of the self. " What is the soul of man ? A composition of various faculties, passions, sentiments, ideas ; united, indeed, into one self or person, but still distinct from each other. When it reasons, the ideas, which are the parts of its discourse, arrange themselves in a certain form or order ; which is not preserved entire for a moment, but immediately gives place to another arrangement, . . . How is this compatible with that perfect immutability and simplicity which all true theists ascribe to the Deity ? " (p. 159).

This brings Cleanthes back into the discussion, to uphold the analogy between the human and the divine ; and in order to preserve it he makes his first break with the traditional theology. Those, he says, who maintain the simplicity of the supreme Being are atheists without knowing it. " A mind whose acts and sentiments and ideas are not distinct and successive . . . is no mind at all " (p. 159). To this extent, therefore, his analogy between the human and the divine mind still holds.

And now we come to Philo's reinforcement of his previous criticisms developing the suggestions which Hume has taken over from Bayle's account of Strato's teaching (*cf.* above, pp. 35–6, and Appendix B, above, p. 80). " I shall prove that there is no ground to suppose a plan of the world to be formed in the divine mind, consisting of distinct ideas . . . in the same manner as an architect forms in his head the plan of a house which he intends to execute " (p. 160). For what is gained by this supposition ? If there be a plan of nature, it must be an all-inclusive plan, specified down to the minutest detail. There will be nothing in nature which does not have its parallel in the plan ; neither, therefore, will be any simpler than the other ; and if either needs a cause, so also must the other. " In an abstract view, they are entirely [*i.e.* in their detail] alike ; and no difficulty attends the one supposition, which is not common to both of them " (p. 160).

Has not Cleanthes' appeal been to experience ? But experience supports us in requiring that the two kinds of world—real and ideal —should have parity of treatment. Experience gives us specimens of both kinds of world. " Our own mind resembles the one : A vegetable or animal body the other " (p. 161). And as experience further shows, both kinds " depend upon an equal variety of causes." " Nothing seems more delicate with regard to its causes than thought. . . . As far as we can judge, vegetables and animal bodies are not more delicate in their motions, nor depend upon a greater variety or more curious adjustment of springs and principles."

If, therefore, we trace the natural world into an exactly parallel, and no less detailed, ideal world in the mind of God, what have we gained ? Have we not the same reason to trace this ideal world into yet another ideal world ? And if we stop, and go no farther, why go so far ? Why not stop at the material world ? Can we go behind it in this manner, without being thereby committed to a regress *in infinitum* ?

[Philo's argument may, with profit, be amplified. In the ' designing ' of a house, we have to distinguish between the parts played by the architect and by the contractor and manual workers. The architect supplies the contractor with a plan. The contractor's task is to embody it in stone and mortar. The plan tells him in detail what he has to do ; from the very start he plans his work with foresight of the end to be achieved. The architect's problem is very different ; his task is to discover a plan. But in doing so, he cannot work according to plan. He works indeed purposively, but without complete foresight (*cf.* above, pp. 102–3). He *creates* his plan ; he does not ' plan ' it— not, at least, in the manner of a contractor, guided at every step by an antecedent fully detailed plan that governs his activities. Hume's treatment (in this and the following sections) of what may perhaps not improperly be entitled the *factual* features of the argument from design, as distinguished from its more strictly logical features, is therefore, in substance, as follows : (1) If there be the same complexity and detail in the plan of nature as in nature itself, is not the true problem how God obtains his plan ? (2) If it be further agreed that God cannot be conceived as planning his plan, but as creating it, why may he not be conceived as creating nature without the intervention of any such intermediary? (3) Lastly—though this is a point which Hume treats only by implication—if God does indeed act *creatively*, can we hope to find in any of our human activities, even in those that we entitle ' creative,' the key to the mystery? Our activities, in proportion as they are creative, and not merely repetitive, proceed by trial and failure, and even so demand for their possibility an independently existing environment to supply the ideas and materials through which the activities operate and by which they are at once directed and inspired. As Philo (in Part VIII) points out, *all our ideas are ectypal before they can become archetypal. Not only does the argument from design reverse this order, it also views the divine activities as if they were of the inferior contractual type.*

This criticism is at once independent of, and supplementary to, Hume's other main criticism of the argument from design that it rests on the illegitimate assumption that the ' form ' of nature originates independently of its ' matter.' This assumption, Hume suggests, is responsible for its other chief assumptions, as covertly made by means of its insufficiently analysed concepts of ' design ' and ' creation.']

If, then, the ideal world into which the argument from design traces the material world is as much in need of explanation as the material world itself, if we have still to postulate a principle of order, on what ground can we claim that this must be mental and cannot be material? That is, indeed, what Cleanthes claims. Mind, he contends, is not only *a* principle of order, but the *only* principle of order. In this thesis he professes to have the support of experience ; and it is against this position that Philo directs his batteries.

" We have, indeed, experience of ideas, which fall into order, of themselves, and without any *known* cause : But, I am su~~, we have a much larger experience of matter, which does the same ; as in all instances of generation and vegetation, where the accurate analysis of the cause exceeds all human comprehension " (p. 162). Secondly, " we have also experience of particular systems of thought and of matter, which have no order ; of the first, in madness, of the second, in corruption. Why then should we think, that order is more essential to one than the other? And if it requires a cause in both, what do we gain . . . in tracing the universe of objects into a similar [equally detailed] universe of ideas ? " (p. 162). We are merely disguising our ignorance which is equally great in both worlds. If when it is asked what cause produces order in the ideas of the Supreme Being, it be legitimate to assign it to a *rational faculty*, and to say that such is the nature of the Deity, why is not a similar answer equally satisfactory in accounting for the order of the world, namely, by saying that *this* is the nature of material bodies, and that they are originally possessed of a *faculty of order and proportion*. " These are only more learned and elaborate ways of confessing our ignorance ; nor has the one hypothesis any real advantage above the other, except in its greater conformity to vulgar prejudices " (p. 163).

In replying to this criticism Cleanthes reaffirms his previous contention (with which Philo has *not* so far dealt), that the immediate impression made by nature upon the mind is irresistible, whatever abstruse doubts and objections may be raised. Incidentally he also makes a further point. Ultimate causes, he urges—and must not Philo agree?—are totally unknown ; the causes of phenomena are to philosophers as inexplicable as the phenomena themselves are to the vulgar. If, then, the order and arrangement of nature bespeak an intelligent cause, why may we not rest in it ? " I have found a Deity ; and here I stop my enquiry " (p. 163).

[Cleanthes, it may be noted, while speaking of the impression made upon us by nature in terms which imply that it is an *immediate* impression " with a force like that of sensation " (p. 154), none the less still continues to assume that it is by *inference* that it carries us to a Deity.]

This gives Philo the opportunity—he still ignores Cleanthes' point regarding the *immediate* impression made by nature—to complete his previous criticism through a return upon his initial statement of it. Philo, it may be recalled, has urged (and Cleanthes has not attempted to make any kind of reply) that inference to a cause is in order only when we have experienced the conjunction of two *species* of objects ; and as he now adds, all that we actually do in such inference is to " explain particular effects by more general causes," the general causes remaining totally inexplicable. There is a genuine gain in this process of ' explanation.' For the newly experienced particular, however unfamiliar in character it may at first have seemed to be, is thereby shown to be an instance of a *species* already known to us in past experience. There can be no such advantage in ' explaining ' a particular effect by a *particular* cause—even granting that this could ever be done by way of inference Yet this is what is attempted in the argument from design. *The particular effect to be accounted for is the universe ; the alleged cause is an ideal system, not itself designed.* Since this cause conforms to no previously experienced type, it is reached (so far as it can be reached at all) only by sheer hypothesis, not by inference. And, moreover, it is just as mysterious as that for which it professes to account. *An ideal system, not itself designed, is just as mysterious as a material system of nature, not itself designed. If the one can possess its order without a precedent design, why not also the other ?* There is no more difficulty in the one supposition than in the other. *Consequently*, in assuming an ideal plan, *we are merely*, as already said, *conceding our ignorance, by a supposition for which we can offer no justification, either evidential or logical.*

PART V

Philo, continuing his argument, elaborates his previous criticism that the universe is *not* of the same species with buildings and machines. As he has just said at the close of Part IV, it is *unique*, and of its mode of origin we have no experience.

Cleanthes, in replying, merely reasserts his first thesis. The new discoveries in anatomy, chemistry, botany, &c., are only, he declares, so many new instances of art and contrivance, reflecting on us from innumerable objects a mind *like the human*. And thus in the endeavour to uphold the argument from design, as an argument by *analogy*, he is driven to make yet a second departure from the traditional theology. *The divine mind is*, he says, *a mind like the human, and " the liker the better "* (p. 166). God is *finite*—a doctrine by which he also endeavours, later (in Part XI), to escape from another set of difficulties.

" The liker the better." With this doctrine of a finite God, limited by external necessities, Philo proceeds to deal very faithfully, on the lines of his argument in Section XI of the *Enquiry*. If, in argument by analogy, the cause must be proportioned to the effect, then on the supposition that God is finite, we have no ground for ascribing perfection to him, " even in his finite capacity " ; **or** for supposing him so different from man as to be free from every error, mistake, or incoherence in his undertakings (p. 166). If we allow a perfect Author of nature to be proved *a priori*, many defects in nature may be viewed as only seeming defects. But on Cleanthes' method of reasoning these defects may be insisted on as new instances of likeness to human art and contrivance. At least it is not possible to decide which of the two interpretations is the more correct. The universe being unique, we have no independent means of discrimination. " Could a peasant, if the *Aeneid* were read to him, pronounce the poem to be absolutely faultless, or even assign to it its proper rank among the productions of human wit ; he, who had never seen any other production ? "

Nor, on such an hypothesis, can we even be certain how far such excellences as we find are justly to be ascribed to its Author. Its Author may be copying an art which has gradually been improving, through a long succession of ages, " after multiplied trials, mistakes, corrections, deliberations, and controversies " (p. 167). Many worlds may have been botched and bungled ; many fruitless trials made. Also, if God be not infinite, but only an angelic being of transcendent power, there may be other such beings ; and it may be to their co-operative contrivance that nature is due. When there are so many hypotheses, how are we to determine the truth, or even conjecture where the probability lies ?

" The liker the better." But men are animals, of two sexes, and renew the species by generation. Why must this circumstance, so universal, so essential, be left out of account ? Is not the theogony of ancient times back on our hands ? Are not gods corporeal and of the human figure ? " From the moment the attributes of the Deity are supposed finite, all these [suppositions] have place. And I cannot, for my part, think, that so wild and unsettled a system of theology is, in any respect, preferable to none at all " (p. 169).

Cleanthes' only reply is that each and all of these wild suppositions admits something like design ; to this concession he adheres, and in it finds a sufficient foundation for religion.

PART VI

Philo makes direct reply to Cleanthes. There *is* an hypothesis alternative to design ; and one which is much more in harmony with Cleanthes' own professed method of argument. For though Cleanthes has rightly insisted upon the principle that like effects arise from like causes, he has omitted to give equal weight to a principle of the same kind, no less certain, and having its source

in the same experience, namely, " that where several known circumstances are *observed* to be similar, the unknown will also be *found*
similar " (p. 170). " Thus, if we see the limbs of a human body,
we conclude, that it is also attended with a human head, though
hid from us. Thus, if we see, through a chink in a wall, a small
part of the sun, we conclude, that, were the wall removed, we
should see the whole body." No method of reasoning is more
familiar, and none more reliable.

Cleanthes has already, by implication, conceded this in his
principle " the liker the better " ; but, as Philo now proceeds to
point out, this principle has consequences very different from those
for which Cleanthes has been arguing. For, as already noted in
Part IV, man is an *animal* ; and the universe itself is more like an
organized body than a work of art and contrivance. " It seems
actuated with a like principle of life and motion. A continual
circulation of matter in it produces no disorder : A continual waste
in every part is incessantly repaired : The closest sympathy is
perceived throughout the entire system ; And each part or member,
in performing its proper offices, operates both to its own preservation
and to that of the whole. The world, therefore, I infer, is an animal "
(pp. 170–1).

If analogy is ever, with any propriety, to be the basis of argument, is not this the inference which experience supports, and not
the hypothesis of design ? *What can be more repugnant to common
experience than mind without body ? Mere spiritual substance is never found
by us.* If, therefore, it be analogy, and analogy alone, that is to
justify our inferences, must we not conclude that " the divine mind
and body [are] also coeval, and [that] both of them [have] order
and arrangement naturally inherent in them, and inseparable from
them " ? (p. 171). If our limited experience is an unequal standard
by which to judge of the universe, then Cleanthes' hypothesis is
entirely abandoned. If, on the other hand, it is to be in any degree
relied upon, this is the conclusion which it supports, not that of
design.

On Cleanthes' admitting that these are considerations which
have never occurred to him, and which he would not like to attempt
to answer without further thought, compliments are paid to him
on his scrupulous caution and reserve. This makes it possible for
Hume to cover Cleanthes' failure to reply, by meantime putting
into his mouth only two minor comments : (*a*) that the universe
has no organs of sense, no seat of thought and reason, no one precise
organ of action and motion ; and that it therefore bears a stronger
resemblance to a vegetable than to an animal. [Thus Philo's main
point that the universe bears stronger resemblance to an organized
body than to a machine is left untouched] : (*b*) that Philo's hypothesis implies the eternity of the world, which is inconsistent with the
late origin of arts and sciences. Nothing less than a total convulsion

of the elements will ever destroy all the European animals and vegetation, which are now to be found in the Western world.

Philo, in this Part, replies only to the second point ; later (in Part VII) he concedes the first. What argument, he asks, is there against such convulsions ? There is sufficient evidence that every part of the earth has continued for many ages entirely covered with water. The supposition that order is inseparable from matter is not inconsistent with our supposing matter to be also susceptible of many and great revolutions through the endless periods of eternal duration. The world, in all its parts, is subject to constant transformation ; and yet all these changes and corruptions are but passages from one order to another. Matter never rests in any one form, but also it never rests in total deformity and confusion.

Philo, in confirmation of this assertion, proceeds to propound the thesis, to the support of which his argument throughout the remaining Parts of the *Dialogues* is directed (the thesis of Strato, *cf.* above, pp. 35–6, 80 *sqq.*), that in nature matter and form are inseparable. " Were I obliged to defend any particular system . . . I esteem none more plausible than that which ascribes an eternal, inherent principle of order to the world ; though attended with great and continual revolutions and alterations. This at once solves all difficulties ; and if the solution, by being so general, is not entirely complete and satisfactory, it is, at least, a theory, that we must, sooner or later, have recourse to, whatever system we embrace " (p. 174). Now also Philo is allowed to indicate the sceptical implications of this thesis. " *How could things have been as they are, were there not an original, inherent principle of order somewhere, in thought or in matter ? And it is very indifferent to which of these we give the preference.* Chance has no place, on any hypothesis, sceptical or religious. Everything is surely governed by steady, inviolable laws. And were the inmost essence of things laid open to us, we should then discover a scene, of which, at present, we can have no idea. Instead of admiring the order of natural beings, we should clearly see, that it was absolutely impossible for them, in the smallest article, ever to admit of any other disposition " (pp. 174–5). This thesis, as befits its central importance, in Philo's teaching, is repeated by him, in almost the same words, in Part IX (*cf.* pp. 189–90).

PART VII

Philo is now in a position to develop the third of his three criticisms (*cf.* above, p. 100) of the argument from design. The argument, as stated by Cleanthes, rests on the fundamental thesis that experience shows mind to be the *sole* ultimate principle of order. Cleanthes has been brought to recognize (p. 172)—or at least not to deny—that the universe bears a greater likeness to an organized body, in the *vegetable* form, than to works of human art. Now we know by experience the causes of vegetable and animal organisms. The cause of animals is generation ; and this cause is as well, or rather as little, known to us as mind or reason. " When I see an animal, I infer, that it sprang from generation ; and that with as great certainty as you conclude a house to have been reared by design " (p. 178). " Nor is it less intelligible, or less comfortable to experience to say, that the world arose by vegetation from a seed sown by another world, than to say that it arose from a divine reason or contrivance, according to the sense in which Cleanthes understands it " (p. 178).

Demea asks whether this power is not ultimately itself an argument for design in the Author of nature. Could so wonderful a faculty as this vegetative quality arise otherwise than from design ? Can order spring from anything which perceives not the order which it bestows ?

Philo brings this question to the test of experience [*cf.* Cicero, *de Natura Deorum*, Bk. II, 8 *sqq.* ; Bk. III, 9 *sqq.*]. A tree bestows order on that tree which springs from it, an animal on its offspring, a bird on its nest. *Instances of this kind are more frequent in the world than those of order which arise from reason and contrivance.* Experience, therefore, affords no justification for Cleanthes' thesis, that thought is the *only* source of order. If that is to be proved, it will have to be proved *a priori.*

There are also two further objections to which, consistently with his principles, Cleanthes can make no effective reply. He has admitted (in Part IV, p. 163) that ultimate causes are always inexplicable—reason as truly as vegetation or generation. " *It is sufficient,*" he has admitted, " *if the steps, so far as we go, are supported by experience and observation* " (p. 179). Now *undeniably*, generation, as well as reason, is a principle of order in nature. If we rest our cosmology on reason, preferably to generation, it is at our own choice ; and moreover—what is still more to the point—the choice runs *counter* to experience. For " *judging by our limited and imperfect experience, generation has some privileges above reason* " (pp. 179–80). *Every day we see reason arise from organization, never organization from reason. In deciding, therefore, for generation as the more ultimate cause, experience is so far on the side of generation.* If Cleanthes professes to carry this hypothesis a step farther, and to be able to infer design from the great principle of generation, we can, *with better authority,* use the same freedom to go behind his hypothesis, inferring a divine generation or theogony from his principle of reason. " I have at least some faint shadow of experience, which is the utmost that can ever be attained in the present subject. Reason, in innumerable instances, is observed to arise from the principle of generation [*i.e.* to be conditioned by animal organization], and never to arise from any other principle."

PART VIII

[To these specific criticisms Cleanthes does not even attempt to reply, either here, or in any later Part of the *Dialogues*. Philo, as already noted (above, p. 65) is made at the close of his argument (p. 180) to expound it in a somewhat outrageous manner, in terms of the Brahmin theory that the world arose from the belly of an infinite spider—and so provides Cleanthes with an excuse for not caring to refute " such out-of-the-way difficulties."]

PART VIII

Philo, tranquilly continuing his argument, points out that the difficulties are not ' invented ' by him, but are native to the questions discussed. In subjects adapted to the narrow compass of human reason there is commonly but one determination that carries probability or conviction with it ; whereas in these ultimate questions a hundred contradictory views may preserve a kind of imperfect analogy, and " it is a thousand, a million to one, if either yours or any one of mine be the true system " (p. 182).

To enforce this thesis, and incidentally to mark his sense of the inadequacy of any merely atomistic metaphysics, Philo takes the Epicurean hypothesis—" commonly, and I believe, justly, esteemed the most absurd system that has yet been proposed " (p. 182), for the purpose of showing that, with a few alterations, even it can be " brought to bear a faint appearance of probability." The modifications which Hume proceeds to suggest are all in the direction of recognizing the inseparability of matter and form in natural processes ; and as he might have added, in view of his statements elsewhere (*cf.* p. 174), of ceasing to place reliance on what we have no grounds for assuming, chance or accident. " The beginning of motion in matter itself is as conceivable *a priori* as its communication from mind and intelligence " (p. 183). If there be a fixed stock of motion which is propagated by impulse through all eternity, which is lost in its composition being gained by its resolution, and if there be also a fixed number of particles susceptible only of finite transpositions, we then ' stumble on ' " a new hypothesis of cosmogony, that is not absolutely absurd and improbable," namely, that there is " a system, an order, an economy of things, by which matter can preserve that perpetual agitation which seems essential to it, and yet maintain a constancy in the forms which it produces " (p. 183). In all its states, when " so poised, arranged, and adjusted as to continue in perpetual motion " it will have the same appearance of art and contrivance which we observe at present.

This, Philo contends, affords a plausible, if not a true, explanation of the order and curious contrivances in nature. It is vain to insist upon the uses of the parts in animals and plants, or the mutual adjustment of the animals and plants to one another and to the world as a whole. How could an animal subsist unless its parts were so adjusted? In the absence of the adjustments it perishes, and its matter in perishing takes some other form. For if the corrupted matter be not laid claim to by some other form, the world must itself dissolve, passing through new positions, until it falls into the present or some other order.

Cleanthes allows that by this last argument we may account for there being necessarily, from time to time, some sort of order, but cannot account for the present order. Men, and all animals, have conveniences and advantages beyond what is necessary for mere survival. Are *two* eyes and *two* ears necessary? Man is supplied with domestic animals and with fruits.

Philo allows the force of Cleanthes' objection. It shows Epicurus' hypothesis to be incomplete and imperfect. This, he says, he has no scruple in allowing. For the hypothesis has been brought forward precisely in order to show that though justly esteemed the most absurd system that has ever been proposed, it can yet, with a few alterations, be brought to bear a faint appearance of probability, and in this respect to compare favourably with any other, not excepting Cleanthes' own hypothesis of design.

To complete the comparison, Philo again states the much more serious objections to which Cleanthes' argument from design has (in Parts IV, V, VI, and VII, in development of Philo's *third* criticism (above, p. 100)) been shown to lie open—notwithstanding that Cleanthes has "run into anthropomorphism" (p. 186) the better to preserve an analogy to common experience. (1) *In all instances which we have ever seen, ideas are copied from real objects, and are ectypal, not archetypal. The hypothesis of design reverses this order, and gives thought the precedence.* (2) *In all instances which we have ever seen, thought has no influence upon matter, except where that matter is so conjoined with it as to have an equal reciprocal influence upon it.* No animal can move immediately anything but the members of that body which makes it possible as a conscious being. *With this uniform and universal experience the design hypothesis is in direct conflict.*

In short, the empirical analogies do not suffice to justify any 'religious system.' Each disputant triumphs in exhibiting the defects in the counter-theories; but all of them together prepare a complete triumph for the sceptic. A suspense of judgment is our only reasonable resource.

PART IX

This brief section, shorter than any of the others, is of the nature of a digression. Demea, who in Part I has dwelt on "the obscurity of all philosophy" (pp. 130-1) and in Part II on "the infirmities of human understanding" and "the temerity of prying into [God's] nature and essence, decrees and attributes" (p. 141), now comes forward as a supporter of the *a priori* argument. It alone, Demea maintains, can afford an infallible demonstration of the infinity of the divine attributes. As Cleanthes has recognized, an effect which is, or may be, finite, cannot prove an infinite cause ; and as Philo has argued, the *unity* of the divine nature is also left undetermined.

[The argument which Demea has in view is a combination of the cosmological and ontological arguments, and is, in fact, a brief restatement of the argument formulated by Clarke (*cf.* above, p. 26), who is referred to by name on p. 190.]

In the chain of causes and effects, each effect is determined by a cause which precedes it, and the chain, taken as a whole, requires a cause or reason as much as any one member of it (p. 189). For the question is reasonable, and has to be met, why this particular succession of causes has existed from eternity, and not any other succession, or no succession at all. Why has something—and this particular something, exclusive of all other possibilities—been determined to exist rather than nothing ? External causes there are supposed to be none. Chance is a word without meaning. The cause cannot be nothing, for that can never produce anything. We must therefore resort to a *necessarily* existent Being, who carries the *reason* of his existence in himself ; and who, as necessarily existent, cannot be supposed not to exist without an express contradiction.

Hume, following his usual procedure of having as much as possible of Philo's case expounded by one of the other protagonists, places his main criticisms of this *a priori* argument in the mouth of Cleanthes.

A matter of fact can never be proved by arguments *a priori*. Nothing is demonstrable unless the contrary implies a contradiction ; and nothing that is distinctly conceivable implies a contradiction ; whatever we conceive as existent, we can also conceive as non-existent. That is to say, there is no being whose non-existence implies a contradiction ; and consequently no being whose existence is demonstrable. This argument is by itself decisive. The words ' necessary *existence* ' have no meaning ; or what is the same thing, none that is consistent (p. 190).

Further, on this pretended ' explication ' of necessity, may not the material universe be the necessarily existent Being ? We do not know all the qualities of matter, and for aught we can determine, it may contain some qualities which, were they known, would make its non-existence appear as great a contradiction as that twice two is five (p. 190).

Lastly, in tracing an eternal succession of objects it seems absurd to inquire for ' a general cause or first Author.' How can anything that exists from eternity have a cause ? That relation implies a priority in time and a beginning of existence. When we have shown the particular cause of each individual in a collection of twenty particles of matter, it is unreasonable to ask what was the cause of the whole twenty. This is sufficiently explained in explaining the cause of the parts (pp. 190–1).

[The last two arguments, it may be noted, sound very strangely in the mouth of Cleanthes.]

Philo, as he well may, approves Cleanthes' reasonings. Hume is careful, however, to pass lightly over Cleanthes' inconsistency in propounding them. All that Philo is permitted to do is to draw attention to the manner in which they support his own previous argument in Part VI (pp. 174–5) ; and again to commend for favourable consideration—almost in the same form of words—the hypothesis that in nature matter and form are inseparable. " Instead of admiring the order of natural beings, may it not happen, that, could we penetrate into the intimate nature of bodies, we should clearly see why it was absolutely impossible, they could ever admit of any other disposition ? So dangerous is it to introduce this idea of necessity into the present question ! And so naturally does it afford an inference directly opposite to the religious hypothesis ! " (p. 191).

PART X

Demea makes no attempt to reply of any kind. Instead, he now declares that it is " from a consciousness of his imbecility and misery, rather than from any reasoning [that each man] is led to seek protection from that Being, on whom he and all nature is dependent " (p. 193) ; and so directs the discussion to new ground. " The whole earth, believe me, Philo, is cursed and polluted. . . . Necessity, hunger, want, stimulate the strong and courageous : Fear, anxiety, terror, agitate the weak and infirm " (p. 194).

Philo gives Demea free rein ; and mischievously agrees that this is " the best and indeed the only method of bringing every one to a due sense of religion." Reason and argument are not needed, only eloquence and strong imagery. " For is it necessary to prove, what every one feels within himself ? It is only necessary to make us feel it, if possible, more intimately and sensibly " (p. 193). " Observe too the curious artifices of nature, in order to embitter the life of every living being. . . . On each hand, before and behind, above and below, every animal is surrounded with enemies, which incessantly seek his misery and destruction" (pp. 194–5). Nor is man an exception. For though he " can, by combination, surmount all his *real* enemies . . . does he not immediately raise up to himself *imaginary* enemies, the daemons of his fancy, who haunt him with superstitious terrors, and blast every enjoyment of life ?. . . . His very sleep and dreams furnish new materials to anxious fear : And even death, his refuge from every other ill, presents only the dread of endless and innumerable woes " (p. 194). " And is it possible, Cleanthes, . . . that after all these reflections, and infinitely more, which might be suggested, you can still persevere in your anthropomorphism, and assert the moral attributes of the Deity, his justice, benevolence, mercy, and rectitude, to be of the same nature with these virtues in human creatures ? " (p. 198).

Cleanthes has appealed to purpose and intention in nature, as displayed in the curious artifices and machinery of animal life. What, Philo asks, is this intention ? The *preservation* only of the species ? " It seems enough for her purpose, if such a rank be barely upheld in the universe, without any care or concern for the happiness of the members, that compose it " (p. 198).

Cleanthes, while expressing dissent (p. 199), yet agrees that Philo has now fallen upon a subject worthy of his " noble spirit of opposition and controversy." If he can make good his present contention, there is an end at once of all religion. " For to what purpose establish the natural attributes of the Deity, while the moral are still doubtful and uncertain ? "

Demea intervenes to suggest the ' probation ' or ' porch ' view of human destiny, as the solution of all difficulties. " This world is but a point in comparison of the universe : This life but a moment in comparison of eternity. The present evil phenomena, therefore, are rectified in other regions, and in some future period of existence " (p. 199). The eyes of men being then opened to a larger view of things, will trace, with adoration, the benevolence and rectitude of the Deity, through the mazes and intricacies of his providence. [*Cf. Enquiry*, S.-B., p. 141 ; *Essays*, G. & G., vol. ii, p. 116.]

Cleanthes, though himself sharing in this ' porch ' view of human life (*cf.* pp. 219, 224), is here brought forward to criticize Demea's methods of advocacy. [He is made to voice against Demea those very objections which Philo has been arguing against his own modes of formulating the argument from design, and the cogency of which he refuses to recognize when they are again urged against him by Philo (*cf.* pp. 203 *sqq.*) in this and the later Parts.] " These arbitrary suppositions "—Cleanthes is speaking—" can never be admitted contrary to matter of fact, visible and incontroverted. Whence can any cause be known but from its known effects ? Whence can any hypothesis be proved but from the apparent phenomena ? To establish one hypothesis upon another, is building entirely in the air " (p. 199). The only method of supporting divine benevolence is " to deny absolutely the misery and wickedness of man." Health is more common than sickness ; and for one vexation we attain a hundred enjoyments.

Philo agrees that pain is less frequent than pleasure, but urges that it is more violent and durable, rising, how often, to torture and agony. But such considerations apart, and even allowing that human happiness in this life exceeds its misery, is this, he asks, all that we expect from infinite power, wisdom, and goodness? Why is there any misery at all in the world? Do not such subjects exceed all human capacity? Are our common measures of truth and falsity applicable to them?

Also, even if it be allowed that pain or misery in man is *compatible* with infinite power and goodness in the Deity, does even this concession advance Cleanthes' argument? [Philo here retorts on Cleanthes the criticism which Cleanthes has passed on Demea.] " A mere possible *compatibility* is not sufficient. You must *prove* these pure, unmixed . . . attributes from the present mixed and confused phenomena, and from these alone. A hopeful undertaking ! " (p. 201).

" Here, Cleanthes, I find myself at ease in my argument. Here I triumph. Formerly, when we argued concerning the natural attributes of intelligence and design, I needed all my sceptical and metaphysical subtilty to elude your grasp. In many views of the universe, and of its parts, particularly the latter, the beauty and fitness of final causes strike us with such irresistible force, that all objections appear (what I believe they really are) mere cavils and sophisms ; nor can we then imagine how it was ever possible for us to repose any weight on them. But there is no view of human life or of the condition of mankind, from which, without the greatest violence, we can infer the moral attributes, or learn that infinite benevolence, conjoined with infinite power and infinite wisdom, which we must discover by the eyes of faith alone. It is your turn now to tug the labouring oar, and to support your philosophical subtilties against the dictates of plain reason and experience " (p. 202).

[Philo's reference here to the manner in which the beauty and fitness of final causes strikes us ' with irresistible force,' antecedently to all abstruse reasoning, and also ultimately in spite of all such reasoning, is his first recognition of this very important part of Cleanthes' argument (*cf.* p. 154 and above, p. 87) ; and prepares the way for its discussion in Part XII.]

PART XI

To abandon all human analogy, as Demea would do, is, Cleanthes declares, to abandon all religion. To preserve the human analogy he " inclines to suppose " the Author of nature to be " finitely perfect, though far exceeding mankind " (p. 203). He invites Philo to comment on " this new theory," " at length, without interruption."

Philo has already (in Parts IV and V) stated the metaphysical and theological objections to the hypothesis of a finite God ; and proceeding he limits his present discussion to the question whether the phenomena of good and evil justify the inference to a Deity, whether finite or infinite, with benevolence and other moral attributes. Philo also takes it as agreed—Cleanthes has himself urged this against Demea—that we have " to reason merely from the known phenomena, and to drop every arbitrary supposition or conjecture." In particular, no such appeal as that of Demea can be made to the narrow limits of our understanding. For the more our weakness and ignorance are exaggerated, the more diffident we must become, and the greater must be the objection to departing from or conjecturally supplementing the phenomena as given in experience.

In support of his previous thesis Philo therefore argues " that, however consistent the world may be, *allowing certain suppositions and conjectures*, with the idea of such a Deity, it can never afford us an inference concerning his existence. *The consistence is not absolutely denied, only the inference.* Conjectures, especially when infinity is excluded from the divine attributes, may perhaps be sufficient to prove a consistence ; but can never be foundations for any inference " (p. 205).

There seem to be *four* causes of evil, no one of which appears to human reason to be in the least degree necessary or unavoidable (p. 205).

Philo goes out of his way to repeat that if the goodness of the Deity could be independently established, by *a priori* argument, " these phenomena, however untoward, would not be sufficient to subvert that principle ; but might easily, in some unknown manner, be reconcilable to it " (p. 211). " I am sceptic enough to allow, that the bad appearances, notwithstanding all my reasonings, may be compatible with such attributes as you suppose : But surely they can never prove these attributes." " Look round this universe. . . . The whole presents nothing but the idea of a blind nature, impregnated by a great vivifying principle ; and pouring forth from her lap, without discernment or parental care, her maimed and abortive children."

The Manichean hypothesis Philo rejects as not in keeping with the uniformity and agreement of the parts of the universe ; there seems to be neither goodness nor malice in the first causes of the universe.

Demea now accuses Philo of being false to their alliance, and of being " secretly a more dangerous enemy [to religion] than Cleanthes himself " (pp. 212-3). Cleanthes remarks that he has been amusing himself at both our expense ; and it must be confessed that the injudicious reasoning of our vulgar theology has given him but too just a handle of ridicule."

Demea departs before the opening of the next, concluding, Part.

PART XII

Philo now reaffirms the confession of faith made at the close of Part X ; and does so in the following terms : " You, in particular, Cleanthes, with whom I live in unreserved intimacy ; you are sensible, that, notwithstanding the freedom of my conversation, and my love of singular arguments, no one has a deeper sense of religion impressed on his mind, or pays more profound adoration to the divine Being, as he discovers himself to reason, in the inexplicable contrivance and artifice of nature. A purpose, an intention, a design strikes everywhere the most careless, the most stupid thinker ; and no man can be so hardened in absurd systems, as at all times to reject it " (p. 214).

[Philo's terms, in this second confession of faith, are, to use Hume's own expression, ' artfully ' chosen. The God here avowed is an object of adoration, *transcending* our powers of comprehension ; the contrivance and artifice of nature are *inexplicable* ; and Philo adds the phrase " *as he discloses himself to reason* " in order, as the sequel shows, to point out that the Deity thus revealed is not to be equated with ' God ' as ordinarily understood in religion, and so to withdraw nearly all that he has seemed to allow. For now, at last, Philo—the preparatory stages of his argument having been completed—defines his attitude to Cleanthes' contention that the impression of design in nature is immediately felt and survives opposing argument. Philo's method of dealing with this contention is not to deny the authenticity of the feeling—he himself, he declares, experiences it strongly—but to question Cleanthes' manner of describing it. Is it as unambiguous and as immediate as Cleanthes suggests ? Is it due to nature acting alone ? Has not the influence of custom, and of the traditional beliefs to which nurture and education give the force of custom, intervened, infusing into the impression a definiteness of meaning, which it does not in itself possess ? Is not reason, which alone is in a position to distinguish the impression from all acquired beliefs, in its rights in insisting on a hearing ? And lastly, has not Cleanthes himself, by implication, recognized the jurisdiction of reason in this regard ? His thesis, as propounded in Part III (pp. 154–5), is not that feeling here supersedes reason, but that it *supports* it.]

This second confession of faith is no sooner made, than Philo, with mischievous intent, describes the contrivance and artifice of nature in a manner quite out of keeping with the views which he is about to expound in the immediately following paragraphs. His evident purpose in introducing this passage (pp. 215–6, *cf.* above,

p. 71) is to afford Cleanthes the opportunity of renewing his original thesis, that " the comparison of the universe to a machine of human contrivance is so obvious and natural, and is justified by so many instances of order and design in nature, that it must immediately strike all unprejudiced apprehensions, and procure *universal appro-bation* " (p. 216). The utmost that can be done, in opposition to this theory, Cleanthes declares, is " to start doubts and difficulties," and so, at most, to cause " suspense of judgment."

[' Universal approbation ' : this extreme contention on the part of Cleanthes—as also in the preceding paragraph on the part of Philo—is, it may be noted, required for the purposes of the thesis to which Hume is carefully leading up, that the dispute is about something which is not really being questioned by any of the disputants, however opposite their other views ; and in which therefore, as Philo contends, they can differ only because of the ambiguity of their terms. Cleanthes' reference (p. 216) to the contributory predisposing influence of ' early education ' may also be noted.]

Suspense of judgment, Philo agrees, is not possible. But what this leads him to suspect is that " there enters somewhat of a dispute of words into this controversy, more than is usually imagined " (p. 216). This, he points out, is particularly apt to happen in controversies regarding the degrees of any quality or circumstance —the degree of greatness in Hannibal, or of beauty in Cleopatra. " The degrees of these qualities are not, like quantity or number, susceptible of any exact mensuration, which may be the standard in the controversy. That the dispute concerning theism is of this nature . . . will appear upon the slightest enquiry. I ask the theist, if he does not allow, that there is a great and immeasurable, because incomprehensible, difference between the *human* and the *divine* mind : The more pious he is, . . . the more will he be disposed to magnify the difference. . . . I next turn to the atheist, who, I assert, is only nominally so, and can never possibly be in earnest ; and I ask him whether . . . there be not a certain degree of analogy among all the operations of nature . . . whether the rotting of a turnip, the generation of an animal, and the structure of human thought be not energies that probably bear some remote analogy to each other : It is impossible he can deny it. . . . Where then, cry I to both these antagonists, is the subject of your dispute ? The theist allows, that the original intelligence is very different from human reason : The atheist allows, that the original principle of order bears some remote analogy to it. Will you quarrel, Gentle-men, about the degrees, and enter into a controversy, which admits not of any precise meaning, nor consequently of any determina-tion ? " (p. 218).

[The above passage has been added in the final revision, in conformity with the new (third) ending of the *Dialogues. Cf.* above, pp. 94–6.]

One further step completes Philo's formulation of the positions in which he so greatly differs from the teaching of Cleanthes. " As the works of nature have a much greater analogy to the effects of *our* art and contrivance, than to those of *our* benevolence and justice ; we have reason to infer that the natural attributes of the Deity have a greater resemblance to those of man, than his moral have to human virtues " (p. 219). [*Cf.* above, p. 72.] " These, Cleanthes, are my unfeigned sentiments on this subject ; and these sentiments, you know, I have ever cherished and maintained. But in proportion to my veneration for true religion, is my abhorrence of vulgar superstitions ; and I indulge a peculiar pleasure, I confess, in pushing such principles sometimes into absurdity, sometimes into impiety. And you are sensible, that all bigots, notwithstanding their great aversion to the latter above the former, are commonly equally guilty of both " (p. 219).

" My inclination," Cleanthes replies, " lies, I own, a contrary way. Religion, however corrupted, is still better than no religion at all " (p. 219). It is, he adds, most truly itself, when " its operation is silent, and only enforces the motives of morality and justice. . . . When it distinguishes itself, and acts as a separate principle over men, it has departed from its proper sphere, and has become only a cover to faction and ambition."

Even with this view of religion Philo is unable to agree, and the next eight pages are occupied (save for Cleanthes' one intervention (pp. 224–5), to advocate the ' porch ' view of human destiny) by Philo's exposition of Hume's view of ' true ' religion as being ' philosophical and rational,' with no claim to influence conduct. Should it claim to do so, it takes the form either of superstition or of enthusiasm, with all the many evils which follow in their train. These evils he describes at length, in the manner which we have already elsewhere considered (above, pp. 11 *sqq.*).

What, then, Philo finally asks—in a paragraph added in the final revision of the *Dialogues*—is the conclusion to which we are brought ? " The whole of natural theology . . . resolves itself into one simple, though somewhat ambiguous, at least undefined proposition, *that the cause or causes of order in the universe probably bear some remote analogy to human intelligence* " (p. 227). This proposition, he adds, is not capable of extension, variation, or more particular explication, and it affords " no inference that affects human life or can be the source of any action or forbearance." And lastly, " the analogy, imperfect as it is . . . cannot be transferred, with any appearance of probability, to the other [*i.e.* moral] qualities of the mind " (p. 227).

Philo, in closing, makes the conventionally prescribed avowal that the disabilities of reason only make revelation and faith the more needful ; and in recommending this lesson to the attention of Pamphilus, hopes that Cleanthes will forgive him " for interposing so far in the education and instruction of his pupil." Pamphilus then comments upon the discussion. " Upon a serious review of the whole " he " cannot but think " that Cleanthes has come nearest to the truth.

DIALOGUES

CONCERNING

NATURAL RELIGION.

BY

DAVID HUME, Eſq;

———

Printed in 1779.

DIALOGUES

CONCERNING

NATURAL RELIGION

PAMPHILUS TO HERMIPPUS

IT has been remarked, my HERMIPPUS, that, though the ancient philosophers conveyed most of their instruction in the form of dialogue, this method of composition has been little practised in later ages, and has seldom succeeded in the hands of those who have attempted it. Accurate and regular argument, indeed, such as is now expected of philosophical enquirers, naturally throws a man into the methodical and didactic manner ; where he can immediately, without preparation, explain the point at which he aims ; and thence proceed, without interruption, to deduce the proofs, on which it is established. To deliver a SYSTEM in conversation scarcely appears natural ; and while the dialogue-writer desires, by departing from the direct style of composition, to give a freer air to his performance, and avoid the appearance of *author* and *reader*, he is apt to run into a worse inconvenience, and convey the image of *pedagogue* and *pupil*. Or if he carries on the dispute in the natural spirit of good company, by throwing in a variety of topics, and preserving a proper balance among the speakers ; he often loses so much time in preparations and transitions, that the reader will scarcely think himself compensated, by all the graces of dialogue, for the order, brevity, and precision, which are sacrificed to them.

There are some subjects, however, to which dialogue-writing is peculiarly adapted, and where it is still preferable to the direct and simple method of composition.

Any point of doctrine, which is so *obvious*, that it scarcely admits of dispute, but at the same time so *important*, that it cannot be too often inculcated, seems to require some such method of handling it ; where the novelty of the manner may compensate the triteness of the subject, where the vivacity of conversation may enforce the precept, and where the variety of lights, presented by various personages and characters, may appear neither tedious nor redundant.

Any question of philosophy, on the other hand, which is so *obscure* and *uncertain*, that human reason can reach no fixed determination with regard to it ; if it should be treated at all ; seems to lead us naturally into the style of dialogue and conversation. Reasonable men may be allowed to differ, where no one can reasonably be positive : Opposite sentiments, even without any decision, afford an agreeable amusement : And if the subject be curious and interesting, the book carries us, in a manner, into company ; and unites the two greatest and purest pleasures of human life, study and society.

Happily, these circumstances are all to be found in the subject of NATURAL RELIGION. What truth so obvious, so certain, as the *being* of a God, which the most ignorant ages have acknowledged, for which the most refined geniuses have ambitiously striven to produce new proofs and arguments ? What truth so important as this, which is the ground of all our hopes, the surest foundation of morality, the firmest support of society, and the only principle which ought never to be a moment absent from our thoughts and meditations ? But in treating of this obvious and important truth ; what obscure questions occur, concerning the *nature* of that divine Being ; his attributes, his decrees, his plan of providence ? These have been always subjected to the disputations of men : Concerning these, human reason has not reached any certain determination : But these are topics so interesting, that we cannot restrain our restless enquiry with regard to them ; though nothing but doubt, uncertainty, and contradiction, have, as yet, been the result of our most accurate researches.

This I had lately occasion to observe, while I passed, as usual, part of the summer season with CLEANTHES, and was present at those conversations of his with PHILO and DEMEA, of which I gave you lately some imperfect account. Your curiosity, you then told me, was so excited, that I must of necessity enter into a more exact detail of their reasonings, and display those various systems which they advanced with regard to so delicate a subject as that of natural religion. The remarkable contrast in their characters still farther raised your expectations ; while you opposed the accurate philosophical turn of CLEANTHES to the careless scepticism of PHILO, or compared either of their dispositions with the rigid inflexible orthodoxy of DEMEA. My youth rendered me a mere auditor

128

of their disputes ; and that curiosity, natural to the early season of life, has so deeply imprinted in my memory the whole chain and connection of their arguments, that, I hope, I shall not omit or confound any considerable part of them in the recital.

PART I

AFTER I joined the company, whom I found sitting in
Cleanthes's library, Demea paid Cleanthes some compliments, on the great care which he took of my education,
and on his unwearied perseverance and constancy in all his
friendships. The father of Pamphilus, said he, was your
intimate friend : The son is your pupil, and may indeed be
regarded as your adopted son ; were we to judge by the pains
which you bestow in conveying to him every useful branch
of literature and science. You are no more wanting, I am persuaded, in prudence than in industry. I shall, therefore,
communicate to you a maxim, which I have observed with
regard to my own children, that I may learn how far it agrees
with your practice. The method I follow in their education
is founded on the saying of an ancient, " That students of
philosophy ought first to learn logics, then ethics, next physics,
last of all, of the nature of the Gods." [1] This science of natural
theology, according to him, being the most profound and
abstruse of any, required the maturest judgment in its students ;
and none but a mind, enriched with all the other sciences, can
safely be entrusted with it.

Are you so late, says Philo, in teaching your children the
principles of religion ? Is there no danger of their neglecting
or rejecting altogether, those opinions, of which they have
heard so little during the whole course of their education ?
It is only as a science, replied Demea, subjected to human
reasoning and disputation, that I postpone the study of natural
theology. To season their minds with early piety is my chief
care ; and by continual precept and instruction, and I hope
too, by example, I imprint deeply on their tender minds an
habitual reverence for all the principles of religion. While
they pass through every other science, I still remark the uncertainty of each part, the eternal disputations of men, the
obscurity of all philosophy, and the strange, ridiculous conclusions, which some of the greatest geniuses have derived
from the principles of mere human reason. Having thus tamed

[1] Chrysippus apud Plut. *de repug. Stoicorum* [ch. 9, 1035 *a, b*]

their mind to a proper submission and self-diffidence, I have no longer any scruple of opening to them the greatest mysteries of religion, nor apprehend any danger from that assuming arrogance of philosophy, which may lead them to reject the most established doctrines and opinions.

Your precaution, says PHILO, of seasoning your children's minds with early piety, is certainly very reasonable ; and no more than is requisite, in this profane and irreligious age. But what I chiefly admire in your plan of education, is your method of drawing advantage from the very principles of philosophy and learning, which, by inspiring pride and self-sufficiency, have commonly, in all ages, been found so destructive to the principles of religion. The vulgar, indeed, we may remark, who are unacquainted with science and profound enquiry, observing the endless disputes of the learned, have commonly a thorough contempt for philosophy ; and rivet themselves the faster, by that means, in the great points of theology, which have been taught them. Those who enter a little into study and enquiry, finding many appearances of evidence in doctrines the newest and most extraordinary, think nothing too difficult for human reason ; and presumptuously breaking through all fences, profane the inmost sanctuaries of the temple. But CLEANTHES will, I hope, agree with me, that, after we have abandoned ignorance, the surest remedy, there is still one expedient left to prevent this profane liberty. Let DEMEA's principles be improved and cultivated : Let us become thoroughly sensible of the weakness, blindness, and narrow limits of human reason : Let us duly consider its uncertainty and needless contrarieties, even in subjects of common life and practice : Let the errors and deceits of our very senses be set before us ; the insuperable difficulties, which attend first principles in all systems ; the contradictions, which adhere to the very ideas of matter, cause and effect, extension, space, time, motion ; and in a word, quantity of all kinds, the object of the only science, that can fairly pretend to any certainty or evidence. When these topics are displayed in their full light, as they are by some philosophers and almost all divines ; who can retain such confidence in this frail faculty of reason as to pay any regard to its determinations in points so sublime, so abstruse, so remote from common life and experience?[1] When the coher-

---

[1] [experience *for* practice]

ence of the parts of a stone, or even that composition of parts, which renders it extended ; when these familiar objects, I say, are so inexplicable, and contain circumstances so repugnant and contradictory ; with what assurance can we decide concerning the origin of worlds, or trace their history from eternity to eternity ?

While PHILO pronounced these words, I could observe a smile in the countenances both of DEMEA and CLEANTHES. That of DEMEA seemed to imply an unreserved satisfaction in the doctrines delivered : But in CLEANTHES's features, I could distinguish an air of finesse ; [1] as if he perceived some raillery or [2] artificial malice in the reasonings of PHILO.

You propose then, PHILO, said CLEANTHES, to erect religious faith on philosophical scepticism ; and you think that if certainty or evidence be expelled from every other subject of enquiry, it will all retire to these theological doctrines, and there acquire a superior force and authority. Whether your scepticism be as absolute and sincere as you pretend, we shall learn bye and bye, when the company breaks up : We shall then see, whether you go out at the door or the window ; and whether you really doubt, if your body has gravity, or can be injured by its fall ; according to popular opinion, derived from our fallacious senses and more fallacious experience. And this consideration, DEMEA, may, I think, fairly serve to abate our ill-will to this humourous [3] sect of the sceptics. If they be thoroughly in earnest, they will not long trouble the world with their doubts, cavils, and disputes : If they be only in jest, they are, perhaps, bad railliers, but can never be very dangerous, either to the state, to philosophy, or to religion.

In reality, PHILO, continued he, it seems certain, that though a man, in a flush of humour, after intense reflection on the many contradictions and imperfections of human reason, may entirely renounce all belief and opinion ; it is impossible for him to persevere in this total scepticism, or make it appear in his conduct for a few hours. External objects press in upon him : Passions solicit him : His philosophical melancholy dissipates ; and even the utmost violence upon his own temper will not be able, during any time, to preserve the poor appearance of scepticism. And for what

[1] [finesse *for* finesse and raillery]   [2] [raillery or *added*]
[3] [humourous *for* pleasant]

reason impose on himself such a violence? This is a point
in which it will be impossible for him ever to satisfy himself,
consistently with his sceptical principles : So that upon the
whole nothing could be more ridiculous than the principles
of the ancient PYRRHONIANS ; if in reality they endeavoured,
as is pretended, to extend throughout,[1] the same scepticism,
which they had learned from the declamations of their school,[2]
and which they ought to have confined to them.

In this view, there appears a great resemblance between
the sects of the STOICS and PYRRHONIANS, though perpetual
antagonists : And both of them seem founded on this erroneous
maxim, that what a man can perform sometimes, and in some
dispositions, he can perform always, and in every disposition.
When the mind, by Stoical reflections, is elevated into a sublime enthusiasm of virtue, and strongly smit with any *species*
of honour or public good, the utmost bodily pain and sufferance
will not prevail over [3] such a high sense of duty ; and it is
possible, perhaps, by its means, even to smile and exult in the
midst of tortures. If this sometimes may be the case in fact
and reality, much more may a philosopher, in his school, or
even in his closet, work himself up to such an enthusiasm, and
support in imagination the acutest pain or most calamitous
event which he can possibly conceive. But how shall he
support this enthusiasm itself? The bent of his mind relaxes,
and cannot be recalled at pleasure : Avocations lead him
astray [4] : Misfortunes attack him unawares : And the
philosopher sinks by degrees into the *plebeian*.

I allow of your comparison between the STOICS and SCEPTICS,
replied PHILO. But you may observe, at the same time, that
though the mind cannot, in Stoicism, support the highest
flights of philosophy, yet even when it sinks lower, it still retains
somewhat of its former disposition ; and the effects of the
Stoic's reasoning will appear in his conduct in common life,
and through the whole tenor of his actions. The ancient
schools, particularly that of ZENO, produced examples of
virtue and constancy which seem astonishing to present
times.

[1] [extend throughout *for* introduce into common life]
[2] [from the declamations of their school *for* from the sciences]
[3] [not prevail over *for* make small impression in opposition to]
[4] [lead him astray *for* call him aside]

Vain Wisdom all and false Philosophy.
Yet with a pleasing sorcery could charm
Pain, for a while, or anguish, and excite
Fallacious Hope, or arm the obdurate breast
With stubborn Patience, as with triple steel.[1]

In like manner, if a man has accustomed himself to sceptical considerations on the uncertainty and narrow limits of reason, he will not entirely forget them when he turns his reflections on other subjects ; [2] but in all his philosophical [3] principles and reasoning, I dare not say, in his common conduct,[4] he will be found different from those, who either never formed any opinions in the case, or have entertained sentiments more favourable to human reason.

To whatever length any one may push his speculative principles of scepticism, he must act, I own, and live, and converse like other men ; and for this conduct he is not obliged to give any other reason than the absolute necessity he lies under of so doing. If he ever carries his speculations farther than this necessity constrains him, and philosophises, either on natural or moral subjects, he is allured by a certain pleasure and satisfaction, which he finds in employing himself after that manner. He considers besides, that every one, even in common life, is constrained to have more or less of this philosophy ; that from our earliest infancy we make continual advances in forming more general principles of conduct and reasoning ; that the larger experience we acquire, and the stronger reason we are endowed with, we always render our principles the more general and comprehensive ; and that what we call *philosophy* is nothing but a more regular and methodical operation of the same kind. To philosophise on such subjects is nothing essentially different from reasoning on common life ; and we may only expect greater stability, if not greater truth, from our philosophy, on account of its exacter and more scrupulous method of proceeding.

But when we look beyond human affairs and the properties of the surrounding bodies : When we carry our speculations into the two eternities, before and after the present state of

[1] [*Paradise Lost,* ii]
[2] [turns . . . subjects *for* leaves his closet]
[3] [philosophical *added*]
[4] [I dare not say, in his common conduct *added*]

things ; into the creation and formation of the universe ; the existence and properties of spirits ; the powers and operations of one universal spirit, existing without beginning and without end ; omnipotent, omniscient, immutable, infinite, and incomprehensible : We must be far removed from the smallest tendency to scepticism not to be apprehensive, that we have here got quite beyond the reach of our faculties. So long as we confine our speculations to trade, or morals, or politics, or criticism, we make appeals, every moment, to common sense and experience, which strengthen our philosophical conclusions, and remove (at least, in part) the suspicion, which we so justly entertain with regard to every reasoning that is very subtile and refined. But in theological reasonings, we have not this advantage ; while at the same time we are employed upon objects, which, we must be sensible, are too large for our grasp, and of all others, require most to be familiarised to our apprehension. We are like foreigners in a strange country, to whom everything must seem suspicious, and who are in danger every moment of transgressing against the laws and customs of the people with whom they live and converse. We know not how far we ought to trust our vulgar methods of reasoning in such a subject ; since, even in common life and in that province which is peculiarly appropriated to them, we cannot account for them, and are entirely guided by a kind of instinct or necessity in employing them.[1]

All sceptics pretend, that, if reason be considered in an abstract view, it furnishes invincible arguments against itself, and that we could never retain any conviction or assurance, on any subject,[2] were not the sceptical reasonings so refined and subtile, that they are not able to counterpoise the more solid and more natural arguments, derived from the senses and experience. But it is evident, whenever our arguments lose this advantage, and run wide of common life, that the most refined scepticism comes to be upon a footing with them, and is able to oppose and counterbalance them. The one has no more weight than the other. The mind must remain in sus-

---

[1] [At the close of this paragraph Hume adds on the margin, and then scores out, the following : " A very small part of this great system, during a very small time, is very imperfectly discovered to us : And do we thence pronounce decisively concerning the whole ? " This passage is transferred by Hume to p. 149, where it is rewritten on the margin.]

[2] [on any subject *for* even in the most common affairs of life]

pense between them ; and it is that very suspense or balance, which is the triumph of scepticism.

But I observe, says CLEANTHES, with regard to you, PHILO, and all speculative sceptics, that your doctrine and practice are as much at variance in the most abstruse points of theory as in the conduct of common life. Wherever evidence discovers itself, you adhere to it, notwithstanding your pretended scepticism ; and I can observe, too, some of your sect to be as decisive as those who make greater professions of certainty and assurance.[1] In reality, would not a man be ridiculous, who pretended to reject NEWTON's explication of the wonderful phenomenon of the rainbow, because that explication gives a minute anatomy of the rays of light ; a subject, forsooth, too refined for human comprehension ? And what would you say to one, who having nothing particular to object to the arguments of COPERNICUS and GALILÆO for the motion of the earth, should withhold his assent, on that general principle, that these subjects were too magnificent and remote to be explained by the narrow and fallacious reason of mankind ?

There is indeed a kind of brutish and ignorant scepticism, as you well observed, which gives the vulgar a general prejudice against what they do not easily understand, and makes them reject every principle which requires elaborate reasoning to prove and establish it. This species of scepticism is fatal to knowledge, not to religion ; since we find, that those who make greatest profession of it, give often their assent, not only to the great truths of theism, and natural theology,[2] but even to the most absurd tenets, which a traditional superstition has recommended to them. They firmly believe in witches ; though they will not believe nor attend to the most simple proposition of Euclid. But the refined and philosophical sceptics fall into an inconsistence of an opposite nature. They push their researches into the most abstruse corners of science ; and their assent attends them in every step, proportioned to the evidence which they meet with. They are even obliged to acknowledge, that the most abstruse and remote objects are those which are best explained by philosophy. Light is in reality anatomized : The true system of the heavenly bodies is discovered and ascertained. But the nourishment of bodies by food [3] is still

---

[1] [assurance *for* dogmatism]   [2] [theology *for* religion]
[3] [nourishment of bodies by food *for* falling of a stone]

an inexplicable mystery : The cohesion of the parts of matter is still incomprehensible. These sceptics, therefore, are obliged, in every question, to consider each particular evidence apart, and proportion their assent to the precise degree of evidence which occurs. This is their practice in all natural, mathematical, moral, and political science. And why not the same, I ask, in the theological and religious? Why must conclusions of this nature be alone rejected on the general presumption of the insufficiency of human reason, without any particular discussion of the evidence? Is not such an unequal conduct a plain proof of prejudice and passion?

Our senses, you say, are fallacious, our understanding erroneous, our ideas even of the most familiar objects, extension, duration, motion, full of absurdities and contradictions. You defy me to solve the difficulties, or reconcile the repugnancies, which you discover in them. I have not capacity for so great an undertaking : I have not leisure for it : I perceive it to be superfluous. Your own conduct, in every circumstance, refutes your principles ; and shows the firmest reliance on all the received maxims of science, morals, prudence, and behaviour.

I shall never assent to so harsh an opinion as that of a celebrated writer,[1] who says that the sceptics are not a sect of philosophers : They are only a sect of liars. I may, however, affirm (I hope without offence), that they are a sect of jesters or railliers. But for my part, whenever I find myself disposed to mirth and amusement, I shall certainly choose my entertainment of a less perplexing and abstruse nature. A comedy, a novel, or at most a history, seems a more natural recreation than such metaphysical subtilties and abstractions.

In vain would the sceptic make a distinction between science and common life, or between one science and another. The arguments employed in all, if just, are of a similar nature, and contain the same force and evidence. Or if there be any difference among them, the advantage lies entirely on the side of theology and natural religion. Many principles of mechanics

---

[1] *L'Art de penser.* [*La Logique ou l'art de penser*, by Antoine Arnauld (1612–94), published in 1662. The passage here referred to is in the *Premier discours* (1843 edition, p. 26) : " Personne ne douta jamais sérieusement qu'il y a une terre, un soleil et une lune, ni si le tout est plus grand que sa partie. On peut bien faire dire extérieurement à sa bouche qu'on en doute, parce que l'on peut mentir ; mais on ne peut pas le faire dire à son esprit. Ainsi le Pyrrhonisme n'est pas une secte de gens qui soient persuadés de ce qu'ils disent, mais c'est une secte de menteurs."]

are founded on very abstruse reasoning ; yet no man, who has any pretensions to science, even no speculative sceptic, pretends to entertain the least doubt with regard to them. The COPER-NICAN system contains the most surprising paradox, and the most contrary to our natural conceptions, to appearances, and to our very senses : Yet even monks and inquisitors are now constrained to withdraw their opposition to it. And shall PHILO, a man of so liberal a genius, and extensive knowledge, entertain any general undistinguished scruples with regard to the religious hypothesis, which is founded on the simplest and most obvious arguments, and, unless it meet with artificial obstacles, has such easy access and admission into the mind of man ?

And here we may observe, continued he, turning himself towards DEMEA, a pretty curious circumstance in the history of the sciences. After the union of philosophy with the popular religion, upon the first establishment of Christianity, nothing was more usual, among all religious teachers, than declamations against reason, against the senses, against every principle, derived merely from human research and enquiry. All the topics of the ancient Academics [1] were adopted by the Fathers ; and thence propagated for several ages in every school and pulpit throughout Christendom. The Reformers embraced the same principles of reasoning, or rather declamation ; and all panegyrics on the excellency of faith were sure to be inter-larded with some severe strokes of satire against natural reason. A celebrated prelate too,[2] of the Romish communion, a man of the most extensive learning, who wrote a demonstration of Christianity, has also composed a treatise, which contains all the cavils of the boldest and most determined PYRRHONISM. LOCKE seems to have been the first Christian, who ventured openly to assert, that *faith* was nothing but a species of *reason*, that religion was only a branch of philosophy, and that a chain of arguments, similar to that which established any truth in morals, politics, or physics, was always employed in dis-covering all the principles of theology, natural and revealed. The ill use, which BAYLE and other libertines made of the philosophical scepticism of the Fathers and first Reformers,

Cleanthes

---

[1] [and sceptics *omitted*]
[2] Mons. Huet. [Peter Daniel Huet (1630–1721), Bishop of Afranches. The treatise here referred to, *Traité philosophique de la faiblesse de l'esprit humain*, was published posthumously in 1723. *Cf.* Mark Pattison's *Essays*, vol. i, p. 299.]

still farther propagated the judicious sentiment of Mr. LOCKE :
And it is now, in a manner, avowed, by all pretenders to reasoning and philosophy, that atheist and sceptic are almost synony-
mous. And as it is certain, that no man is in earnest, when
he professes the latter principle ; I would fain hope that there
are as few, who seriously maintain the former.

Don't you remember, said PHILO, the excellent saying of
Lord BACON on the head ? That a little philosophy, replied
CLEANTHES, makes a man an atheist : A great deal converts
him to religion. That is a very judicious remark too, said
PHILO. But what I have in my eye is another passage, where,
having mentioned DAVID's fool, who said in his heart there
is no God, this great philosopher observes, that the atheists
now a days have a double share of folly : For they are not
contented to say in their hearts there is no God, but they also
utter that impiety with their lips, and are thereby guilty of
multiplied indiscretion and imprudence. Such people, though
they were ever so much in earnest, cannot, methinks, be very
formidable.

But though you should rank me in this class of fools, I cannot forbear communicating a remark that occurs to me from
the history of the religious and irreligious scepticism with
which you have entertained us. It appears to me, that there
are strong symptoms of priestcraft in the whole progress of this
affair. During ignorant ages, such as those which followed
the dissolution of the ancient schools, the priests perceived,
that atheism, deism, or heresy of any kind, could only proceed
from the presumptuous questioning of received opinions, and
from a belief that human reason was equal to everything.
Education had then a mighty influence over the minds of men,
and was almost equal in force to those suggestions of the senses
and common understanding, by which the most determined
sceptic must allow himself to be governed. But at present,
when the influence of education is much diminished, and men,
from a more open commerce of the world, have learned to compare the popular principles of different nations and ages, our
sagacious divines have changed their whole system of philosophy, and talk the language of STOICS, PLATONISTS, and
PERIPATETICS, not that of PYRRHONIANS and ACADEMICS. If
we distrust human reason, we have now no other principle to
lead us into religion. Thus, sceptics in one age, dogmatists

in another ; whichever system best suits the purpose of these reverend gentlemen,[1] in giving them an ascendant over mankind, they are sure to make it their favourite principle, and established tenet.

It is very natural, said CLEANTHES, for men to embrace those principles, by which they find they can best defend their doctrines ; nor need we have any recourse to priestcraft to account for so reasonable an expedient. And surely, nothing can afford a stronger presumption, that any set of principles are true, and ought to be embraced, than to observe, that they tend to the confirmation of true religion, and serve to confound the cavils of atheists, libertines, and freethinkers of all denominations.

[1] [these reverend gentlemen *for* the clergy]

PART II

I MUST own, CLEANTHES, said DEMEA, that nothing can more surprise me, than the light, in which you have, all along, put this argument. By the whole tenor of your discourse, one would imagine that you were maintaining the being of a God, against the cavils of atheists and infidels; and were necessitated to become a champion for that fundamental principle of all religion. But this, I hope, is not by any means a question among us. No man; no man, at least, of common sense, I am persuaded, ever entertained a serious doubt with regard to a truth so certain and self-evident. The question is not concerning the *being* but the *nature* of God. This, I affirm, from the infirmities of human understanding, to be altogether incomprehensible and unknown to us. The essence of that supreme mind, his attributes, the manner of his existence, the very nature of his duration; these and every particular, which regards so divine a Being, are mysterious to men. Finite, weak, and blind creatures, we ought to humble ourselves in his august presence, and, conscious of our frailties, adore in silence his infinite perfections, which eye hath not seen, ear hath not heard, neither hath it entered into the heart of man to conceive them. They are covered in a deep cloud from human curiosity: It is profaneness to attempt penetrating through these sacred obscurities: And next to the impiety of denying his existence, is the temerity of prying into his nature and essence, decrees and attributes.

But lest you should think, that my *piety* has here got the better of my *philosophy*, I shall support my opinion, if it needs any support, by a very great authority. I might cite all the divines almost, from the foundation of Christianity, who have ever treated of this or any other theological subject: But I shall confine myself, at present, to one equally celebrated for piety and philosophy. It is Father MALEBRANCHE, who, I remember, thus expresses himself.[1] "One ought not so much (says he) to call God a spirit, in order to express positively what he is, as in order to signify that he is not matter. He is a Being infinitely perfect: Of this we cannot doubt. But in the same

---

[1] *Recherche de la vérité, liv.* 3, chap. 9

manner as we ought not to imagine, even supposing him corporeal, that he is cloathed with a human body, as the ANTHRO-
POMORPHITES asserted, under colour that that figure was the
most perfect of any ; so neither ought we to imagine, that the
Spirit of God has human ideas, or bears *any* resemblance to
our spirit ; under colour that we know nothing more perfect
than a human mind. We ought rather to believe, that as he
comprehends the perfections of matter without being material
. . . he comprehends also the perfections of created spirits,
without being spirit, in the manner we conceive spirit : That
his true name is, *He that is,* or in other words, Being without
restriction, All Being, the Being infinite and universal."

After so great an authority, DEMEA, replied PHILO, as that
which you have produced, and a thousand more, which you
might produce, it would appear ridiculous in me to add my
sentiment, or express my approbation of your doctrine. But
surely, where reasonable men treat these subjects, the question
can never be concerning the *being,* but only the *nature* of the
Deity. The former truth, as you well observe, is unquestion-
able and self-evident. Nothing exists without a cause ; and
the original cause of this universe (whatever it be) we call
GOD ; and piously ascribe to him every species of perfection.
Whoever scruples this fundamental truth deserves every
punishment, which can be inflicted among philosophers, to
wit, the greatest ridicule, contempt and disapprobation. But
as all perfection is entirely relative, we ought never to imagine,
that we comprehend the attributes of this divine Being, or to
suppose, that his perfections have any analogy or likeness to
the perfections of a human creature. Wisdom, thought, design,
knowledge ; these we justly ascribe to him ; because these
words are honourable among men, and we have no other
language or other conceptions, by which we can express our
adoration of him. But let us beware, lest we think, that our
ideas any wise correspond to his perfections, or that his attributes have any resemblance to these qualities among men. He
is infinitely superior to our limited view and comprehension ;
and is more the object of worship in the temple, than of disputation in the schools.   *Philo*

In reality, CLEANTHES, continued he, there is no need of
having recourse to that affected scepticism, so displeasing to
you, in order to come at this determination. Our ideas reach

that
God is mysterious

no farther than our experience : We have no experience of divine attributes and operations : I need not conclude my syllogism : You can draw the inference yourself. And it is a pleasure to me (and I hope to you too) that just reasoning and sound piety here concur in the same conclusion, and both of them establish the adorably mysterious and incomprehensible nature of the supreme Being.

Not to lose any time in circumlocutions, said CLEANTHES, addressing himself to DEMEA, much less in replying to the pious declamations of PHILO ; I shall briefly explain how I conceive this matter. Look round the world : Contemplate the whole and every part of it : You will find it to be nothing but one great machine, subdivided into an infinite number of lesser machines, which again admit of subdivisions, to a degree beyond what human senses and faculties can trace and explain. All these various machines, and even their most minute parts, are adjusted to each other with an accuracy, which ravishes into admiration all men, who have ever contemplated them. The curious adapting of means to ends, throughout all nature, resembles exactly, though it much exceeds, the productions of human contrivance ; of human design, thought, wisdom, and intelligence. Since therefore the effects resemble each other, we are led to infer, by all the rules of analogy, that the causes also resemble ; and that the Author of nature is somewhat similar to the mind of man ; though possessed of much larger faculties, proportioned to the grandeur of the work, which he has executed. By this argument *a posteriori*, and by this argument alone, we do prove at once the existence of a Deity, and his similarity to human mind and intelligence.

I shall be so free, CLEANTHES, said DEMEA, as to tell you, that from the beginning, I could not approve of your conclusion concerning the similarity of the Deity to men ; still less can I approve of the mediums, by which you endeavour to establish it. What ! No demonstration of the being of a God ! No abstract arguments ! No proofs *a priori* ! Are these, which have hitherto been so much insisted on by philosophers, all fallacy, all sophism ? Can we reach no farther in this subject than experience [1] and probability ? I will not say, that this is betraying the cause of a Deity : But surely, by this affected

---

[1] [moral evidence *substituted for* experience, and *then* experience *restored*]

candour, you give advantage to atheists, which they never could obtain, by the mere dint of argument and reasoning.

What I chiefly scruple in this subject, said PHILO, is not so much, that all religious arguments are by CLEANTHES reduced to experience, as that they appear not to be even the most certain and irrefragable of that inferior kind. That a stone will fall, that fire will burn, that the earth has solidity, we have observed a thousand and a thousand times ; and when any new instance of this nature is presented, we draw without hesitation the accustomed inference. The exact similarity of the cases gives us a perfect assurance of a similar event ; and a stronger evidence is never desired nor sought after. But wherever you depart, in the least, from the similarity of the cases, you diminsh proportionably the evidence ; and may at last bring it to a very weak *analogy*, which is confessedly liable to error and uncertainty. After having experienced the circulation of the blood in human creatures, we make no doubt that it takes place in Titius and Mævius : But from its circulation in frogs and fishes, it is only a presumption, though a strong one, from analogy, that it takes place in men and other animals. The analogical reasoning is much weaker, when we infer the circulation of the sap in vegetables from our experience that the blood circulates in animals ; and those, who hastily followed that imperfect analogy, are found, by more accurate experiments, to have been mistaken.

If we see a house, CLEANTHES, we conclude, with the greatest certainty, that it had an architect or builder ; because this is precisely that species of effect, which we have experienced to proceed from that species of cause. But surely you will not affirm, that the universe bears such a resemblance to a house, that we can with the same certainty infer a similar cause, or that the analogy is here entire and perfect. The dissimilitude is so striking, that the utmost you can here pretend to is a guess, a conjecture, a presumption concerning a similar cause ; and how that pretension will be received in the world, I leave you to consider.

It would surely be very ill received, replied CLEANTHES ; and I should be deservedly blamed and detested, did I allow that the proofs of a Deity amounted to no more than a guess or conjecture. But is the whole adjustment of means to ends in a house and in the universe so slight a resemblance ? The

œconomy of final causes ? The order, proportion, and arrangement of every part ? Steps of a stair are plainly contrived,
that human legs may use them in mounting ; and this inference
is certain and infallible. Human legs are also contrived for
walking and mounting ; and this inference, I allow, is not altogether so certain, because of the dissimilarity which you remark ;
but does it, therefore, deserve the name only of presumption
or conjecture ?

Good God ! cried DEMEA, interrupting him, where are we ?
Zealous defenders of religion allow, that the proofs of a Deity
fall short of perfect evidence ! And you, PHILO, on whose
assistance I depended, in proving the adorable mysteriousness
of the divine nature, do you assent to all these extravagant
opinions of CLEANTHES ? For what other name can I give
them ? Or why spare my censure, when such principles are
advanced, supported by such an authority, before so young
a man as PAMPHILUS ?

You seem not to apprehend, replied PHILO, that I argue
with CLEANTHES in his own way ; and by showing him the
dangerous consequences of his tenets, hope at last to reduce
him to our opinion. But what sticks most with you, I observe,
is the representation which CLEANTHES has made of the argument *a posteriori* ; and finding that that argument is likely to
escape your hold and vanish into air, you think it so disguised
that you can scarcely believe it to be set in its true light. Now,
however much I may dissent, in other respects, from the dangerous principles of CLEANTHES, I must allow, that he has fairly
represented that argument ; and I shall endeavour so to state
the matter to you, that you will entertain no farther scruples
with regard to it.

Were a man to abstract from every thing which he knows
or has seen, he would be altogether incapable, merely from
his own ideas, to determine what kind of scene the universe
must be, or to give the preference to one state or situation of
things above another. For as nothing, which he clearly conceives, could be esteemed impossible or implying a contradiction, every chimera of his fancy would be upon an equal footing ;
nor could he assign any just reason, why he adheres to one idea
or system, and rejects the others, which are equally possible.

Again ; after he opens his eyes, and contemplates the world,
as it really is, it would be impossible for him, at first, to assign

the cause of any one event ; much less, of the whole of things or of the universe. He might set his fancy a rambling ; and she might bring him in an infinite variety of reports and representations. These would all be possible ; but being all equally possible, he would never, of himself, give a satisfactory account for his preferring one of them to the rest. Experience alone can point out to him the true cause of any phenomenon.

Now according to this method of reasoning, DEMEA, it follows (and is, indeed, tacitly allowed by CLEANTHES himself) that order, arrangement, or the adjustment of final causes is not, of itself, any proof of design ; but only so far as it has been experienced to proceed from that principle. For aught we can know *a priori*, matter may contain the source or spring of order originally, within itself, as well as mind does ; and there is no more difficulty in conceiving, that the several elements, from an internal unknown cause, may fall into the most exquisite arrangement, than to conceive that their ideas, in the great, universal mind, from a like internal, unknown cause, fall into that arrangement. The equal possibility of both these suppositions is allowed. By experience we find (according to CLEANTHES), that there is a difference between them. Throw several pieces of steel together, without shape or form ; they will never arrange themselves so as to compose a watch : Stone, and mortar, and wood, without an architect, never erect a house. But the ideas in a human mind, we see, by an unknown, inexplicable œconomy, arrange themselves so as to form the plan of a watch or house. Experience, therefore, proves, that there is an original principle of order in mind, not in matter. From similar effects we infer similar causes. The adjustment of means to ends [1] is alike in the universe, as in a machine of human contrivance. The causes, therefore, must be resembling.

I was from the beginning scandalised, I must own, with this resemblance, which is asserted, between the Deity and human creatures ; and must conceive it to imply such a degradation of the supreme Being as no sound theist could endure. With your assistance, therefore, DEMEA, I shall endeavour to defend what you justly call the adorable mysteriousness of the divine nature, and shall refute this reasoning of CLEANTHES ; provided he allows, that I have made a fair representation of it.

---

[1] [means to ends *for* final causes]

When CLEANTHES had assented, PHILO, after a short pause, proceeded in the following manner.

That all inferences, CLEANTHES, concerning fact, are founded on experience, and that all experimental reasonings are founded on the supposition, that similar causes prove similar effects, and similar effects similar causes ; I shall not, at present, much dispute with you. But observe, I entreat you, with what extreme caution all just reasoners proceed in the transferring of experiments to similar cases. Unless the cases be exactly similar, they repose no perfect confidence in applying their past observation to any particular phenomenon. Every alteration of circumstances occasions a doubt concerning the event ; and it requires new experiments to prove certainly, that the new circumstances are of no moment or importance. A change in bulk, situation, arrangement, age, disposition of the air, or surrounding bodies ; any of these particulars may be attended with the most unexpected consequences : And unless the objects be quite familiar to us, it is the highest temerity to expect with assurance, after any of these changes, an event similar to that which before fell under our observation. The slow and deliberate steps of philosophers, here, if any where, are distinguished from the precipitate march of the vulgar, who, hurried on by the smallest similitude, are incapable of all discernment or consideration.

But can you think, CLEANTHES, that your usual phlegm and philosophy have been preserved in so wide a step as you have taken, when you compared to the universe houses, ships, furniture, machines ; and from their similarity in some circumstances inferred a similarity in their causes ? Thought, design, intelligence, such as we discover in men and other animals, is no more than one of the springs and principles of the universe, as well as heat or cold, attraction or repulsion, and a hundred others, which fall under daily observation. It is an active cause, by which some particular parts of nature, we find, produce alterations on other parts. But can a conclusion, with any propriety, be transferred from parts to the whole ? Does not the great disproportion bar all comparison and inference ? From observing the growth of a hair, can we learn any thing concerning the generation of a man ? Would the manner of a leaf's blowing, even though perfectly known, afford us any instruction concerning the vegetation of a tree ?

But allowing that we were to take the *operations* of one part of nature upon another for the foundation of our judgment concerning the *origin* of the whole (which never can be admitted) yet why select so minute, so weak, so bounded a principle as the reason and design of animals is found to be upon this planet? What peculiar privilege has this little agitation of the brain which we call thought, that we must thus make it the model of the whole universe? Our partiality in our own favour does indeed present it on all occasions: But sound philosophy ought carefully to guard against so natural an illusion.

So far from admitting, continued PHILO, that the operations of a part can afford us any just conclusion concerning the origin of the whole, I will not allow any one part to form a rule for another part, if the latter be very remote from the former. Is there any reasonable ground to conclude, that the inhabitants of other planets possess thought, intelligence, reason, or any thing similar to these faculties in men? When nature has so extremely diversified her manner of operation in this small globe; can we imagine, that she incessantly copies herself throughout so immense a universe? And if thought, as we may well suppose, be confined merely to this narrow corner, and has even there so limited a sphere of action; with what propriety can we assign it for the original cause of all things? The narrow views of a peasant, who makes his domestic œconomy the rule for the government of kingdoms, is in comparison a pardonable sophism.

But were we ever so much assured, that a thought and reason, resembling the human, were to be found throughout the whole universe, and were its activity elsewhere vastly greater and more commanding than it appears in this globe: Yet I cannot see, why the operations of a world, constituted, arranged, adjusted, can with any propriety be extended to a world, which is in its embryo-state, and is advancing towards that constitution and arrangement. By observation, we know somewhat of the œconomy, action, and nourishment of a finished animal; but we must transfer with great caution that observation to the growth of a fœtus in the womb, and still more, to the formation of an animalcule in the loins of its male parent. Nature, we find, even from our limited experience, possesses an infinite number of springs and principles, which incessantly discover themselves on every change of her position

see Cleanthes rebuke p 153

and situation. And what new and unknown principles would actuate her in so new and unknown a situation as that of the formation of a universe, we cannot, without the utmost temerity, pretend to determine.

[A very small part of this great system, during a very short time, is very imperfectly discovered to us : And do we thence pronounce decisively concerning the origin of the whole ?] [1]

Admirable conclusion ! Stone, wood, brick, iron, brass have not, at this time, in this minute globe of earth, an order or arrangement without human art and contrivance : Therefore the universe could not originally attain its order and arrangement, without something similar to human art. But is a part of nature a rule for another part very wide of the former ? Is it a rule for the whole ? [2] Is a very small part a rule for the universe ? Is nature in one situation, a certain rule for [3] nature in another situation, vastly different from the former ?

And can you blame me, CLEANTHES, if I here imitate the prudent reserve of SIMONIDES, who, according to the noted story,[4] being asked by HIERO, *What God was ?* desired a day to think of it, and then two days more ; and after that manner continually prolonged the term, without ever bringing in his definition or description ? Could you even blame me, if I had answered at first, *that I did not know*, and was sensible that this subject lay vastly beyond the reach of my faculties ? You might cry out sceptic and raillier as much as you pleased : But having found, in so many other subjects, much more familiar, the imperfections and even contradictions of human reason, I never should expect any success from its feeble conjectures, in a subject, so sublime, and so remote from the sphere of our observation. When two *species* of objects have always been observed to be conjoined together, I can *infer*, by custom, the existence of one wherever I *see* the existence of the other : And this I call an argument from experience. But how this argument can have place, where the objects, as in the present case,[5] are single, individual, without parallel, or specific resemblance, may be difficult to explain. And will any man

---

[1] [This paragraph transferred from p. 135]
[2] [whole *for* world]
[3] [a certain rule for *for* precisely similar to]
[4] [*Cf.* Cicero, *De Natura Deorum*, Bk. 1, 22]
[5] [concerning the origin of the world *omitted*]

tell me with a serious countenance, that an orderly universe must arise from some thought and art, like the human ; because we have experience of it ? To ascertain this reasoning, it were requisite, that we had experience of the origin of worlds ; and it is not sufficient surely, that we have seen ships and cities arise from human art and contrivance. . . .

PHILO was proceeding in this vehement manner, somewhat between jest and earnest, as it appeared to me ; when he observed some signs of impatience in CLEANTHES, and then immediately stopped short. What I had to suggest, said CLEANTHES, is only that you would not abuse terms, or make use of popular expressions to subvert philosophical reasonings. You know, that the vulgar often distinguish reason from experience, even where the question relates only to matter of fact and existence ; though it is found, where that *reason* is properly analysed, that it is nothing but a species of experience. To prove by experience the origin of the universe from mind is not more contrary to common speech than to prove the motion of the earth from the same principle. And a caviller might raise all the same objections to the COPERNICAN system, which you have urged against my reasonings. Have you other earths, might he say, which you have seen to move ? Have. . . .

Yes ! cried PHILO, interrupting him, we have other earths. Is not the moon another earth, which we see to turn round its centre ? Is not Venus another earth, where we observe the same phenomenon ? Are not the revolutions of the sun also a confirmation, from analogy, of the same theory ? All the planets, are they not earths, which revolve about the sun ? Are not the satellites moons, which move round Jupiter and Saturn, and along with these primary planets, round the sun ? These analogies and resemblances, with others, which I have not mentioned, are the sole proofs of the COPERNICAN system : And to you it belongs to consider, whether you have any analogies of the same kind to support your theory. *Philo*

In reality, CLEANTHES, continued he, the modern system of astronomy is now so much received by all enquirers, and has become so essential a part even of our earliest education, that we are not commonly very scrupulous in examining the reasons upon which it is founded. It is now become a matter of mere curiosity to study the first writers on that subject, who had the full force of prejudice to encounter, and were obliged to turn their arguments on every side, in order to render them popular and convincing. But if we peruse GALILÆO's famous Dialogues concerning the system of the world, we shall find, that that great genius, one of the sublimest that ever existed, first bent all his endeavours to prove, that there was no foundation for the distinction commonly made between elementary and celestial substances. The schools, proceeding from the illusions of sense, had carried this distinction very far ; and had established the latter substances to be ingenerable, incorruptible, unalterable, impassible ; and had assigned all the opposite qualities to the former. But GALILÆO, beginning with the moon, proved its similarity in every particular to the earth ; its convex figure, its natural darkness when not illuminated, its density, its distinction into solid and liquid, the variations of its phases, the mutual illuminations of the earth and moon, their mutual eclipses, the inequalities of the lunar surface, &c. After many instances of this kind, with regard to all the planets, men plainly saw, that these bodies became proper objects of experience ; and that the similarity of their nature enabled us to extend the same arguments and phenomena from one to the other.

In this cautious proceeding of the astronomers, you may read your own condemnation, CLEANTHES ; or rather may see, that the subject in which you are engaged exceeds all human reason and enquiry. ꝫ Can you pretend to show any such similarity between the fabric of a house, and the generation of a universe ? Have you ever seen nature in any such situation as resembles the first arrangement of the elements ? Have worlds ever been formed under your eye ? and have you had leisure to observe the whole progress of the phenomenon, from the first appearance of order to its final consummation ? If you have, then cite your experience, and deliver your theory.

PART III

NOW the most absurd argument, replied CLEANTHES, in the hands of a man of ingenuity and invention, may acquire an air of [1] probability ! Are you not aware, PHILO, that it became necessary for COPERNICUS and his first disciples to prove the similarity of the terrestrial and celestial matter ; because several philosophers, blinded by old systems, and supported by some sensible appearances,[2] had denied this similarity ? But that it is by no means necessary, that theists should prove the similarity of the works of nature to those of art ; because this similarity is self-evident and undeniable ? The same matter, a like form : What more is requisite to show [3] an analogy between their causes, and to ascertain the origin of all things from a divine purpose and intention ? Your objections, I must freely tell you, are no better than the abstruse cavils of those philosophers, who denied motion ; and ought to be refuted in the same manner, by illustrations, examples, and instances, rather than by serious argument and philosophy.

Suppose, therefore, that an articulate voice were heard in the clouds, much louder and more melodious than any which human art could ever reach : Suppose, that this voice were extended in the same instant over all nations, and spoke to each nation in its own language and dialect : Suppose, that the words delivered not only contain a just sense and meaning, but convey some instruction altogether worthy of a benevolent Being, superior to mankind : Could you possibly hesitate a moment concerning the cause of this voice ? And must you not instantly ascribe it to some design or purpose ? Yet I cannot see but all the same objections (if they merit that appellation) which lie against the system of theism, may also be produced against this inference.

Might you not say, that all conclusions concerning fact were founded on experience : That when we hear an articulate voice in the dark, and thence infer a man, it is only the resem-

[1] [truth and *omitted*]
[2] [some sensible appearances *for* the illusions of sense]
[3] [show *for* prove]

152

blance of the effects, which leads us to conclude that there is
a like resemblance in the cause : But that this extraordinary
voice, by its loudness, extent, and flexibility to all languages,
bears so little analogy to any human voice, that we have no
reason to suppose any analogy in their causes : And consequently, that a rational, wise, coherent speech proceeded,
you knew not whence, from some accidental whistling of the
winds, not from any divine reason or intelligence ? You see
clearly your own objections in these cavils ; and I hope too,
you see clearly, that they cannot possibly have more force in
the one case than in the other.

But to bring the case still nearer the present one of the
universe, I shall make two suppositions, which imply not any
absurdity or impossibility. Suppose, that there is a natural,
universal, invariable language, common to every individual of
human race ; and that books are natural productions, which
perpetuate themselves in the same manner with animals and
vegetables, by descent and propagation. Several expressions
of our passions contain a universal language : All brute [1]
animals have a natural speech, which, however limited, is very
intelligible to their own species. And as there are infinitely
fewer parts and less contrivance in the finest composition of
eloquence, than in the coarsest organized body, the propagation
of an *Iliad* or *Æneid* is an easier supposition than that of any
plant or animal.

Suppose, therefore, that you enter into your library, thus
peopled by natural [2] volumes, containing the most refined
reason and most exquisite beauty : Could you possibly open
one of them, and doubt, that its original cause bore the strongest analogy to mind and intelligence ? When it reasons and
discourses ; when it expostulates, argues, and enforces its views
and topics ; when it applies sometimes to the pure intellect,
sometimes to the affections ; when it collects, disposes, and
adorns every consideration suited to the subject : could you
persist in asserting, that all this, at the bottom, had really no
meaning, and that the first formation of this volume in the
loins of its original [3] parent proceeded not from thought and
design ? Your obstinacy, I know, reaches not that degree of
firmness : Even your sceptical play and wantonness would
be abashed at so glaring an absurdity.

[1] [brute *added*]   [2] [vegetating animal *omitted*]   [3] [original *added*]

But if there be any difference, PHILO, between this supposed case and the real one of the universe, it is all to the advantage of the latter. The anatomy of an animal affords many stronger instances of design than the perusal of LIVY or TACITUS : [1] And any objection which you start in the former case, by carrying me back to so unusual and extraordinary a scene as the first formation of worlds, the same objection has place on the supposition of our vegetating library. Choose, then, your party, PHILO, without ambiguity or evasion : Assert either that a rational volume is no proof of a rational cause, or admit of a similar cause to all the works of nature.

Let me here observe too, continued CLEANTHES, that this religious argument, instead of being weakened by that scepticism, so much affected by you, rather acquires force from it, and becomes more firm and undisputed. To exclude all argument or reasoning of every kind is either affectation or madness. The declared profession of every reasonable sceptic is only to reject abstruse, remote and refined arguments ; to adhere to common sense and the plain instincts of nature ; and to assent, wherever any reasons strike him with so full a force, that he cannot, without the greatest violence, prevent it. Now the arguments for natural religion are plainly of this kind ; and nothing but the most perverse, obstinate metaphysics can reject them. Consider, anatomize the eye : Survey its structure and contrivance ; and tell me, from your own feeling, if the idea of a contriver does not immediately flow in upon you with a force like that of sensation. The most obvious conclusion surely is in favour of design ; and it requires time, reflection and study, to summon up those frivolous, though abstruse, objections, which can support infidelity. Who can behold the male and female of each species, the correspondence of their parts and instincts, their passions and whole course of life before and after generation, but must be sensible, that the propagation of the species is intended by nature ? Millions and millions of such instances present themselves through every part of the universe ; and no language can convey a more intelligible, irresistible meaning, than the curious adjustment of final causes. To what degree, therefore, of blind dogmatism must one have attained, to reject such natural and such convincing arguments ?

[1] [Livy or Tacitus *for* the Iliad]

[¹ Some beauties in writing we may meet with, which seem contrary to rules, and which gain the affections, and animate the imagination, in opposition to all the precepts of criticism, and to the authority of the established masters of art. And if the argument for theism be, as you pretend, contradictory to the principles of logic : its universal, its irresistible influence proves clearly, that there may be arguments of a like irregular nature. Whatever cavils may be urged ; an orderly world, as well as a coherent, articulate speech, will still be received as an incontestable proof of design and intention.]

It sometimes happens, I own, that the religious arguments have not their due influence on an ignorant savage and barbarian ; not because they are obscure and difficult, but because he never asks himself any question with regard to them. Whence arises the curious structure of an animal ? From the copulation of its parents. And these whence ? From *their* parents. A few removes set the objects at such a distance, that to him they are lost in darkness and confusion ; nor is he actuated by any curiosity to trace them farther. But this is neither dogmatism nor scepticism, but stupidity ; a state of mind very different from your sifting, inquisitive disposition, my ingenious friend. You can trace causes from effects : You can compare the most distant and remote objects : And your greatest errors proceed not from barrenness of thought and invention, but from too luxuriant a fertility, which suppresses your natural good sense, by a profusion of unnecessary scruples and objections.

Here I could observe, HERMIPPUS, that PHILO was a little embarrassed and confounded : But while he hesitated in delivering an answer, luckily for him, DEMEA broke in upon the discourse, and saved his countenance,

Your instance, CLEANTHES, said he, drawn from books and language, being familiar, has, I confess, so much more force on that account ; but is there not some danger too in this very circumstance, and may it not render us presumptuous, by making us imagine we comprehend the Deity, and have some adequate idea of his nature and attributes ? When I read a volume, I enter into the mind and intention of the author : I become him, in a manner, for the instant ; and have an immediate feeling and conception of those ideas, which revolved

---

¹ [This paragraph in brackets is added on the last page of Part III, with marks to indicate point of insertion.]

in his imagination, while employed in that composition. But so near an approach we never surely can make to the Deity. His ways are not our ways. His attributes are perfect, but incomprehensible. And this volume of nature contains a great and inexplicable riddle, more than any intelligible discourse or reasoning.

The ancient PLATONISTS, you know, were the most religious and devout of all the pagan philosophers : Yet many of them, particularly PLOTINUS, expressly declare, that intellect or understanding is not to be ascribed to the Deity, and that our most perfect worship of him consists, not in acts of veneration, reverence, gratitude or love ; but in a certain mysterious self-annihilation or total extinction of all our faculties. These ideas are, perhaps, too far stretched ; but still it must be acknowledged, that, by representing the Deity as so intelligible, and comprehensible, and so similar to a human mind,[1] we are guilty of the grossest and most narrow partiality, and make our selves the model of the whole universe.

[[2] All the *sentiments* of the human mind, gratitude, resentment, love, friendship, approbation, blame, pity, emulation, envy, have a plain reference to the state and situation of man, and are calculated for preserving the existence, and promoting the activity of such a being in such circumstances. It seems therefore unreasonable to transfer such sentiments to a supreme existence, or to suppose him actuated by them ; and the phenomena, besides, of the universe will not support us in such a theory. All our *ideas*, derived from the senses, are confessedly false and illusive ; and cannot, therefore, be supposed to have place in a supreme intelligence : And as the ideas of internal sentiment, added to those of the external senses, compose the whole furniture of human understanding, we may conclude, that none of the *materials* of thought are in any respect similar in the human and in the divine intelligence. Now, as to the *manner* of thinking ; how can we make any comparison between them, or suppose them any wise resembling ? Our thought is fluctuating, uncertain, fleeting, successive, and compounded ; and were we to remove these circumstances, we

---

[1] [and so similar to a human mind *added*]

[2] [This concluding paragraph in brackets is added, with marks to indicate point of insertion, on lower part of the last page of Part III, and continued on an otherwise blank sheet.]

absolutely annihilate its essence, and it would, in such a case, be an abuse of terms to apply to it the name of thought or reason. At least, if it appear more pious and respectful (as it really is still to retain these terms, when we mention the supreme Being, we ought to acknowledge, that their meaning, in that case, is totally incomprehensible ; and that the infirmities of our nature do not permit us to reach any ideas, which in the least [1] correspond to the ineffable sublimity of the divine attributes.]

[1] [in the least *added*]

PART IV

IT seems strange to me, said CLEANTHES, that you, DEMEA, who are so sincere in the cause of religion, should still maintain the mysterious, incomprehensible nature of the Deity, and should insist so strenuously, that he has no manner of likeness or resemblance to human creatures.[1] The Deity, I can readily allow, possesses many powers and attributes, of which we can have no comprehension : But if our ideas, so far as they go, be not just and adequate, and correspondent to his real nature, I know not what there is in this subject worth insisting on. Is the name, without any meaning, of such mighty importance ? Or how do you MYSTICS, who maintain the absolute incomprehensibility of the Deity, differ from sceptics or atheists, who assert, that the first cause of All is unknown and unintelligible ? Their temerity must be very great, if, after rejecting the production by a mind ; I mean, a mind resembling the human (for I know of no other), they pretend to assign, with certainty, any other specific, intelligible cause : And their conscience must be very scrupulous indeed, if they refuse to call the universal, unknown cause a God or Deity ; and to bestow on him as many sublime eulogies and unmeaning epithets, as you shall please to require of them.

Who could imagine, replied DEMEA, that CLEANTHES, the calm, philosophical CLEANTHES, would attempt to refute his antagonists, by affixing a nick-name to them ; and like the common bigots and inquisitors of the age, have recourse to invective and declamation, instead of reasoning ? Or does he not perceive, that these topics are easily retorted, and that *anthropomorphite* is an appellation as invidious, and implies as dangerous consequences, as the epithet of *mystic*, with which he has honoured us ? In reality, CLEANTHES, consider what it is you assert, when you represent the Deity as similar to a human

---

[1] [At this point in Hume's MS. a passage scored out reads as follows : " Are you unacquainted with that principle of philosophy, that we have no idea of anything which has no likeness to ourselves, or to those objects that have been exposed to our senses and experience ? " Omission of this sentence is obviously occasioned by the insertion of the new concluding paragraph of Part III. But first Hume has tried to retain it by changing the beginning of the sentence to : " Reflect a moment on that principle of philosophy which you at present allege, . . ."]

mind and understanding. <u>What is the soul of man</u> ? A composition of various faculties, passions, sentiments, ideas ; united,
indeed, into one self or person, but still distinct from each other.
When it reasons, the ideas, which are the parts of its discourse,
arrange themselves in a certain form or order ; which is not
preserved entire for a moment, but immediately gives place to
another arrangement. New opinions, new passions, new affections, new feelings arise, which continually diversify the mental
scene, and produce in it the greatest variety, and most rapid
succession imaginable. <u>How is this compatible with that
perfect immutability and simplicity, which all true theists
ascribe to the Deity ?</u> By the same act, say they, he sees past,
present, and future : His love and his hatred, his mercy and
his justice are one individual operation : He is entire in every
point of space ; and complete in every instant of duration.
No succession, no change, no acquisition, no diminution. What
he is implies not in it any shadow of distinction or diversity.
And what he is, this moment, he ever has been, and ever will
be, without any new judgment, sentiment, or operation. He
stands fixed in one simple, perfect state ; nor can you ever say,
with any propriety, that this act of his is different from that
other, or that this judgment or idea has been lately formed,
and will give place, by succession, to any different judgment
or idea.

I can readily allow, <u>said CLEANTHES,</u> that those who maintain the perfect simplicity of the supreme Being, to the extent
in which you have explained it, are complete *mystics*, and
chargeable with all the consequences which I have drawn from
their opinion. They are, in a word, atheists, without knowing
it. For though it be allowed, that the Deity possesses attributes,
of which we have no comprehension ; yet ought we never
to ascribe to him any attributes, which are absolutely incompatible with that intelligent nature, essential to him. <u>A mind,
whose acts and sentiments and ideas are not distinct and
successive ; one, that is wholly simple, and totally immutable ;
is a mind which has no thought, no reason, no will, no sentiment, no love, no hatred ; or in a word, is no mind at all.</u>
It is an abuse of terms to give it that appellation ; and we may
as well speak of limited extension without figure, or of number
without composition.

Pray consider, <u>said PHILO,</u> whom you are at present in-

veighing against. You are honouring with the appellation of
atheist all the sound, orthodox divines almost, who have treated
of this subject ; and you will, at last, be, yourself, found, according to your reckoning, the only sound theist in the world. But
if idolaters be atheists, as, I think may justly be asserted, and
Christian theologians [1] the same ; what becomes of the argument, so much celebrated, derived from the universal consent
of mankind ?

But because I know you are not much swayed by names
and authorities, I shall endeavour to show you, a little more
distinctly, the inconveniences of that anthropomorphism, which
you have embraced ; and shall prove, that there is no ground
to suppose a plan of the world to be formed in the divine mind,
consisting of distinct ideas, differently arranged ; in the same
manner as an architect forms in his head the plan of a house
which he intends to execute.

It is not easy, I own, to see, what is gained by this supposition, whether we judge of the matter by *reason* or by *experience*.
We are still obliged to mount higher, in order to find the cause
of this cause, which you had assigned as satisfactory and
conclusive.

[If *reason* (I mean abstract reason, derived from enquiries
a priori) be not alike mute with regard to all questions concerning cause and effect ; this sentence at least it will venture to
pronounce, That a mental [2] world or universe of ideas requires
a cause as much as does a material world or [3] universe of objects ;
and if similar in its arrangement must require a similar cause.
For what is there in this subject, which should occasion a different
conclusion or inference ? In an abstract view, they are entirely
alike ; and no difficulty attends the one supposition, which is
not common to both of them.] [4]

---

[1] [Christian theologians *for* Christians]
[2] [mental *added*]
[3] [material world or *added*]
[4] [Paragraph in brackets substituted for : " When we consult reason, all causes
and effects seem equally explicable *a priori* ; nor is it possible to assign either of
them, by the mere abstract contemplation of their nature, without consulting
experience, or considering what we have found to result from the operation of
objects. And if this proposition be true in general, that *reason, judging* a priori,
finds all causes and effects alike explicable ; it must appear more so, when we compare
the external world of objects with that world of thought, which is represented as
its cause. If *reason* tells us, that the world of objects requires a cause, it must give
us the same information concerning the world of thought : And if the one seems
to reason to require a cause of any particular kind, the other must require a cause

Again, when we will needs force _experience_ to pronounce some sentence, even on these subjects, which lie beyond her sphere; neither can she perceive any material difference in this particular, between these two kinds of worlds, but finds them to be governed by similar principles, and to depend upon an equal variety of causes in their operations. We have specimens in miniature of both of them. Our own mind resembles the one : A vegetable or animal body the other. Let experience, therefore, judge from these samples. Nothing seems more delicate with regard to its causes than thought; and as these causes never operate in two persons after the same manner, so we never find two persons, who think exactly alike. Nor indeed does the same person think exactly alike at any two different periods of time. A difference of age, of the disposition of his body, of weather, of food, of company, of books, of passions; any of these particulars or others more minute, are sufficient to alter the curious machinery of thought, and communicate to it very different movements and operations. As far as we can judge, vegetables and animal bodies are not more delicate in their motions, nor depend upon a greater variety or more curious adjustment of springs and principles.

How therefore shall we satisfy ourselves concerning the cause of that Being,[1] whom you suppose the Author of nature, or, according to your system of anthropomorphism, the ideal world, into which you trace the material? Have we not the same reason to trace that ideal world into another ideal world, or new intelligent principle? But if we stop, and go no farther; why go so far? Why not stop at the material world? How can we satisfy ourselves without going on _in infinitum_? And after all, what satisfaction is there in that infinite progression? Let us remember the story of the INDIAN philosopher and his elephant. It was never more applicable than to the present subject. If the material world rests upon a similar ideal world,

of a like kind. Any proposition, therefore, which we can form concerning the cause of the former, if it be consistent, or intelligible, or necessary, must also appear to reason consistent or intelligible or necessary, when apply'd to the latter, such as you have described it; and _vice versa_. It is evident, then, that as far as abstract reason can judge, it is perfectly indifferent, whether we rest on the universe of matter or on that of thought; nor do we gain any thing by tracing the one into the other." Hume has scored out this passage; then added twice on the margin : " Print these lines, though eraz'd " ; and then, in both cases, scored through the instruction. The paragraph substituted for it is written on the last page of Part IV.]

[1] [the cause of that Being, _for_ that Deity]

this ideal world must rest upon some other ; and so on, without end. It were better, therefore, never to look beyond the
present material world. By supposing it to contain the principle
of its order within itself, we really assert it to be God ; and the
sooner we arrive at that divine Being so much the better.
When you go one step beyond the mundane system [1] you only
excite an inquisitive humour, which it is impossible ever to
satisfy.

To say, that the different ideas, which compose the reason
of the supreme Being, fall into order, of themselves, and by
their own nature, is really to talk without any precise meaning.[2] If it has a meaning, I would fain know, why it is not as
good sense to say, that the parts of the material world fall into
order, of themselves, and by their own nature ? Can the one
opinion be intelligible, while the other is not so ?

We have, indeed, experience of ideas, which fall into order,
of themselves, and without any *known* cause : But, I am sure,
we have a much larger experience of matter, which does the
same ; as in all instances of generation and vegetation, where
the accurate analysis of the cause exceeds all human comprehension. We have also experience of particular systems of
thought and of matter, which have no order ; of the first, in
madness, of the second, in corruption. Why then should we
think, that order is more essential to one than the other ? And
if it requires a cause in both, what do we gain by your system,
in tracing the universe of objects into a similar universe of ideas ?
The first step, which we make, leads us on for ever. It were,
therefore, wise in us, to limit all our enquiries to the present
world, without looking farther. No satisfaction can ever be
attained by these speculations, which so far exceed the narrow
bounds of human understanding.

It was usual with the PERIPATETICS, you know, CLEANTHES,
when the cause of any phenomenon was demanded, to have
recourse to their *faculties* or *occult qualities*, and to say, for
instance, that bread nourished by its nutritive faculty, and
senna purged by its purgative : But it has been discovered,
that this subterfuge was nothing but the disguise of ignorance ;
and that these philosophers, though less ingenuous, really said
the same thing with the sceptics or the vulgar, who fairly

---

[1] [mundane system *for* universe]
[2] [any precise meaning *for* a meaning]

confessed, that they knew not the cause of these phenomena. In like manner, when it is asked, what cause produces order in the ideas of the supreme Being, can any other reason be assigned by you, anthropomorphites, than that it is a *rational* faculty, and that such is the nature of the Deity? But why a similar answer will not be equally satisfactory in accounting for the order of the world, without having recourse to any such intelligent Creator as you insist on, may be difficult to determine. It is only to say, that *such* is the nature of material objects, and that they are all originally possessed of a *faculty* of order and proportion. These are only more learned and elaborate ways of confessing our ignorance ; nor has the one hypothesis any real advantage above the other, except in its greater conformity to vulgar prejudices.

You have displayed this argument with great emphasis, replied CLEANTHES : You seem not sensible, how easy it is to answer it. Even in common life, if I assign a cause for any event ; is it any objection, PHILO, that I cannot assign the cause of that cause, and answer every new question, which may incessantly be started? And what philosophers could possibly submit to so rigid a rule? philosophers, who confess ultimate causes to be totally unknown, and are sensible, that the most refined principles, into which they trace the phenomena, are still to them as inexplicable as these phenomena themselves are to the vulgar. The order and arrangement of nature, the curious adjustment of final causes, the plain use and intention of every part and organ ; all these bespeak in the clearest language an intelligent cause or Author. The heavens and the earth join in the same testimony : The whole chorus of nature raises one hymn to the praises of its Creator : You alone, or almost alone, disturb this general harmony. You start abstruse doubts, cavils, and objections : You ask me, what is the cause of this cause? I know not ; I care not ; that concerns not me. I have found a Deity ; and here I stop my enquiry. Let those go farther, who are wiser or more enterprising.

[I pretend to be neither, replied PHILO : And for that very reason, I should never perhaps have attempted to go so far ; especially when I am sensible, that I must at last be contented to sit down with the same answer, which, without farther trouble, might have satisfied me from the beginning.

If I am still to remain in utter ignorance of causes, and can absolutely give an explication of nothing, I shall never esteem it any advantage to shove off for a moment a difficulty, which, you acknowledge, must immediately, in its full force, recur upon me. Naturalists indeed very justly explain particular effects by more general causes ; though these general causes themselves should remain in the end totally inexplicable : But they never surely thought it satisfactory to explain a particular effect by a particular cause, which was no more to be accounted for than the effect itself.] [1] An ideal system, arranged of itself,[2] without a precedent design, it not a whit more explicable than a material one, which attains its order in a like manner ; nor is there any more difficulty in the latter supposition than in the former. ⟵

___

[1] [Passage in brackets substituted for : " Your answer may, perhaps, be good, said Philo, upon your principles, that the religious system can be proved by experience, and by experience alone ; and that the Deity arose from some external cause. But these opinions, you know, will be adopted by very few. And as to all those, who reason upon other principles, and yet deny the mysterious simplicity of the divine nature, my objection still remains good. An ideal system, &c." The new passage is written on the lower part of the last page of Part IV, with marks to indicate point of insertion.]

[2] [of itself *added*]

PART V

BUT to show you still more inconveniences, continued PHILO, in your anthropomorphism ; please to take a new survey of your principles. _Like effects prove like causes._ This is the experimental argument ; and this, you say too, is the sole theological [1] argument. Now it is certain, that the liker the effects are, which are seen, and the liker the causes, which are inferred, the stronger is the argument. Every departure on either side diminishes the probability, and renders the experiment less conclusive. You cannot doubt of [2] this principle : Neither ought you to reject its consequences.

All the new discoveries in astronomy, which prove the immense grandeur and magnificence of the works of nature, are so many additional arguments for a Deity, according to the true system of theism : But according to your hypothesis of experimental theism, [3] they become so many objections, by removing the effect still farther from all resemblance to the effects of human art and contrivance. For if Lucretius, [4] even following the old system of the world, could exclaim,

> Quis regere immensi summam, quis habere profundi
> Indu manu validas potis est moderanter habenas ?
> Quis pariter cœlos omnes convertere ? et omnes
> Ignibus ætheriis terras suffire feraces ?
> Omnibus inve locis esse omni tempore præsto ?

If _Tully_ [5] esteemed this reasoning so natural, as to put it into the mouth of his EPICUREAN. _Quibus enim oculis animi intueri potuit vester Plato fabricam illam tanti operis, qua construi a Deo_

---

[1] [theological _for_ religious]
[2] [doubt of _for_ deny]
[3] [of experimental theism _added_]
[4] Lib. II, 1095 [" Who can rule the sum, who hold in his hand with controlling force the strong reins, of the immeasurable deep ? who can at once make all the different heavens to roll and warm with ethereal fires all the fruitful earths, or be present in all places at all times " (Munro's translation).]
[5] _De Nat[ura] Deor[um]_, Lib. I [8. " For with what eyes of the mind could your Plato have beheld that workshop of such stupendous toil, in which he represents the world as having been put together and built by God ? How was so vast an undertaking set about ? What tools, what levers, what machines, what servants, were employed in so great a work ? How came air, fire, water, and earth to obey and submit to the architect's will ? "]

*atque ædificari mundum facit ? quæ molitio ? quæ ferramenta ? qui
vectes ? quæ machinæ ? qui ministri tanti muneris fuerunt ? quemad-
modum autem obedire et arere voluntati architecti aer, ignis, aqua,
terra potuerunt ?* If this argument, I say, had any force in former
ages ; how much greater must it have at present ; when the
bounds of nature are so infinitely enlarged, and such a magnificent scene is opened to us ? It is still more unreasonable to
form our idea of so unlimited a cause from our experience
of the narrow productions of human design and invention.

The discoveries by microscopes, as they open a new universe
in miniature, are still objections, according to you ; arguments,
according to me. The farther we push our researches of this
kind, we are still led to infer the universal cause of All to be
vastly different from mankind, or from any object of human
experience and observation.

And what say you to the discoveries in anatomy, chemistry,
botany ?. . . . These surely are no objections, replied CLEAN-
THES : They only discover new instances of art and contrivance.
It is still the image of mind reflected on us from unnumerable
objects. Add, a mind *like the human*, said PHILO. I know of
no other, replied CLEANTHES. And the liker the better, insisted PHILO. To be sure, said CLEANTHES.

Now, CLEANTHES, said PHILO, with an air of alacrity and
triumph, mark the consequences. *First* By this method of
reasoning, you renounce all claim to infinity in any of the
attributes of the Deity. For as the cause ought only to be
proportioned to the effect, and the effect, so far as it falls under
our cognisance, is not infinite ; what pretensions have we,
upon your suppositions,[1] to ascribe that attribute to the divine
Being ? You will still insist, that, by removing him so much
from all similarity to human creatures, we give into the most
arbitrary hypothesis, and at the same time weaken all proofs
of his existence.

Secondly, You have no reason, on your theory, for ascribing
perfection to the Deity, even in his finite capacity ; or for
supposing him free from every error, mistake, or incoherence
in his undertakings. There are many inexplicable difficulties
in the works of nature, which, if we allow a perfect Author
to be proved *a priori*, are easily solved, and become only seeming difficulties, from the narrow capacity of man, who cannot

---

[1] [upon your suppositions *added*]

trace infinite relations. But according to your method of reasoning, these difficulties become all real ; and perhaps will be insisted on, as new instances of likeness to human art and contrivance. At least, you must acknowledge, that it is impossible for us to tell, from our limited views, whether this system contains any great faults, or deserves any considerable praise, if compared to other possible, and even real systems. Could a peasant, if the ÆNEID were read to him, pronounce that poem to be absolutely faultless, or even assign to it its proper rank among the productions of human wit ; he, who had never seen any other production ?

[1 But were this world ever so perfect a production, it must still remain uncertain, whether all the excellencies of the work can justly be ascribed to the workman. If we survey a ship, what an exalted idea must we form of the ingenuity of the carpenter, who framed so complicated, useful, and beautiful a machine ? And what surprise must we entertain, when we find him a stupid mechanic, who imitated others, and copied an art, which, through a long succession of ages, after multiplied trials, mistakes, corrections, deliberations, and controversies, had been gradually improving ? Many worlds might have been botched and bungled, throughout an eternity, ere this system was struck out : Much labour lost : Many fruitless trials made : And a slow, but continued improvement carried on during infinite ages in the art of world-making. In such subjects, who can determine, where the truth ; nay, who can conjecture where the probability, lies ; amidst a great number of hypotheses which may be proposed, and a still greater number which may be imagined ?]

And what shadow of an argument, continued PHILO, can you produce, from your hypothesis, to prove the unity of the Deity ? A great number of men join in building a house or ship, in rearing a city, in framing a commonwealth : Why may not several Deities combine in contriving and framing a world ? This is only so much greater similarity to human affairs. By sharing the work among several, we may so much farther limit the attributes of each, and get rid of that extensive power and knowledge, which must be supposed in one Deity, and which, according to you, can only serve to weaken the

---

1 [This paragraph, and the paragraph on p. 168, in square brackets, are added on the last page of Part V, with marks to indicate points of insertion.]

proof of his existence. And if such foolish, such vicious creatures
as man can yet often unite in framing and executing one plan ;
how much more those Deities or Dæmons, whom we may suppose several degrees more perfect ?

[To multiply causes, without necessity, is indeed contrary
to true philosophy : But this principle applies not to the present
case. Were one Deity antecedently _proved_ by your theory,
who were possessed of every attribute requisite to the production
of the universe ; it would be needless, I own (though not
absurd) to suppose any other Deity existent. But while it is
still a question, whether all these attributes are united in one
subject, or dispersed among several independent Beings : By
what phenomena in nature can we pretend to decide the
controversy ? Where we see a body raised in a scale, we are
sure that there is in the opposite scale, however concealed from
sight, some counterpoising weight equal to it : But it is still
allowed to doubt, whether that weight be an aggregate of
several distinct bodies, or one uniform united mass. And if
the weight requisite very much exceeds any thing which we
have ever seen conjoined in any single body, the former supposition becomes still more probable and natural. An intelligent
Being of such vast power and capacity, as is necessary to produce the universe, or, to speak in the language of ancient
philosophy, so prodigious an animal, exceeds all analogy, and
even comprehension.]

But farther, CLEANTHES ; men are mortal, and renew their
species by generation ; and this is common to all living creatures.
The two great sexes of male and female, says MILTON, animate
the world. Why must this circumstance, so universal, so
essential, be excluded from those numerous and limited Deities ?
Behold then the theogony of ancient times brought back upon us.

And why not become a perfect anthropomorphite ? Why
not assert the Deity or Deities to be corporeal, and to have
eyes, a nose, mouth, ears, &c. ? EPICURUS maintained, that
no man had ever seen reason but in a human figure ; therefore the gods must have a human figure. And this argument,
which is deservedly so much ridiculed by Cicero,[1] becomes,
according to you, solid and philosophical.

In a word, CLEANTHES, a man, who follows your hypothesis,
is able, perhaps, to assert, or conjecture, that the universe,

[1] [Cicero *for* Divines]

sometime, arose from something like [1] design : But beyond
that position he cannot ascertain one single circumstance, and
is left afterwards to fix every point of his theology, by the
utmost licence of fancy and hypothesis. This world, for aught
he knows, is very faulty and imperfect, compared to a superior
standard ; and was only the first rude essay of some infant
Deity, who afterwards abandoned it, ashamed of his lame
performance ; it is the work only of some dependent, inferior
Deity ; and is the object of derision to his superiors : it is the
production of old age and dotage in some superannuated Deity ;
and ever since his death, has run on at adventures, from the
first impulse and active force, which it received from him. . . .
You justly give signs of horror, DEMEA, at these strange suppositions : But these, and a thousand more of the same kind, are
CLEANTHES's suppositions, not mine. From the moment the
attributes of the Deity are supposed finite, all these have place.
And I cannot, for my part, think, that so wild and unsettled
a system of theology is, in any respect, preferable to none at all.

These suppositions I absolutely disown, cried CLEANTHEs :
They strike me, however, with no horror ; especially, when
proposed in that rambling way in which they drop from you.
On the contrary, they give me pleasure, when I see, that, by
the utmost indulgence of your imagination, you never get rid
of the hypothesis of design in the universe ; but are obliged,
at every turn, to have recourse to it. To this concession I
adhere steadily ; and this I regard as a sufficient foundation
for religion.

[1] [something like *for* some kind of]

IT must be a slight fabric, indeed, <u>said DEMEA</u>, which can be erected on so tottering a foundation. While we are uncertain, whether there is one Deity or many ; whether the Deity or Deities, to whom we owe our existence, be perfect or imperfect, subordinate or supreme, dead or alive ; what trust or confidence can we repose in them ? What devotion or worship address to them ? What veneration or obedience pay them ? To all the purposes of life, the theory of religion becomes altogether useless : And even with regard to speculative consequences, its uncertainty, according to you, must render it totally precarious and unsatisfactory.

To render it still more unsatisfactory, <u>said PHILO</u>, there occurs to me another hypothesis, which must acquire an air of probability from the method of reasoning so much insisted on by CLEANTHES. <u>That like effects arise from like causes</u> : <u>This principle he supposes the foundation of all religion.</u> But there is another principle of the same kind, no less certain, and derived from the same source of [1] experience ; <u>that where several known circumstances are</u> *observed* <u>to be similar, the unknown will</u> [2] <u>also be</u> *found* similar. Thus, if we see the limbs of a human body, we conclude, that it is also attended with a human head, though hid from us. Thus, if we see, through a chink in a wall, a small part of the sun, we conclude, that, were the wall removed, we should see the whole body.[3] In short, this method of reasoning is so obvious and familiar, that no scruple can ever be made with regard to its solidity.

Now if we survey the universe, so far as it falls under our knowledge, it bears a great resemblance to an animal or organized body, and seems actuated with a like principle of life and motion. A continual circulation of matter in it produces no disorder : A continual waste in every part is incessantly

---

[1] [practice and *omitted*]   [2] [will *for* must]
[3] [*This sentence has been substituted for :* Thus, if we hear, in the dark, reason and sense delivered in an articulate voice, we infer, that there is also present a human figure, which we shall discover on the return of light. *There is also, on the margin, scored out, the words :* If we see from a distance the buildings of a city, we infer that they contain inhabitants whom we shall discover on our approach to them.]

repaired : The closest sympathy is perceived throughout the entire system : And each part or member, in performing its proper offices, operates both to its own preservation and to that of the whole. The world, therefore, I infer, is an animal, and the Deity is the SOUL of the world, actuating it, and actuated by it.

You have too much learning, CLEANTHES, to be at all surprised at this opinion, which, you know, was maintained by almost all the theists of antiquity, and chiefly prevails in their discourses and reasonings. For though sometimes the ancient philosophers reason from final causes, as if they thought the world the workmanship of God ; yet it appears rather their favourite notion to consider it as his body, whose organization renders it subservient to him. And it must be confessed, that as the universe resembles more a human body than it does the works of human art and contrivance ; if our limited analogy could ever, with any propriety, be extended to the whole of nature, the inference seems juster in favour of the ancient than the modern theory.

There are many other advantages too, in the former theory, which recommended it to the ancient theologians. Nothing more repugnant to all their notions, because nothing more repugnant to common experience, than mind without body ; a mere spiritual substance, which fell not under their senses nor comprehension, and of which they had not observed one single instance throughout all nature. Mind and body they knew, because they felt both : An order, arrangement, organization, or internal machinery in both they likewise knew, after the same manner : And it could not but seem reasonable to transfer this experience to the universe, and to suppose the divine mind and body to be also coeval, and to have, both of them, order and arrangement naturally inherent in them, and inseparable from them.

Here therefore is a new species of anthropomorphism, CLEANTHES, on which you may deliberate ; and a theory which seems not liable to any considerable difficulties. You are too much superior surely to *systematical prejudices*, to find any more difficulty in supposing an animal body to be, originally, of itself, or from unknown causes, possessed of order and organization, than in supposing a similar order to belong [1] to

1 [order to belong *for* principle belonging]

mind. But the *vulgar prejudice*, that body and mind ought always to accompany each other, ought not, one should think, to be entirely neglected ; since it is founded on *vulgar experience*, the only guide which you profess to follow in all these theological inquiries. And if you assert, that our limited experience is an unequal standard, by which to judge of the unlimited extent of nature ; you entirely abandon your own hypothesis, and must thenceforward adopt our mysticism, as you call it, and admit of the absolute incomprehensibility of the divine nature.[1]

This theory, I own, replied CLEANTHES, has never before occurred to me, though a pretty natural one ; and I cannot readily, upon so short an examination and reflection, deliver any opinion with regard to it. You are very scrupulous, indeed, said PHILO ; were I to examine any system of yours, I should not have acted with half that caution and reserve, in starting objections and difficulties to it. However, if any thing occur to you, you will oblige us by proposing it.

Why then, replied CLEANTHES, it seems to me that, though the world does, in many circumstances, resemble an animal body ; yet is the analogy also effective in many circumstances, the most material : No organs of sense ; no seat of thought or reason ; no one precise origin of motion and action. In short, it seems to bear a stronger resemblance to a vegetable than to an animal ; and your inference would be so far inconclusive in favour of the soul of the world.

But in the next place, your theory seems to imply the eternity of the world ; and that is a principle which, I think, can be refuted by the strongest reasons and probabilities. I shall suggest an argument to this purpose, which, I believe, has not been insisted on by any writer. Those, who reason from the late origin of arts and sciences, though their inference wants not force, may perhaps be refuted by considerations derived from the nature of human society, which is in continual revolution between ignorance and knowledge, liberty and slavery, riches and poverty ; so that it is impossible for us, from our limited experience, to foretell with assurance what events may or may not be expected. Ancient learning and history seem to have been in great danger of entirely perishing

---

[1] [This last sentence scored out, with note on the margin : " Print this sentence though eraz'd."]

after the inundation of the barbarous nations ; and had these convulsions continued a little longer, or been a little more violent, we should not probably have now known what passed in the world a few centuries before us. Nay, were it not for the superstition of the Popes, who preserved a little jargon of LATIN, in order to support the appearance of an ancient and universal church, that tongue must have been utterly lost. In which case, the Western world, being totally barbarous, would not have been in a fit disposition for receiving the GREEK language and learning, which was conveyed to them after the sacking of CONSTANTINOPLE. When learning and books had been [1] extinguished, even the mechanical arts would have fallen considerably to decay ; and it is easily imagined, that fable or tradition might ascribe to them a much later origin than the true one. This vulgar [2] argument, therefore, against the eternity of the world, seems a little precarious.

But here appears to be the foundation of a better argument. LUCULLUS was the first that brought cherry-trees from ASIA to EUROPE ; though that tree thrives so well in many EUROPEAN climates, that it grows in the woods without any culture. Is it possible, that, throughout a whole eternity, no EUROPEAN had ever passed into ASIA, and thought of transplanting so delicious a fruit into his own country ? Or if the tree was once transplanted and propagated, how could it ever afterwards perish ? Empires may rise and fall ; liberty and slavery succeed alternately ; ignorance and knowledge give place to each other ; but the cherry-tree will still remain in the woods of GREECE, SPAIN and ITALY, and will never be affected by the revolutions of human society.

It is not two thousand years since vines were transplanted into FRANCE ; though there is no climate in the world more favourable to them. It is not three centuries since horses, cows, sheep, swine, dogs, corn, were known in AMERICA. Is it possible, that, during the revolutions of a whole eternity, there never arose a COLUMBUS, who might open the communication between EUROPE and that continent ? We may as well imagine, that all men would wear stockings for ten thousand years, and never have the sense to think of garters to tie them. All these seem convincing proofs of the youth, or rather infancy, of the world ; as being founded on the operation of principles more

---

[1] [totally *omitted*]   [2] [vulgar *for* common]

constant and steady than those by which human society is governed and directed. Nothing less than a total convulsion of the elements will ever destroy all the Europeaɴ animals and vegetables, which are now to be found in the Western world.

And what argument have you against such convulsions? replied Phiʟo. Strong and almost incontestable proofs may be traced over the whole earth, that every part of this globe has continued for many ages entirely covered with water. And though order were supposed inseparable from matter, and inherent in it; yet may matter be susceptible of many and great revolutions, through the endless periods of eternal duration. The incessant changes, to which every part of it is subject, seem to intimate some such general transformations; though at the same time, it is observable, that all the changes and corruptions, of which we have ever had experience, are but passages from one state of order to another; nor can matter ever rest in total deformity and confusion. What we see in the parts, we may infer in the whole; at least, that is the method of reasoning on which you rest your whole theory. And were I obliged to defend any particular system of this nature (which I never willingly should do), I esteem none more plausible than that which ascribes an eternal, inherent principle of order to the world;[1] though attended with great and continual revolutions and alterations. This at once solves all difficulties;[2] and if the solution, by being so general,[3] is not entirely complete and satisfactory, it is, at least, a theory, that we must, sooner or later, have recourse to, whatever system we embrace. How could things have been as they are, were there not an original, inherent principle of order somewhere, in thought or in matter? And it is very[4] indifferent to which of these we give the preference. Chance has no place, on any hypothesis, sceptical or religious.[5] Every thing is surely governed by steady, inviolable laws. And were the inmost essence of things laid open to us, we should then discover a scene, of

---

[1] [to the world *for* in matter]
[2] [solves all difficulties *for* answers all questions]
[3] [by being so general, is not *for* be not]
[4] [is very *for* seems]
[5] [(1) *Originally :* Chance it is ridiculous to maintain on any hypothesis, (2) *Altered to :* Chance, or what is the same thing liberty, seems not to have place on any hypothesis, sceptical or religious. (3) *Finally revised as above.*]

which, at present, we can have no idea. Instead of admiring
the order of natural beings, we should clearly see, that it was
absolutely impossible for them, in the smallest article, ever to
admit of any other disposition.

Were any one inclined to revive the ancient Pagan Theology,
which maintained, as we learn from Hesiod,[1] that this globe
was governed by 30,000 Deities, who arose from the unknown
powers of nature : You would naturally object, CLEANTHES,
that nothing is gained by this hypothesis, and that it is as easy
to suppose all men and animals, beings more numerous, but
less perfect, to have sprung immediately from a like origin.
Push the same inference a step farther ; and you will find
a numerous society of Deities as explicable as one universal
Deity, who possesses, within himself, the powers and perfections
of the whole society. All these systems, then, of scepticism,
polytheism, and theism, you must allow, on your principles,
to be on a like footing,[2] and that no one of them has any
advantages over the others. You may thence learn the fallacy
of your principles.

[1] [which maintained . . . Hesiod *for* mentioned by Varro]
[2] [on a like footing *for* alike explicable]

BUT here, continued PHILO, in examining the ancient system of the soul of the world, there strikes me, all on a sudden, a new idea, which, if just, must go near to subvert all your reasoning, and destroy even your first inferences, on which you repose such confidence. If the universe bears a greater likeness to animal bodies and to vegetables, than to the works of human art, it is more probable that its cause resembles the cause of the former than that of the latter, and its origin ought rather to be ascribed to generation or vegetation than to reason or design. Your conclusion, even according to your own principles, is therefore lame and defective.

Pray open up this argument a little farther, said DEMEA. For I do not rightly apprehend it, in that concise manner in which you have expressed it. (Dim wit!)

Our friend, CLEANTHES, replied PHILO, as you have heard, asserts, that since no question of fact can be proved otherwise than by experience, the existence of a Deity admits not of proof from any other medium. The world, says he, resembles the works of human contrivance : Therefore its cause must also resemble that of the other. Here we may remark, that the operation of one very small part of nature, to wit man, upon another very small part, to wit that inanimate matter lying within his reach, is the rule by which CLEANTHES judges of the origin of the whole ; and he measures objects, so widely disproportioned, by the same individual standard. But to waive all objections drawn from this topic ; I affirm, that there are other parts of the universe (besides the machines of human invention) which bear still a greater resemblance to the fabric of the world, and which therefore afford a better conjecture concerning the universal origin of this system.[1] These parts are animals and vegetables. The world plainly resembles more an animal or a vegetable, than it does a watch or a knitting-loom. Its cause, therefore, it is more probable, resembles the cause of the former. The cause of the former is generation or vegetation. The cause, therefore, of the world,

---

[1] [this system *for* the whole of nature]

we may infer to be some thing similar or analogous to generation or vegetation.

But how is it conceivable, said DEMEA, that the world can
arise from any thing similar to vegetation or generation ?

Very easily, replied PHILO. In like manner as a tree sheds
its seed into the neighbouring fields, and produces other trees ;
so the great vegetable, the world, or this planetary system,
produces within itself certain seeds, which, being scattered
into the surrounding chaos, vegetate into new worlds. A
comet, for instance, is the seed of a world ; and after it has
been fully ripened, by passing from sun to sun, and star to star,
it is at last tossed into the unformed elements, which everywhere surround this universe, and immediately sprouts up
into a new system.

Or if, for the sake of variety (for I see no other advantage),
we should suppose this world to be an animal ; a comet is the
egg of this animal ; and in like manner as an ostrich lays its
egg in the sand, which, without any farther care, hatches the
egg, and produces a new animal ; so. . . .

I understand you, says DEMEA : But what wild, arbitrary
suppositions are these ? What *data* have you for such extraordinary conclusions ? And is the slight, imaginary resemblance
of the world to a vegetable or an animal sufficient to establish
the same inference with regard to both ? Objects, which are
in general so widely different ; ought they to be a standard
for each other ?

Right, cries PHILO : This is the topic on which I have all
along insisted. I have still asserted, that we have no *data* to
establish any system of cosmogony. Our experience, so imperfect in itself, and so limited both in extent and duration,
can afford us no probable conjecture concerning the whole
of things. But if we must needs fix on some hypothesis ; by
what rule, pray, ought we to determine our choice ? Is there
any other rule than the greater similarity of the objects compared ? And does not a plant or an animal, which springs
from vegetation or generation, bear a stronger resemblance to
the world, than does any artificial machine, which arises from
reason and design ?

But what is this vegetation and generation of which you
talk ? said DEMEA. Can you explain their operations, and
anatomize that fine internal structure, on which they depend ?

As much, at least, replied PHILO, as CLEANTHES can explain
the operations of reason, or anatomize that internal structure,
on which *it* depends. But without any such elaborate disquisi-
tions, when I see an animal, I infer, that it sprang from generation ; and that with as great certainty as you conclude a house
to have been reared by [1] design. *[*These words, *generation,
reason,* mark only certain powers and energies in nature, whose
effects are known, but whose essence is incomprehensible ; and
one of these principles, more than the other, has no privilege
for made being a standard to the whole of nature.*]*

In reality, DEMEA, it may reasonably be expected, that the
larger the views are which we take of things, the better will
they conduct us in our conclusions concerning such extraordinary and such magnificent subjects. In this little corner
of the world alone, there are four principles, *reason, instinct,
generation, vegetation,* which are similar to each other, and are
the causes of similar effects. What a number of other principles
may we naturally suppose in the immense extent and variety
of the universe, could we travel from planet to planet and
from system to system, in order to examine each part of this
mighty fabric ? [2] Any one of these four principles above
mentioned (and a hundred others which lie open to our conjecture) may afford us a theory,[3] by which to judge of the origin
of the world ; and it is a palpable and egregious partiality,
to confine our view entirely to that principle, by which our
own minds [4] operate. Were this principle more intelligible
on that account, such a partiality might be somewhat excusable :
But reason, in its internal fabric and structure, is really as little
known to us as instinct or vegetation ; and perhaps even that
vague, undeterminate word, nature, to which the vulgar refer
every thing, is not at the bottom more inexplicable   The effects
of these principles are all known to us from experience : But
the principles themselves, and their manner of operation, are
totally unknown : Nor is it less intelligible, or less conformable to experience to say, that the world arose by vegetation
from a seed shed by another world, than to say that it arose
from a divine reason or contrivance, according to the sense
in which CLEANTHES understands it.

But methinks, said DEMEA, if the world had a vegetative

---

[1] [reason and *omitted*]   [2] [fabric *for* whole]
[3] [theory *for* standard]   [4] [our own minds *for* we ourselves]

quality, and could sow the seeds of new worlds into the infinite chaos, this power would be still an additional argument for design in its Author. For whence could arise so wonderful a faculty but from design? Or how can order spring from any thing, which perceives not that order which it bestows?

You need only look around you, replied PHILO, to satisfy yourself with regard to this question. A tree bestows order and organization on that tree which springs from it, without knowing the order : an animal, in the same manner, on its offspring : a bird, on its nest : And instances of this kind are even more frequent in the world, than those of order, which arise from reason and contrivance.[1] To say that all this order in animals and vegetables proceeds ultimately from design is begging the question ; nor can that great point be ascertained otherwise than by proving *a priori*, both that order is, from its nature,[2] inseparably attached to thought,[3] and that it can never, of itself, or from original unknown principles, belong to matter.

But farther, DEMEA ; this objection, which you urge, can never be made use of by CLEANTHES, without renouncing a defence which he has already made against one of my objections. When I enquired concerning the cause of that supreme reason and intelligence, into which he resolves every thing ; he told me, that the impossibility of satisfying such enquiries could never be admitted as an objection in any species of philosophy. *We must stop somewhere*, says he ; *nor is it ever within the reach of human capacity to explain ultimate causes, or show the last connections of any objects. It is sufficient, if the steps, so far as we go, are supported by experience and observation.* Now that vegetation and generation, as well as reason, are experienced to be principles of order in nature, is undeniable. If I rest my system of cosmogony on the former, preferably to the latter, it is at my choice. The matter seems entirely arbitrary. And when CLEANTHES asks me what is the cause of my great vegetative or generative faculty, I am equally entitled to ask him the cause of his great reasoning principle.[4] These questions we have agreed to forbear on both sides ; and it is chiefly his interest on the present occasion to stick to this agreement. Judging by our limited and imperfect experience, generation has some privileges above

---

[1] [contrivance *for* perception]   [2] [from its nature *added*]
[3] [thought *for* perception]   [4] [principle *for* faculty]

reason : For we see every day the latter arise from the former, never the former from the latter.

Compare, I beseech you, the consequences on both sides. The world, say I, resembles an animal, therefore it is an animal, therefore it arose from generation. The steps, I confess, are wide ; yet there is some small appearance of analogy in each step. The world, says CLEANTHES, resembles a machine, therefore it is a machine, therefore it arose from design. The steps are here equally wide, and the analogy less striking. And if he pretends to carry on *my* hypothesis a step farther, and to infer design or reason from the great principle of generation, on which I insist ; I may, with better authority, use the same freedom to push farther *his* hypothesis, and infer a divine genera- tion or theogony from his principle of reason. I have at least some faint shadow of experience, which is the utmost that can ever be attained in the present subject. Reason, in in- numerable instances, is observed to arise from the principle of generation, and never to arise from any other principle.

[¹ HESIOD, and all the ancient mythologists, were so struck with this analogy, that they universally explained the origin of nature from an animal birth, and copulation. PLATO too, so far as he is intelligible, seems to have adopted some such notion in his TIMÆUS.]

[² The BRAHMINS assert, that the world arose from an infinite spider, who spun this whole complicated mass from his bowels, and annihilates afterwards the whole or any part of it, by absorbing it again, and resolving it into his own essence. Here is a species of cosmogony, which appears to us ridiculous ; because a spider is a little contemptible animal, whose opera- tions we are never likely to take for a model of the whole universe. But still here is a new species of analogy, even in our globe. And were there a planet wholly inhabited by spiders (which is very possible), this inference would there appear as natural and irrefragable as that which in our planet ascribes the origin of all things to design and intelligence, as explained by CLEAN- THES. Why an orderly system may not be spun from the belly

---

¹ [This paragraph, written on the margin, with marks to show that it was intended to continue the preceding paragraph, originally began : " And Hesiod, you know, as well as all the " &c. It has later been altered as above, and in- struction inserted " New Paragraph."]

² [This paragraph is also a later edition. It is written on the last page of Part VII, with marks to indicate point of insertion.]

as well as from the brain, it will be difficult for him to give a satisfactory reason.]

I must confess, PHILO, replied CLEANTHES, that of all men living, the task which you have undertaken, of raising doubts and objections, suits you best, and seems, in a manner, natural and unavoidable to you. So great is your fertility of invention, that I am not ashamed to acknowledge myself unable, in a sudden, to solve regularly such out-of-the-way difficulties as you incessantly start upon me : Though I clearly see, in general, their fallacy and error. And I question not, but you are yourself, at present, in the same case, and have not the solution so ready as the objection ; while you must be sensible, that common sense and reason is entirely against you, and that such whimsies, as you have delivered, may puzzle, but never can convince us.

PART VIII

WHAT you ascribe to the fertility of my invention, replied PHILO, is entirely owing to the nature of the subject. In subjects, adapted to the narrow compass of human reason, there is commonly but one determination, which carries probability or conviction with it ; and to a man of sound judgment, all other suppositions, but that one, appear entirely absurd and chimerical. But in such questions as the present, a hundred contradictory views may preserve a kind of imperfect analogy ; and invention has here full scope to exert itself. Without any great effort of thought, I believe that I could, in an instant, propose other systems of cosmogony, which would have some faint appearance of truth ; though it is a thousand, a million to one, if either yours or any one of mine be the true system.

For instance ; what if I should revive the old EPICUREAN hypothesis ? This is commonly, and I believe, justly, esteemed the most absurd system, that has yet been proposed ; yet, I know not, whether, with a few alterations, it might not be brought to bear a faint appearance of probability. Instead of supposing matter infinite, as EPICURUS did ; let us suppose it finite. A finite number of particles is only susceptible of finite transpositions : And it must happen, in an eternal duration, that every possible order or position must be tried an infinite number of times. This world, therefore, with all its events, even the most minute, has before been produced and destroyed, and will again be produced and destroyed, without any bounds and limitations. No one, who has a conception of the powers of infinite, in comparison of finite, will ever scruple this determination.

But this supposes, said DEMEA, that matter can acquire motion, without any voluntary agent or first mover.

And where is the difficulty, replied PHILO, of that supposition ? Every event, before experience, is equally difficult and incomprehensible ; and every event, after experience, is equally easy and intelligible. Motion, in many instances, from gravity, from elasticity, from electricity, begins in matter, without any known voluntary agent ; and to suppose always, in these cases,

an unknown voluntary agent, is mere hypothesis ; and hypothesis attended with no advantages. The beginning of motion
in matter itself is as conceivable *a priori* as its communication
from mind and intelligence.

Besides, why may not motion have been propagated by
impulse through all eternity, and the same stock of it, or nearly
the same, be still upheld in the universe ? As much as is lost
by the composition of motion, as much is gained by its resolution.
And whatever the causes are, the fact is certain, that matter is,
and always has been in continual agitation, as far as human
experience or tradition reaches. There is not probably, at
present, in the whole universe, one particle of matter at absolute
rest.

And this very consideration too, continued PHILO, which
we have stumbled on in the course of the argument, suggests
a new hypothesis [1] of cosmogony, that is not absolutely absurd
and improbable. Is there a system, an order, an œconomy
of things, by which matter can preserve that perpetual agitation, which seems essential to it, and yet maintain a constancy
in the forms, which it produces ? There certainly is such an
œconomy : For this is actually the case with the present world.
The continual motion of matter, therefore, in less than infinite
transpositions, must produce this œconomy or order ; and by
its very nature, that order, when once established, supports
itself, for many ages, if not to eternity. But wherever matter
is so poised, arranged, and adjusted as to continue in perpetual
motion, and yet preserve a constancy in the forms, its situation
must, of necessity, have all the same appearance of art and
contrivance which we observe at present. All the parts of each
form must have a relation to each other, and to the whole :
And the whole itself must have a relation to the other parts
of the universe ; to the element, in which the form subsists ;
to the materials, with which it repairs its waste and decay ;
and to every other form, which is hostile or friendly. A defect
in any of these particulars destroys the form ; and the matter,
of which it is composed, is again set loose, and is thrown into
irregular motions and fermentations, till it unite itself to some
other regular form. If no such form be prepared to receive it,
and if there be a great quantity of this corrupted matter in
the universe, the universe itself is entirely disordered ; whether

[1] [hypothesis *for* system]

it be the feeble embryo of a world in its first beginnings, that is thus destroyed, or the rotten carcass of one, languishing in old age and infirmity. In either case, a chaos ensures ; till finite, though innumerable revolutions produce at last some forms, whose parts and organs are so adjusted as to support the forms amidst a continued succession of matter.

[¹ Suppose (for we shall endeavour to vary the expression), that matter were thrown into any position, by a blind, unguided force ; it is evident that this first position must in all probability be the most confused and most disorderly imaginable, without any resemblance to those works of human contrivance, which, along with a symmetry of parts, discover an adjustment of means to ends and a tendency to self-preservation. If the actuating force cease after this operation, matter must remain for ever in disorder, and continue an immense chaos, without any proportion or activity. But suppose, that the actuating force, whatever it be, still continues in matter, this first position will immediately give place to a second, which will likewise in all probability be as disorderly as the first, and so on, through many successions of changes and revolutions. No particular order or position ever continues a moment unaltered. The original force, still remaining in activity, gives a perpetual restlessness to matter. Every possible situation is produced, and instantly destroyed. If a glimpse or dawn of order appears for a moment, it is instantly hurried away, and confounded, by that never-ceasing force, which actuates every part of matter.

Thus the universe goes on for many ages in a continued succession of chaos and disorder. But is it not possible that it may settle at last, so as not to lose its motion and active force (for that we have supposed inherent in it), yet so as to preserve an uniformity of appearance, amidst the continual motion and fluctuation of its parts ? This we find to be the case with the universe at present. Every individual is perpetually changing, and every part of every individual, and yet the whole remains, in appearance, the same. May we not hope for such a position, or rather be assured of it, from the eternal revolutions of unguided matter, and may not this account for all the appearing wisdom and contrivance which is in the universe ? Let us

¹ [This and the next paragraph in brackets are written, with marks to indicate point of insertion, on the last page of Part VIII.]

contemplate the subject a little, and we shall find, that this adjustment, if attained by matter, of a seeming stability in the forms, with a real and perpetual revolution or motion of parts, affords a plausible, if not a true solution of the difficulty.]

It is in vain, therefore, to insist upon the uses of the parts in animals or vegetables, and their curious adjustment to each other. I would fain know how an animal could subsist, unless its parts were so adjusted ? Do we not find, that it immediately perishes whenever this adjustment ceases, and that its matter corrupting tries some new form ? It happens, indeed, that the parts of the world are so well adjusted, that some regular form immediately lays claim to this corrupted matter : And if it were not so, could the world subsist ? Must it not dissolve as well as the animal, and pass through new positions and situations ; till in a great, but finite succession, it fall at last into the present or some such order ?

It is well, replied CLEANTHES, you told us, that this hypothesis was suggested on a sudden, in the course of the argument. Had you had leisure to examine it, you would soon have perceived the insuperable objections, to which it is exposed. No form, you say, can subsist, unless it possess those powers and organs,[1] requisite for its subsistence : Some new order or œconomy must be tried, and so on, without intermission ; till at last some order, which can support and maintain itself, is fallen upon. But according to this hypothesis, whence arise the many conveniences and advantages which men and all animals possess ? Two eyes, two ears, are not absolutely necessary for the subsistence of the species. Human race might have been propagated and preserved, without horses, dogs, cows, sheep, and those innumerable fruits and products which serve to our satisfaction and enjoyment. If no camels had been created for the use of man in the sandy deserts of AFRICA and ARABIA, would the world have been dissolved ? If no loadstone had been framed to give that wonderful and useful direction to the needle, would human society and the human kind have been immediately extinguished ? Though the maxims of nature be in general very frugal, yet instances of this kind are far from being rare ; and any one of them is a sufficient proof of design, and of a benevolent design, which gave rise to the order and arrangement of the universe.

[1] [organs *for* members]

Hmmm.

At least, you may safely infer, said PHILO, that the fore-going hypothesis is so far incomplete and imperfect ; which I shall not scruple to allow. But can we ever reasonably expect greater success in any attempts of this nature ? Or can we ever hope to erect a system of cosmogony, that will be liable to no exceptions, and will contain no circumstance repugnant to our limited and imperfect experience of the [1] analogy of nature ? Your theory itself cannot surely pretend to any such advantage ; even though you have run into *anthropomorphism*, the better to preserve a conformity to common experience. Let us once more put it to trial. In all instances which we have ever seen, ideas are copied from real objects, and are ectypal, not arche-typal, to express myself in learned terms : You reverse this order, and give thought the precedence. In all instances which we have ever seen, thought has no influence upon matter, except where that matter is so conjoined with it, as to have an equal reciprocal influence upon it. No animal can move immediately any thing but the members of its own body ; and indeed, the equality of action and re-action seems to be an universal law of nature : But your theory implies a contradiction to this experience. These instances, with many more, which it were easy to collect (particularly the supposition of a mind or system of thought that is eternal, or in other words, an animal ingener-able and immortal [2]), these instances, I say, may teach, all of us, sobriety in condemning each other, and let us see, that as no system of this kind ought ever to be received from a slight analogy, so neither ought any to be rejected on account of a small incongruity. For that is an inconvenience from which we can justly pronounce no one to be exempted.

All religious systems, it is confessed, are subject to great and insuperable difficulties. Each disputant triumphs in his turn ; while he carries on an offensive war, and exposes the absurdities, barbarities, and pernicious tenets of his antagonist. But all of them, on the whole, prepare a complete triumph for the sceptic, who tells them, that no system ought ever to be embraced with regard to such subjects : For this plain reason, that no absurdity ought ever to be assented to with regard to any subject. A total suspense of judgment is here our only

---

[1] [our limited and imperfect experience of the *for* the usual]
[2] [particularly the supposition . . . immortal *for* particularly the creation from nothing]

atheist

reasonable resource.   And if every attack, as is commonly observed, and no defence, among theologians, is successful ; how complete must be *his* victory, who remains always, with all mankind,[1] on the offensive, and has himself no fixed station or abiding city, which he is ever, on any occasion, obliged to defend ?

[1] [Hume presumably means *against* all mankind.   *Cf.* the concluding words of his *Natural History of Religion*, quoted above, p. 74.]

wrong

PART IX

BUT if so many difficulties attend the argument *a posteriori*, said DEMEA; had we not better adhere to that simple and sublime argument *a priori*, which, by offering to us infallible demonstration, cuts off at once all doubt and difficulty? By this argument, too, we may prove the INFINITY of the divine attributes, which, I am afraid, can never be ascertained with certainty from any other topic. For how can an effect, which either is finite, or, for aught we know, may be so; how can such an effect, I say, prove an infinite cause? The unity too of the divine nature, it is very difficult, if not absolutely impossible, to deduce merely from contemplating the works of nature; nor will the uniformity alone of the plan, even were it allowed, give us any assurance of that attribute. Whereas the argument *a priori* . . . .

You seem to reason, DEMEA, interposed CLEANTHES, as if those advantages and conveniences in the abstract argument were full proofs of its solidity. But it is first proper, in my opinion, to determine what argument of this nature you choose to insist on; and we shall afterwards, from itself, better than from its *useful* consequences, endeavour to determine what value we ought to put upon it.

The argument, replied DEMEA, which I would insist on is the common one. Whatever exists must have a cause or reason of its existence; it being absolutely impossible for any thing to produce itself, or be the cause of its own existence. In mounting up, therefore, from effects to causes, we must either go on in tracing an infinite succession, without any ultimate cause at all, or must at last have recourse to some ultimate cause, that is *necessarily* existent: Now that the first supposition is absurd may be thus proved. In the infinite chain or succession of causes and effects, each single effect is determined to exist by the power and efficacy of that cause which immediately preceded; but the whole eternal chain or succession, taken together, is not determined or caused by any thing: And yet it is evident that it requires a cause or reason, as much as any particular object, which begins to exist in time. The question is still reasonable, why this particular succession of causes existed from eternity, and not any other succession, or no succession at all. If there be no necessarily existent Being, any supposition, which can be formed, is equally possible; nor is there any more absurdity in nothing's having existed from eternity, than there is in that succession of causes, which constitutes the universe. What was it, then, which determined something to exist rather than nothing, and bestowed being on a particular possibility, exclusive of the rest? *External causes*, there are supposed to be none. *Chance* is a word without a meaning. Was it *nothing*? But that can never produce any thing. We must, therefore, have recourse to a necessarily existent Being, who carries the REASON of his existence in himself; and who cannot be supposed not to exist without an express contradiction. There is consequently such a Being, that is, there is a Deity.

I shall not leave it to PHILO, said CLEANTHES (though I know that the starting objections is his chief delight), to point out the weakness of this metaphysical reasoning. It seems to me so obviously ill-grounded, and at the same time of so little consequence to the cause of true piety and religion, that I shall myself venture to show the fallacy of it.

I shall begin with observing, that there is an evident absurdity in pretending to demonstrate a matter of fact, or to prove it by any arguments *a priori*. Nothing is demonstrable, unless the contrary implies a contradiction. Nothing, that is distinctly conceivable, implies a contradiction. Whatever we conceive as existent, we can also conceive as non-existent. There is no Being, therefore, whose non-existence implies a contradiction. Consequently there is no Being, whose existence is demonstrable. I propose this argument as entirely decisive, and am willing to rest the whole controversy upon it.

It is pretended that the Deity is a necessarily existent Being; and this necessity of his existence is attempted to be explained by asserting, that, if we knew his whole essence or nature, we should perceive it to be as impossible for him not to exist as for twice two not to be four. But it is evident, that this can never happen, while our faculties remain the same as at present. It will still be possible for us, at any time, to conceive the non-existence of what we formerly conceived to exist; nor can the mind ever lie under a necessity of supposing any object to remain always in being; in the same manner as we lie under a necessity of always conceiving twice two to be four. The words, therefore, *necessary existence*, have no meaning ; or, which is the same thing, none that is consistent.

But farther ; why may not the material universe be the necessarily existent Being, according to this pretended explication of necessity ? We dare not affirm that we know all the qualities of matter ; and for aught we can determine, it may contain some qualities, which, were they known, would make its non-existence appear as great a contradiction as that twice two is five. I find only one argument employed to prove, that the material world is not the necessarily existent Being ; and this argument is derived from the contingency both of the matter and the form of the world. " Any particle of matter," it is said,[1] " may be *conceived* to be annihilated ; and any form may be *conceived* to be altered. Such an annihilation or alteration, therefore, is not impossible." But it seems a great partiality not to perceive, that the same argument extends equally to the Deity, so far as we have any conception of him ; and that the mind can at least imagine [2] him to be non-existent, or his attributes to be altered. It must be some unknown, inconceivable qualities, which can make his non-existence appear impossible, or his attributes unalterable : And no reason can be assigned, why these qualities may not belong to matter. As they are altogether unknown and inconceivable, they can never be proved incompatible with it.

Add to this, that in tracing an eternal succession of objects, it seems absurd to inquire for a general cause or first Author. How can any thing, that exists from eternity, have a cause, since that relation implies a priority in time and a beginning of existence ?

In such a chain too, or succession of objects, each part is caused by that which preceded it, and causes that which succeeds it. Where then is the difficulty ? But the WHOLE, you say, wants a cause. I answer, that the uniting of these parts into a whole, like the uniting of several distinct counties into one kingdom, or several distinct members into one body, is performed merely by an arbitrary act of the mind, and has no influence on the nature of things. Did I show you the particular causes of each individual in a collection of twenty particles of matter, I should think it very unreasonable, should

[1] Dr. Clarke　　　　　　　[2] [imagine *for* conceive]

you afterwards ask me, what was the cause of the whole twenty. This is sufficiently explained in explaining the cause of the parts.

[¹ Though the reasonings, which you have urged, CLEANTHES, may well excuse me, said PHILO, from starting any farther difficulties ; yet I cannot forbear insisting still upon another topic. It is observed by arithmeticians, that the products of 9 compose always either 9 or some lesser product of 9 ; if you add together all the characters, of which any of the former products is composed. Thus, of 18, 27, 36, which are products of 9, you make 9 by adding 1 to 8, 2 to 7, 3 to 6. Thus 369 is a product also of 9 ; and if you add 3, 6, and 9, you make 18, a lesser product of 9.² To a superficial observer, so wonderful a regularity may be admired as the effect either of chance or design ; but a skilful algebraist immediately concludes it to be the work of necessity, and demonstrates, that it must for ever result from the nature of these numbers. Is it not probable, I ask, that the whole œconomy of the universe is conducted by a like necessity, though no human algebra can furnish a key which solves the difficulty ? And instead of admiring the order of natural beings, may it not happen, that, could we penetrate into the intimate nature of bodies, we should clearly see why it was absolutely impossible, they could ever admit of any other disposition ? So dangerous is it to introduce this idea of necessity into the present question ! And so naturally does it afford an inference directly opposite to the religious hypothesis !

But dropping all these abstractions, continued PHILO ; and confining ourselves to more familiar topics ; I shall venture to add an observation,] ³ that the argument *a priori* has seldom been found very convincing, except to people of a metaphysical head, who have accustomed themselves to abstract reasoning, and who finding from mathematics, that the understanding frequently leads to truth, through obscurity, and contrary to first appearances, have transferred the same habit of thinking

---

¹ [Passage in brackets is written on the reverse side of the last sheet of Part IX with marks to indicate point of insertion. The whole passage is scored out by Hume and then the instruction added, also by Hume, on the margin : " Print this passage."]

² *République des Lettres*, Août, 1685

³ [*The original opening of this concluding paragraph runs :* I shall venture, said PHILO, to add to these reasonings of CLEANTHES an observation.]

to subjects where it ought not to have place.   Other people, even of good sense and the best inclined to religion, feel always some deficiency in such arguments, though they are not perhaps able to explain distinctly where it lies.   A certain proof, that men ever did, and ever will, derive their religion from other sources than from this species of reasoning.

PART X

Here we go again.

IT is my opinion, I own, replied DEMEA, that each man feels, in a manner, the truth of religion within his own breast; and from a consciousness of his imbecility and misery, rather than from any reasoning, is led to seek protection from that Being, on whom he and all nature is dependent. So anxious or so tedious are even the best scenes of life, that futurity is still the object of all our hopes and fears. We incessantly look forward, and endeavour, by prayers, adoration, and sacrifice, to appease those unknown powers, whom we find, by experience, so able to afflict and oppress us. Wretched creatures that we are! What resource for us amidst the innumerable ills of life, did not religion suggest some methods of atonement, and appease those terrors, with which we are incessantly agitated and tormented?

I am indeed persuaded, said PHILO, that the best and indeed the only method of bringing every one to a due sense of religion is by just representations of the misery and wickedness of men. And for that purpose a talent of eloquence and strong imagery is more requisite than that of reasoning and argument. For is it necessary to prove, what every one feels within himself? It is only necessary to make us feel it, if possible, more intimately and sensibly.

The people, indeed, replied DEMEA, are sufficiently convinced of this great and melancholy truth. The miseries of life, the unhappiness of man, the general corruptions of our nature, the unsatisfactory enjoyment of pleasures, riches, honours; these phrases have become almost proverbial in all languages. And who can doubt of what all men declare from their own immediate feeling and experience?

In this point, said PHILO, the learned are perfectly agreed with the vulgar; and in all letters, *sacred* and *profane*, the topic of human misery has been insisted on with the most pathetic eloquence that sorrow and melancholy could inspire. The poets, who speak from sentiment, without a system, and whose testimony has therefore the more authority, abound in images of this nature. From HOMER down to Dr. YOUNG, the whole inspired tribe have ever been sensible, that no other

193

representation of things would suit the feeling and observation of each individual.

As to authorities, replied DEMEA, you need not seek them. Look round this library of CLEANTHES. I shall venture to affirm, that, except authors of particular sciences, such as chemistry or botany, who have no occasion to treat of human life, there scarce is one of those innumerable writers, from whom the sense of human misery has not, in some passage or other, extorted a complaint and confession of it. At least, the chance is entirely on that side ; and no one author has ever, so far as I can recollect, been so extravagant as to deny it.

There you must excuse me, said PHILO : LEIBNITZ has denied it ; and is perhaps the first,[1] who ventured upon so bold and paradoxical an opinion ; at least, the first, who made it essential to his philosophical system.

And by being the first, replied DEMEA, might he not have been sensible of his error ? For is this a subject in which philosophers can propose to make discoveries, especially in so late an age ? And can any man hope by a simple denial (for the subject scarcely admits of reasoning) to bear down the united testimony of mankind, founded on sense and consciousness ?

And why should man, added he, pretend to an exemption from the lot of all other animals ? The whole earth, believe me, PHILO, is cursed and polluted. A perpetual war is kindled amongst all living creatures. Necessity, hunger, want, stimulate the strong and courageous : Fear, anxiety, terror, agitate the weak and infirm. The first entrance into life gives anguish to the new-born infant and to its wretched parent : Weakness, impotence, distress, attend each stage of that life : And it is at last finished in agony and horror.

Observe too, says PHILO, the curious artifices of nature, in order to embitter the life of every living being. The stronger prey upon the weaker, and keep them in perpetual terror and anxiety. The weaker too, in their turn, often prey upon the stronger, and vex and molest them without relaxation. Consider that innumerable race of insects, which either are bred on the body of each animal, or flying about infix their stings in him. These insects have others still less than themselves,

---

[1] That sentiment had been maintained by Dr. King [*De Origine Mali*, 1702] and some few others, before LEIBNITZ, though by none of so great fame as that German philosopher.

which torment them. And thus on each hand, before and behind, above and below, every animal is surrounded with enemies, which incessantly seek his misery and destruction.

Man alone, said DEMEA, seems to be, in part, an exception to this rule. For by combination in society, he can easily master lions, tigers, and bears, whose greater strength and agility naturally enable them to prey upon him.

On the contrary, it is here chiefly, cried PHILO, that the uniform and equal maxims of nature are most apparent. Man, it is true, can, by combination, surmount all his *real* enemies, and become master of the whole animal creation : But does he not immediately raise up to himself *imaginary* enemies, the dæmons of his fancy, who haunt him with superstitious terrors, and blast every enjoyment of life? His pleasure, as he imagines, becomes, in their eyes, a crime : His food and repose give them umbrage and offence : His very sleep and dreams furnish new materials to anxious fear : And even death, his refuge from every other ill, presents only the dread of endless and innumerable woes. Nor does the wolf molest more the timid flock, than superstition does the anxious breast of wretched mortals.

Besides, consider, DEMEA ; this very society, by which we surmount those wild beasts, our natural enemies ; what new enemies does it not raise to us? What woe and misery does it not occasion? Man is the greatest enemy of man. Oppression, injustice, contempt, contumely, violence, sedition, war, calumny, treachery, fraud ; by these they mutually torment each other : And they would soon dissolve that society which they had formed, were it not for the dread of still greater ills, which must attend their separation.

But though these external insults, said DEMEA, from animals, from men, from all the elements, which assault us, form a frightful catalogue of woes, they are nothing in comparison of those, which arise within ourselves, from the distempered condition of our mind and body. How many lie under the lingering torment of diseases? Hear the pathetic enumeration of the great poet.

> Intestine stone and ulcer, colic-pangs,
> Daemoniac frenzy, moping melancholy,
> And moon-struck madness, pining atrophy,
> Marasmus and wide-wasting pestilence.

> Dire was the tossing, deep the groans : DESPAIR
> Tended the sick, busiest from couch to couch.
> And over them triumphant DEATH his dart
> Shook, but delay'd to strike, tho' oft invok'd
> With vows, as their chief good and final hope.[1]

The disorders of the mind, continued DEMEA, though more secret, are not perhaps less dismal and vexatious. Remorse, shame, anguish, rage, disappointment, anxiety, fear, dejection, despair ; who has ever passed through life without cruel inroads from these tormentors ? How many have scarcely ever felt any better sensations ? Labour and poverty, so abhorred by every one, are the certain lot of the far greater number : And those few privileged persons, who enjoy ease and opulence, never reach contentment or true felicity. All the goods of life united would not make a very happy man : But all the ills united would make a wretch indeed ; and any one of them almost (and who can be free from every one), nay often the absence of one good (and who can possess all) is sufficient to render life ineligible.

Were a stranger to drop, in a sudden, into this world, I would show him, as a specimen of its ills, an hospital full of diseases, a prison crowded with malefactors and debtors, a field of battle strowed with carcases, a fleet floundering in the ocean, a nation languishing under tyranny, famine, or pestilence. To turn the gay side of life to him, and give him a notion of its pleasures ; whither should I conduct him ? to a ball, to an opera, to court ? He might justly think, that I was only showing him a diversity of distress and sorrow.

There is no evading such striking instances, said PHILO, but by apologies, which still farther aggravate the charge. Why have all men, I ask, in all ages, complained incessantly of the miseries of life ? . . . They have no just reason, says one : These complaints proceed only from their discontented, repining, anxious disposition . . . And can there possibly, I reply, be a more certain foundation of misery, than such a wretched temper ?

But if they were really as unhappy as they pretend, says my antagonist, why do they remain in life ? . . .

Not satisfied with life, afraid of death.

[1] [Milton : *Paradise Lost*, XI]

This is the secret chain, say I, that holds us. We are terrified, not bribed to the continuance of or existence.

It is only a false delicacy, he may insist, which a few spirits indulge, and which has spread these complaints among the whole race of mankind. . . . And what is this delicacy, I ask, which you blame? Is it any thing but a greater sensibility to all the pleasures and pains of life? and if the man of a delicate, refined temper, by being so much more alive than the rest of the world, is only so much more unhappy; what judgment must we form in general of human life?

Let men remain at rest, says our adversary; and they will be easy. They are willing artificers of their own misery. . . . No! reply I; an anxious languor follows their repose: Disappointment, vexation, trouble, their activity and ambition.

I can observe something like what you mention in some others, replied CLEANTHES: But I confess, I feel little or nothing of it in myself; and hope that it is not so common as you represent it.

If you feel not human misery yourself, cried DEMEA, I congratulate you on so happy a singularity. Others, seemingly the most prosperous, have not been ashamed to vent their complaints in the most melancholy strains. Let us attend to the great, the fortunate Emperor, CHARLES V, when, tired with human grandeur, he resigned all his extensive dominions into the hands of his son. In the last harangue, which he made on that memorable occasion, he publicly avowed, *that the greatest prosperities which he had ever enjoyed, had been mixed with so many adversities, that he might truly say he had never enjoyed any satisfaction or contentment.* But did the retired life, in which he sought for shelter, afford him any greater happiness? If we may credit his son's account, his repentance commenced the very day of his resignation.

CICERO's fortune, from small beginnings, rose to the greatest lustre and renown; yet what pathetic complaints of the ills of life do his familiar letters, as well as philosophical discourses, contain? And suitably to his own experience, he introduces CATO, the great, the fortunate CATO, protesting in his old age, that, had he a new life in his offer, he would reject the present.

Ask yourself, ask any of your acquaintance, whether they would live over again the last ten or twenty years of their life. No! but the next twenty, they say, will be better:

And from the dregs of life, hope to receive
What the first sprightly running could not give.[1]

Thus at last they find (such is the greatness of human misery ;
it reconciles even contradictions) that they complain, at once,
of the shortness of life, and of its vanity and sorrow.

And it is possible, CLEANTHES, said PHILO, that after all
these reflections, and infinitely more, which might be suggested,
you can still persevere in your anthropomorphism, and assert
the moral attributes of the Deity, his justice, benevolence,
mercy, and rectitude, to be of the same nature with these
virtues in human creatures ? His power we allow infinite :
Whatever he wills is executed : But neither man nor any
other animal are happy : Therefore he does not will their
happiness. His wisdom is infinite : He is never mistaken in
choosing the means to any end : But the course of nature tends
not to human or animal felicity : Therefore it is not established for that purpose. Through the whole compass of human
knowledge, there are no inferences more certain and infallible
than these. In what respect, then, do his benevolence and
mercy resemble the benevolence and mercy of men ?

EPICURUS's old questions are yet unanswered. Is he willing
to prevent evil, but not able ? then is he impotent. Is he able,
but not willing ? then is he malevolent. Is he both able and
willing ? whence then is evil ?

You ascribe, CLEANTHES (and I believe justly) a purpose
and intention to nature. But what, I beseech you, is the object
of that curious artifice and machinery, which she has displayed
in all animals ? The preservation alone of individuals and
propagation of the species. It seems enough for her purpose,
if such a rank be barely upheld in the universe, without any
care or concern for the happiness of the members that compose
it. No resource for this purpose : No machinery, in order
merely to give pleasure or ease : No fund of pure joy and contentment : No indulgence without some want or necessity
accompanying it. At least, the few phenomena of this nature
are overbalanced by opposite phenomena of still greater
importance.

Our sense of music, harmony, and indeed beauty of all
kinds, gives satisfaction, without being absolutely necessary to

[1] [Dryden, *Aurengzebe*, Act IV, sc. I. Hume has written ' hope ' *for* ' think ']

the preservation and propagation of the species. But what
racking pains, on the other hand, arise from gouts, gravels,
megrims, tooth-aches, rheumatisms ; where the injury to the
animal-machinery is either small or incurable ? Mirth, laughter,
play, frolic, seem gratuitous satisfactions, which have no farther
tendency : Spleen, melancholy, discontent, superstition, are
pains of the same nature. How then does the divine benevolence
display itself, in the sense of you anthropomorphites ? None
but we mystics, as you were pleased to call us, can account
for this strange mixture of phenomena, by deriving it from
attributes, infinitely perfect, but incomprehensible.

And have you at last, said CLEANTHES smiling, betrayed
your intentions, PHILO ? Your long agreement with DEMEA did
indeed a little surprise me ; but I find you were all the while
erecting a concealed battery against me. And I must confess,
that you have now fallen upon a subject worthy of your noble
spirit of opposition and controversy. If you can make out the
present point, and prove mankind to be unhappy or corrupted,
there is an end at once of all religion. For to what purpose
establish the natural attributes of the Deity, while the moral
are still doubtful and uncertain ?

You take umbrage very easily, replied DEMEA, at opinions
the most innocent, and the most generally received even amongst
the religious and devout themselves : And nothing can be
more surprising than to find a topic like this, concerning the
wickedness and misery of man, charged with no less than
atheism and profaneness. Have not all pious divines and
preachers, who have indulged their rhetoric on so fertile a
subject ; have they not easily, I say, given a solution of any
difficulties which may attend it ? This world is but a point in
comparison of the universe : This life but a moment in comparison of eternity. The present evil phenomena, therefore,
are rectified in other regions, and in some future period of
existence. And the eyes of men, being then opened to larger
views of things, see the whole connection of general laws, and
trace, with adoration, the benevolence and rectitude of the
Deity, through all the mazes and intricacies of his providence.

No ! replied CLEANTHES, No ! These arbitrary suppositions
can never be admitted, contrary to matter of fact, visible and
uncontroverted. Whence can any cause be known but from
its known effects ? Whence can any hypothesis be proved but

from the apparent phenomena ? To establish one hypothesis upon another is building entirely in the air ; and the utmost we ever attain, by these conjectures and fictions, is to ascertain the bare possibility of our opinion ; but never can we, upon such terms, establish its reality.

The only method of supporting divine benevolence (and it is what I willingly embrace) is to deny absolutely the misery and wickedness of man. Your representations are exaggerated : Your melancholy views mostly fictitious : Your inferences contrary to fact and experience. Health is more common than sickness : Pleasure than pain : Happiness than misery. And for one vexation which we meet with, we attain, upon computation, a hundred enjoyments.

Admitting your position, replied PHILO, which yet is extremely doubtful, you must, at the same time, allow, that, if pain be less frequent than pleasure, it is infinitely more violent and durable. One hour of it is often able to outweigh a day, a week, a month of our common insipid enjoyments : And how many days, weeks, and months are passed by several in the most acute torments ? Pleasure, scarcely in one instance, is ever able to reach ecstasy and rapture : And in no one instance can it continue for any time at its highest pitch and altitude. The spirits evaporate ; the nerves relax ; the fabric is disordered ; and the enjoyment quickly degenerates into fatigue and uneasiness. But pain often, Good God, how often ! rises to torture and agony ; and the longer it continues, it becomes still more genuine agony and torture. Patience is exhausted ; courage languishes ; melancholy seizes us ; and nothing terminates our misery but the removal of its cause, or another event, which is the sole cure of all evil, but which, from our natural folly, we regard with still greater horror and consternation.

But not to insist upon these topics, continued PHILO, though most obvious, certain, and important ; I must use the freedom to admonish you, CLEANTHES, that you have put this controversy upon a most dangerous issue, and are unawares introducing a total scepticism into the most essential articles of natural and revealed theology. What ! no method of fixing a just foundation for religion, unless we allow the happiness of human life, and maintain a continued existence even in this world, with all our present pains, infirmities, vexations, and follies, to be eligible and desirable ! But this is contrary to every one's feeling and experience : It is contrary to an authority so established as nothing can subvert : No decisive proofs can ever be produced against this authority ; nor is it possible for you to compute, estimate, and compare all the pains and all the pleasures in the lives of all men and of all animals : And thus by your resting the whole system of religion on a point, which, from its very nature, must for ever be uncertain, you tacitly confess, that that system is equally uncertain.

But allowing you, what never will be believed ; at least, what you never possibly [1] can prove, that animal, or at least,[2] human happiness, in this life, exceeds its misery ; you have yet done nothing : For this is not, by any means, what we expect from infinite power, infinite wisdom, and infinite goodness. Why is there any misery at all in the world ? Not by chance surely. From some cause then. Is it from the intention of the Deity ? But he is perfectly benevolent. Is it contrary to his intention ? But he is almighty. Nothing can shake the solidity of this reasoning, so short, so clear, so decisive ; except we assert, that these subjects exceed all human capacity, and that our common measures of truth and falsehood are not applicable to them ; a topic, which I have all along insisted on, but which you have, from the beginning, rejected with scorn and indignation.

But I will be contented to retire still from this intrenchment : [3] For I deny that you can ever force me in it : I will allow, that pain or misery in man is *compatible* with infinite power and goodness in the Deity, even in your sense of these attributes : What are you advanced by all these concessions ? A mere possible compatibility is not sufficient. You must *prove* these pure, unmixed, and uncontrollable attributes from the present mixed and confused phenomena, and from these alone. A hopeful [4] undertaking ! Were the phenomena ever so pure and unmixed, yet being finite, they would be insufficient for that purpose. How much more, were they are also so jarring and discordant ?

Here, CLEANTHES, I find myself at ease in my argument. Here I triumph. Formerly, when we argued concerning the

---

[1] [possibly *omitted and then restored*]   [2] [animal, or at least *added*]
[3] [retrenchment *for* defence : *altered to* intrenchment *by Hume's nephew*]
[4] [hopeful *for* strange]

natural attributes of intelligence and design, I needed all my
sceptical and metaphysical subtilty to elude your grasp. In
many views of the universe, and of its parts, particularly the
latter, the beauty and fitness of final causes strike us with such
irresistible force, that all objections appear (what I believe [1]
they really are) mere cavils and sophisms ; nor can we then
imagine how it was ever possible for us to repose any weight
on them. But there is no view of human life, or of the condition of mankind, from which, without the greatest violence,
we can infer the moral attributes, or learn that infinite benevolence, conjoined with infinite power and infinite wisdom,
which we must discover by the eyes of faith alone. It is your
turn now to tug the labouring oar, and to support your philosophical subtilties against the dictates of plain reason and
experience.

[1] [I believe *for* perhaps. This alteration may have been made in 1776. *Cf.*
above, Appendix C, p. 95.]

I SCRUPLE not to allow, said CLEANTHES, that I have been apt to suspect the frequent repetition of the word, *infinite*, which we meet with in all theological writers, to savour more of panegyric than of philosophy, and that any purposes of reasoning, and even of religion, would be better served, were we to rest contented with more accurate and more moderate expressions. The terms, *admirable, excellent, superlatively great, wise,* and *holy* ; these sufficiently fill the imaginations of men ; and any thing beyond, besides that it leads into absurdities, has no influence on the affections or sentiments. Thus, in the present subject, if we abandon all human analogy, as seems your intention, DEMEA, I am afraid we abandon all religion, and retain no conception of the great object of our adoration. If we preserve human analogy, we must for ever find it impossible to reconcile any mixture of evil in the universe with infinite attributes ; much less, can we ever prove the latter from the former. But supposing the Author of nature to be finitely perfect, though far exceeding mankind ; a satisfactory account may then be given of natural and moral evil, and every untoward phenomenon be explained and adjusted. A less evil may then be chosen, in order to avoid a greater : Inconveniences be submitted to, in order to reach a desirable end : And in a word, benevolence, regulated by wisdom, and limited by necessity, may produce just such a world as the present. You, PHILO, who are so prompt at starting views, and reflections, and analogies ; I would gladly hear, at length, without interruption, your opinion of this new theory ; and if it deserve our attention, we may afterwards, at more leisure, reduce it into form.

My sentiments, replied PHILO, are not worth being made a mystery of ; and therefore, without any ceremony, I shall deliver what occurs to me with regard to the present subject. It must, I think, be allowed, that, if a very limited intelligence, whom we shall suppose utterly unacquainted with the universe, were assured, that it were the production of a very good, wise, and powerful Being, however finite, he would, from his con-jectures, form *beforehand* a different notion of it from what we find it to be by experience ; nor would he ever imagine, merely from these attributes of the cause, of which he is informed, that the effect could be so full of vice and misery and disorder, as it appears in this life. Supposing now, that this person were brought into the world, still assured, that it was the work-manship of such a sublime and benevolent Being ; he might, perhaps, be surprised at the disappointment ; but would never retract his former belief, if founded on any very solid argument ; since such a limited intelligence must be sensible of his own blindness and ignorance, and must allow, that there may be many solutions of those phenomena, which will for ever escape his comprehension. But supposing, which is the real case with regard to man, that this creature is not antecedently convinced of a supreme intelligence, benevolent, and powerful, but is left to gather such a belief from the appearances of things ; this entirely alters the case, nor will he ever find any reason for such a conclusion. He may be fully convinced of the narrow limits of his understanding ; but this will not help him in forming an inference concerning the goodness of superior powers, since he must form that inference from what he knows, not from what he is ignorant of. The more you exaggerate his weakness and ignorance, the more diffident you render him, and give him the greater suspicion, that such subjects are beyond the reach of his faculties. You are obliged, therefore, to reason with him merely from the known phenomena, and to drop every arbitrary supposition or conjecture.

Did I show you a house or palace, where there was not one apartment convenient or agreeable ; where the windows, doors, fires, passages, stairs, and the whole œconomy of the building were the source of noise, confusion, fatigue, darkness, and the extremes of heat and cold ; you would certainly blame the contrivance, without any farther examination. The architect would in vain display his subtilty, and prove to you, that if this door or that window were altered, greater ills would ensue. What he says, may be strictly true : The alteration of one particular, while the other parts of the building remain, may only augment the inconveniences. But still you would assert in general, that, if the architect had had skill and good intentions, he might have formed such a plan of the whole, and might have adjusted the parts in such a manner, as would have remedied all or most of these inconveniences. His ignorance, or even your own ignorance of such a plan, will never convince you of the impossibility of it. If you find many inconveniences and deformities in the building, you will always, without entering into any detail, condemn the architect.

In short, I repeat the question : Is the world considered in general, and as it appears to us in this life,[1] different from what a man or such a limited being would, *beforehand*, expect from a very powerful, wise, and benevolent Deity ? It must be strange prejudice to assert the contrary. And from thence I conclude, that, however consistent the world may be, allowing certain suppositions and conjectures, with the idea of such a Deity, it can never afford us an inference concerning his existence. The consistence is not absolutely denied, only the inference. Conjectures, especially where infinity is excluded from the divine attributes, may, perhaps, be sufficient to prove a consistence ; but can never be foundations for any inference.

There seem to be *four* circumstances, on which depend all, or the greatest part of the ills, that molest sensible creatures ; and it is not impossible but all these circumstances may be necessary and unavoidable. We know so little beyond common life, or even of common life, that, with regard to the œconomy of a universe, there is no conjecture, however wild, which may not be just ; nor any one, however plausible, which may not be erroneous. All that belongs to human understanding, in this deep ignorance and obscurity, is to be sceptical, or at least cautious ; and not to admit of any hypothesis, whatever ; much less, of any which is supported by no appearance of probability. Now this I assert to be the case with regard to all the causes of evil, and the circumstances on which it depends. None of them appear to human reason, in the least degree, necessary or unavoidable ; nor can we suppose them such, without the utmost licence of imagination.

The *first* circumstance which introduces evil, is that contrivance or œconomy of the animal creation, by which pains, as well as pleasures, are employed to excite all creatures to action, and make them vigilant in the great work of self-preservation. Now pleasure alone, in its various degrees, seems to human understanding sufficient for this purpose. All animals might be constantly in a state of enjoyment ; but when urged by any of the necessities of nature, such as thirst, hunger, weari-

---

[1] [in this life *added*]

ness ; instead of pain, they might feel a diminution of pleasure, by which they might be prompted to seek that object, which is necessary to their subsistence. Men pursue pleasure as eagerly as they avoid pain ; at least, might have been so constituted. It seems, therefore, plainly possible to carry on the business of life without any pain. Why then is any animal ever rendered susceptible of such a sensation ? If animals can be free from it an hour, they might enjoy a perpetual exemption from it ; and it required as particular a contrivance of their organs to produce that feeling, as to endow them with sight, hearing, or any of the senses. Shall we conjecture, that such a contrivance was necessary, without any appearance of reason ? And shall we build on that conjecture as on the most certain truth ?

But a capacity of pain would not alone produce pain, were it not for the *second* circumstance, viz. the conducting of the world by general laws ; and this seems nowise necessary to a very perfect Being. It is true ; if every thing were conducted by particular volitions, the course of nature would be perpetually broken, and no man could employ his reason in the conduct of life. But might not other particular volitions remedy this inconvenience ? In short, might not the Deity exterminate all ill, wherever it were to be found ; and produce all good, without any preparation or long progress of causes and effects ?

Besides, we must consider, that, according to the present œconomy of the world, the course of nature, though supposed exactly regular, yet to us appears not so, and many events are uncertain, and many disappoint our expectations. Health and sickness, calm and tempest, with an infinite number of other accidents, whose causes are unknown and variable, have a great influence both on the fortunes of particular persons and on the prosperity of public societies : And indeed all human life, in a manner, depends on such accidents. A Being, therefore, who knows the secret springs of the universe, might easily, by particular volitions, turn all these accidents to the good of mankind, and render the whole world happy, without discovering himself in any operation. A fleet, whose purposes were salutary to society, might always meet with a fair wind : Good princes enjoy sound health and long life : Persons born to power and authority, be framed with good tempers and virtuous dispositions. A few such events as these, regularly and wisely conducted, would change the face of the world ; and yet would no more seem to disturb the course of nature or confound human conduct, than the present œconomy of things, where the causes are secret, and variable, and com-pounded. Some small touches, given to CALIGULA's brain in his infancy, might have converted him into a TRAJAN : One wave, a little higher than the rest, by burying CÆSAR and his fortune in the bottom of the ocean, might have restored liberty to a considerable part of mankind.] There may, for aught we know, be good reasons, why providence interposes not in this manner ; but they are unknown to us : And though the mere supposition, that such reasons exist, may be sufficient to *save* the conclusion concerning the divine attributes, yet surely it can never be sufficient to *establish* that conclusion.

If every thing in the universe be conducted by general laws, and if animals be rendered susceptible of pain, it scarcely seems possible but some ill must arise in the various shocks of matter, and the various concurrence and opposition of general laws : But this ill would be very rare, were it not for the *third* circumstances, which I proposed to mention, viz. the great frugality with which all powers and faculties are distri-buted to every particular being. So well adjusted are the organs and capacities of all animals, and so well fitted to their preservation, that, as far as history or tradition reaches, there appears not to be any single species which has yet been extin-guished in the universe.[1] Every animal has the requisite endowments ; but these endowments are bestowed with so scrupulous an œconomy, that any considerable diminution must entirely destroy the creature. Wherever one power is increased, there is a proportional abatement in the others. Animals, which excel in swiftness, are commonly defective in force. Those, which possess both, are either imperfect in some of their senses, or are oppressed with the most craving wants. The human species, whose chief excellency is reason and sagacity, is of all others the most necessitous, and the most

[1] [*In Hume's manuscript there is here the following note, scored out :* CÆSAR, speak-ing of the woods in Germany, mentions some animals as subsisting there, which are now utterly extinct. *De Bello Gall :* lib. 6. These, and some few more in-stances, may be exceptions to the proposition here delivered. STRABO (lib. 4) quotes from POLYBIUS an account of an animal about the Tyrol, which is not now to be found. If POLYBIUS was not deceived, which is possible, the animal must have been then very rare, since STRABO cites but one authority, and speaks doubt-fully.]

deficient in bodily advantages ; without clothes, without arms, without food, without lodging, without any convenience of life, except what they owe to their own skill and industry. In short, nature seems to have formed an exact calculation of the necessities of her creatures ; and like a *rigid master*, has afforded them little [1] more powers or endowments, than what are strictly sufficient to supply those necessities. An *indulgent parent* would have bestowed a large stock, in order to guard against accidents, and secure the happiness and welfare of the creature, in the most unfortunate concurrence of circumstances. Every course of life would not have been so surrounded [2] with precipices, that the least departure from the true path, by mistake or necessity, must involve us in misery and ruin. Some reserve, some fund would have been provided to ensure happiness ; nor would the powers and the necessities have been adjusted with so rigid an œconomy. The Author of nature is inconceivably powerful : His force is supposed great, if not altogether inexhaustible : Nor is there any reason, as far as we can judge, to make him observe this strict frugality in his dealings with his creatures. [[3] It would have been better, were his power extremely limited, to have created fewer animals, and to have endowed these with more faculties for their happiness and preservation. A builder is never esteemed prudent, who undertakes a plan, beyond what his stock will enable him to finish.]

[In order to cure most of the ills of human life, I require not that man should have the wings of the eagle, the swiftness of the stag, the force of the ox, the arms of the lion, the scales of the crocodile or rhinoceros ; much less do I demand the sagacity of an angel or cherubim. I am contented to take an increase in one single power of faculty of his soul. Let him be endowed with a greater propensity to industry and labour ; a more vigorous spring and activity of mind ; a more constant bent to business and application. Let the whole species possess naturally an equal diligence with that which many individuals are able to attain by habit and reflection ; and the most beneficial consequences, without any allay of ill,

---

[1] [little *for* no]   [2] [surrounded *for* bordered]
[3] [This passage in brackets is first written on the margin, then scored out and rewritten on the last page of Part XI, with marks to indicate point of insertion. The next paragraph, also here given in brackets, is added, in immediate sequence, on the same page.]

is the immediate and necessary result of this endowment.
Almost all the moral, as well as natural evils of human life
arise from idleness ; and were our species, by the original
constitution of their frame, exempt from this vice or infirmity,
the perfect cultivation of land, the improvement of arts and
manufactures, the exact execution of every office and duty,
immediately follow ; and men at once may fully reach that
state of society, which is so imperfectly attained by the best-
regulated government. But as industry is a power, and the
most valuable of any, nature seems determined, suitably to
her usual maxims, to bestow it on men with a very sparing
hand ; and rather to punish him severely for his deficiency
in it, than to reward him for his attainments. She has so contrived his frame, that nothing but the most violent necessity
can oblige him to labour ; and she employs all his other wants
to overcome, at least in part, the want of diligence, and to
:ndow him with some share of a faculty, of which she has
thought fit naturally to bereave him. Here our demands may
be allowed very humble, and therefore the more reasonable.[1]
If we required the endowments of superior penetration and
judgment, of a more delicate taste of beauty, of a nicer sensibility to benevolence and friendship ; we might be told, that
we impiously pretend to break the order of nature, that we
want to exalt ourselves into a higher rank of being, that the
presents which we require, not being suitable to our state and
condition, would only be pernicious to us. But it is hard ;
I dare to repeat it, it is hard, that being placed in a world so
full of wants and necessities ; where almost every being and
element is either our foe or refuses us their assistance ; we
should also have our own temper to struggle with, and should
be deprived of that faculty which can alone fence against these
multiplied evils.]

The *fourth* circumstance, whence arises the misery and ill
of the universe, is the inaccurate workmanship of all the springs
and principles of the great machine of nature. It must be
acknowledged, that there are few parts of the universe, which
seem not to serve some purpose, and whose removal would
not produce a visible defect and disorder in the whole. The
parts hang all together ; nor can one be touched without
affecting the rest, in a greater or less degree. But at the same

<hr>

[1] [reasonable *for* legitimate]

time, it must be observed, that none of these parts or principles, however useful, are so accurately adjusted, as to keep precisely within those bounds in which their utility consists ; but they are, all of them, apt, on every occasion, to run into the one extreme or the other. One would imagine, that this grand production has not received the last hand of the maker ; so little finished is every part, and so coarse are the strokes, with which it is executed. Thus, the winds are requisite to convey the vapours along the surface of the globe, and to assist men in navigation : But how oft, rising up to tempests and hurricanes, do they become pernicious ? Rains are necessary to nourish all the plants and animals of the earth : But how often are they defective ? how often excessive ? Heat is requisite to all life and vegetation ; but is not always found in the due proportion. On the mixture and secretion of the humours and juices of the body depend the health and prosperity of the animal : But the parts perform not regularly their proper function. What more useful than all the passions of the mind, ambition, vanity, love, anger ? But how oft do they break their bounds, and cause the greatest convulsions in society ? There is nothing so advantageous in the universe, but what frequently becomes pernicious, by its excess or defect ; nor has nature guarded, with the requisite accuracy, against all disorder or confusion. The irregularity is never, perhaps,[1] so great as to destroy any species ; but is often sufficient to involve the individuals in ruin and misery.

On the concurrence, then, of these *four* circumstances does all or the greatest part of natural evil depend. Were all living creatures incapable of pain, or were the world administered by particular volitions, evil never could have found access into the universe : And were animals endowed with a large stock of powers and faculties, beyond what strict necessity requires ; or were the several springs and principles of the universe so accurately framed as to preserve always the just temperament and medium ; there must have been very little ill in comparison of what we feel at present. What then shall we pronounce on this occasion ? Shall we say, that these circumstances are not necessary, and that they might easily have been altered in the contrivance of the universe ? This decision seems too presumptuous for creatures so blind and ignorant. Let

---

[1] [perhaps *added*]

us be more modest in our conclusions. Let us allow, that, if the goodness of the Deity (I mean a goodness like the human) could be established on any tolerable reasons [1] *a priori*, these phenomena, however untoward, would not be sufficient to subvert that principle ; but might easily, in some unknown manner, be reconcilable to it. But let us still assert, that as this goodness is not antecedently established, but must be inferred from the phenomena, there can be no grounds for such an inference, while there are so many ills in the universe, and while these ills might so easily have been remedied, as far as human understanding can be allowed to judge on such a subject. I am sceptic enough to allow, that the bad appearances, notwithstanding all my reasonings, may be compatible with such attributes as you suppose : But surely they can never prove these attributes. Such a conclusion cannot result from scepticism ; but must arise from the phenomena, and from our confidence in the reasonings which we deduce from these phenomena.

[Look round this universe. What an immense profusion of beings, animated and organized, sensible and active ! You admire this prodigious variety and fecundity. But inspect a little more narrowly these living existences, the only beings worth regarding. How hostile and destructive to each other ! How insufficient all of them for their own happiness ! How contemptible or odious to the spectator ! The whole presents nothing but the idea of a blind nature, impregnated by a great [2] vivifying principle, and pouring forth from her lap, without discernment or parental care, her maimed and abortive children. [3]]

Here the MANICHÆAN system occurs as a proper hypothesis to solve the difficulty : And no doubt, in some respects, it is very specious, and has more probability than the common hypothesis, by giving a plausible account of the strange mixture of good and ill which appears in life. But if we consider, on the other hand, the perfect uniformity and agreement of the parts of the universe, we shall not discover in it any marks of the combat of a malevolent with a benevolent Being. There

[1] [on any tolerable reasons *added*]
[2] [a great *for* an infinitely]
[3] [This passage in brackets is written, with marks to indicate point of insertion, on the last sheet of Part XI, immediately prior to the other additions given above, pp. 208-9.]

is indeed an opposition of pains and pleasures in the feelings of sensible creatures : But are not all the operations of nature carried on by an opposition of principles, of hot and cold, moist and dry, light and heavy ? The true conclusion is, that the original source [1] of all things is entirely indifferent to all these principles, and has no more regard to good above ill than to heat above cold, or to drought above moisture, or to light above heavy.

There may *four* hypotheses be framed concerning the first [2] causes of the universe : *that* they are endowed with perfect goodness, *that* they have perfect malice, *that* they are opposite and have both goodness and malice, *that* they have neither goodness nor malice. Mixed phenomena can never prove the two former unmixed principles. And the uniformity and steadiness of general laws seem to oppose the third. The fourth, therefore, seems by far the most probable.

What I have said concerning natural evil will apply to moral, with little or no variation ; and we have no more [3] reason to infer, that the rectitude of the supreme Being resembles human rectitude than that his benevolence resembles the human. Nay, it will be thought, that we have still greater cause to exclude from him moral sentiments, such as we feel them ; since moral evil, in the opinion of many, is much more predominant above moral good than natural evil above natural good.

But even though this should not be allowed, and though the virtue, which is in mankind, should be acknowledged much superior to the vice ; yet so long as there is any vice at all in the universe, it will very much puzzle you anthropomorphites, how to account for it. You must assign a cause for it, without having recourse to the first cause. But as every effect must have a cause, and that cause another ; you must either carry on the progression *in infinitum*, or rest on [4] that original principle, who is the ultimate cause of all things. . . .

Hold ! Hold ! cried DEMEA : Whither does your imagination hurry you ? I joined in alliance with you, in order to prove the incomprehensible nature of the divine Being, and refute the principles of CLEANTHES, who would measure every thing by a human rule and standard. But I now find you

---

[1] [source *for* cause]   [2] [first *for* original]
[3] [no more *for* the same]   [4] [rest on *for* stop at]

running into all the topics of the greatest libertines and infidels;[1] and betraying that holy cause, which you seemingly espoused. Are you secretly, then, a more dangerous enemy than CLEANTHES himself?

And are you so late in perceiving it? replied CLEANTHES. Believe me, DEMEA; your friend PHILO, from the beginning, has been amusing himself at both our expence; and it must be confessed, that the injudicious reasoning of our vulgar theology has given him but too just a handle of ridicule. The total infirmity of human reason, the absolute incomprehensibility of the divine nature, the great and universal misery and and still greater wickedness of men; these are strange topics surely to be so fondly cherished by orthodox divines and doctors. In ages of stupidity and ignorance, indeed, these principles may safely be espoused; and perhaps, no views of things are more proper to promote superstition, than such as encourage the blind amazement, the diffidence, and melancholy of mankind. But at present. . . .

Blame not so much, interposed PHILO, the ignorance of these reverend gentlemen. They know how to change their style with the times. Formerly it was a most popular theological topic to maintain, that human life was vanity and misery, and to exaggerate all the ills and pains which are incident to men. But of late years, divines, we find, begin to retract this position, and maintain, though still with some hesitation, that there are more goods than evils, more pleasures than pains, even in this life. When religion stood entirely upon temper and education, it was thought proper to encourage melancholy; as indeed, mankind never have recourse to superior powers so readily as in that disposition. But as men have now learned to form principles, and to draw consequences, it is necessary to change the batteries, and to make use of such arguments as will endure, at least some scrutiny and examination. This variation is the same (and from the same causes) with that which I formerly remarked with regard to scepticism.

Thus PHILO continued to the last his spirit of opposition, and his censure of established opinions. But I could observe, that DEMEA did not at all relish the latter part of the discourse; and he took occasion soon after, on some pretence or other, to leave the company.

---

[1] [infidels *for* sceptics]

AFTER DEMEA's departure, CLEANTHES and PHILO continued the conversation in the following manner. Our friend, I am afraid, said CLEANTHES, will have little inclination to revive this topic of discourse, while you are in company ; and to tell truth, PHILO, I should rather wish to reason with either of you apart on a subject so sublime and interesting. Your spirit of controversy, joined to your abhorrence of vulgar superstition, carries you strange lengths, when engaged in an argument ; and there is nothing so sacred and venerable, even in your own eyes, which you spare on that occasion.

I must confess, replied PHILO, that I am less cautious on the subject of natural religion than on any other ; both because I know that I can never, on that head, corrupt the principles of any man of common sense, and because no one, I am confident, in whose eyes I appear a man of common sense, will ever mistake my intentions. You, in particular, CLEANTHES, with whom I live in unreserved intimacy ; you are sensible, that, notwithstanding the freedom of my conversation, and my love of singular arguments, no one has a deeper sense of religion impressed on his mind, or pays more profound adoration to the divine Being, as he discovers himself to reason, in the inexplicable contrivance and artifice of nature. A purpose, an intention, or design strikes everywhere the most careless, the most stupid thinker ; and no man can be so hardened in absurd systems, as at all times to reject it. *That nature does nothing in vain,* is a maxim established in all the schools, merely from the contemplation of the works of nature, without any religious purpose ; and, from a firm conviction of its truth, an anatomist, who had observed a new organ or canal, would never be satisfied till he had also discovered its use and intention. One great foundation of the COPERNICAN system is the maxim, *that nature acts by the simplest methods, and chooses the most proper means to any end ;* and astronomers often, without thinking of it, lay this strong foundation of piety and religion. [1 The same thing is observable in other parts of philosophy : And] thus all the sciences almost lead us insensibly to acknowledge

1 [Added on the margin]

a first intelligent Author ; and their authority is often so much the greater, as they do not directly profess that intention.

It is with pleasure I hear GALEN reason concerning the structure of the human body. The anatomy of a man, says he,[1] discovers above 600 different muscles ; and whoever duly considers these, will find, that in each of them nature must have adjusted at least ten different circumstances, in order to attain the end which she proposed ; proper figure, just magnitude, right disposition of the several ends, upper and lower position of the whole, the due insertion of the several nerves, veins, and arteries : So that, in the muscles alone, above 6000 several views and intentions must have been formed and executed. The bones he calculates to be 284 : The distinct purposes, aimed at in the structure of each, above forty. What a prodigious display of artifice, even in these simple and homogeneous parts ? But if we consider the skin, ligaments, vessels, glandules, humours, the several limbs and members of the body ; how must our astonishment rise upon us, in proportion to the number and intricacy of the parts so artificially adjusted ? The farther we advance in these researches, we discover new scenes of art and wisdom : But descry still, at a distance, farther scenes beyond our reach ; in the fine internal structure of the parts, in the œconomy of the brain, in the fabric of the seminal vessels. All these artifices are repeated in every different species of animal, with wonderful variety, and with exact propriety, suited to the different intentions of nature, in framing each species. And if the infidelity of GALEN, even when these natural sciences were still imperfect, could not withstand such striking appearances ; to what pitch of pertinacious obstinacy must a philosopher in this age have attained, who can now doubt of a supreme intelligence ?

Could I meet with one of this species (who, I thank God, are very rare) I would ask him : Supposing there were a God, who did not discover himself immediately to our senses ; were it possible for him to give stronger proofs of his existence, than what appear on the whole face of nature ? What indeed could such a divine Being do, but copy the present œconomy of things ; render many of his artifices so plain, that no stupidity could mistake them ; afford glimpses of still greater artifices,

---

[1] De formatione foetus. [*De Foetuum Formatione Libellus,* cap. vi ; Galeni *Opera* (1822), lib. iv, pp. 691 *sqq.*]

which demonstrate his prodigious superiority above our narrow apprehensions ; and conceal altogether a great many from such imperfect creatures ?   Now according to all rules of just reasoning, every fact must pass for undisputed, when it is supported by all the arguments which its nature admits of, even though these arguments be not, in themselves, very numerous or forcible :   How much more, in the present case, where no human imagination can compute their number, and no understanding estimate their cogency ?

I shall farther add, said CLEANTHES, to what you have so well urged, that one great advantage of the principle of theism, is, that it is the only system of cosmogony which can be rendered intelligible and complete, and yet can throughout preserve a strong analogy to what we every day see and experience in the world.   The comparison of the universe to a machine of human contrivance is so obvious and natural, and is justified by so many instances of order and design in nature,[1] that it must immediately strike all unprejudiced apprehensions, and procure universal approbation.   Whoever attempts to weaken this theory, cannot pretend to succeed by establishing in its place any other that is precise and determinate :   It is sufficient for him, if he start doubts and difficulties ; and by remote and abstract views of things, reach that suspence of judgment, which is here the utmost boundary of his wishes.   But besides that this state of mind is in itself unsatisfactory, it can never be steadily maintained against such striking appearances as continually engage us into the religious hypothesis.[2]   A false, absurd system, human nature, from the force of prejudice, is capable of adhering to with obstinacy and perseverance :   But no system at all, in opposition to a theory, supported by strong and obvious [3] reason, by natural propensity, and by early education, I think it absolutely impossible to maintain or defend.

So little, replied PHILO, do I esteem this suspense of judgment in the present case to be possible, that I am apt to suspect there enters somewhat of a dispute of words into this controversy, more than is usually imagined.   That the works of nature bear a great analogy to the productions of art is evident ; and according to all the rules of good reasoning, we ought to infer,

---

[1] [design in nature *for* contrivance]   [2] [hypothesis *for* theory]
[3] [and obvious *added*]

if we argue at all concerning them, that their causes have a proportional analogy. But as there are also considerable differences, we have reason to suppose a proportional difference in the causes ; and in particular ought to attribute a much higher degree of power and energy to the supreme cause than any we have ever observed in mankind. Here then the existence of a DEITY is plainly ascertained by reason ; and if we make it a question, whether, on account of these analogies, we can properly call him a *mind* or *intelligence,* notwithstanding the vast difference, which may reasonably be supposed between him and human minds ; what is this but a mere verbal controversy ? No man can deny the analogies between the effects : To restrain ourselves from enquiring concerning the causes is scarcely possible : From this enquiry, the legitimate conclusion is, that the causes have also an analogy : And if we are not contented with calling the first and supreme cause a GOD or DEITY, but desire to vary the expression ; what can we call him but MIND or THOUGHT, to which he is justly supposed to bear a considerable resemblance ?

[[1 All men of sound reason are disgusted with verbal disputes, which abound so much in philosophical and theological enquiries ; and it is found, that the only remedy for this abuse must arise from clear definitions, from the precision of those ideas which enter into any argument, and from the strict and uniform use of those terms which are employed. But there is a species of controversy, which, from the very nature of language and of human ideas, is involved in perpetual ambiguity, and can never, by any precaution or any definitions, be able to reach a reasonable certainty or precision. These are the controversies concerning the degrees of any quality or circumstance. Men may argue to all eternity, whether Hannibal be a great, or a very great, or a superlatively great man, what degree of beauty Cleopatra possessed, what epithet of praise Livy or Thucydides is entitled to, without bringing the controversy to any determination. The disputants may here agree in their sense and differ in the terms, or *vice versa* ; yet never be able to define their terms, so as to enter into each

---

1 [This paragraph in double brackets is written on the concluding sheet of the manuscript, with marks to indicate point of insertion. The double bracket is here used to mark this addition as having been made in the final revision, in 1776. *Cf.* above, Appendix C, pp. 94–5.]

other's meaning : Because the degrees of these qualities are not, like quantity or number, susceptible of any exact mensuration, which may be the standard in the controversy. That the dispute concerning theism is of this nature, and consequently is merely verbal, or perhaps, if possible, still more incurably ambiguous, will appear upon the slightest enquiry. I ask the theist, if he does not allow, that there is a great and immeasurable, because incomprehensible, difference between the *human* and the *divine* mind : The more pious he is, the more readily will he assent to the affirmative, and the more will he be disposed to magnify the difference : He will even assert, that the difference is of a nature which cannot be too much magnified. I next turn to the atheist, who, I assert, is only nominally so, and can never possibly be in earnest ; and I ask him, whether, from the coherence and apparent sympathy in all the parts of this world, there be not a certain degree of analogy among all the operations of nature, in every situation and in every age ; whether the rotting of a turnip, the generation of an animal, and the structure of human thought be not energies that probably bear some remote analogy to each other : It is impossible he can deny it : He will readily acknowledge it. Having obtained this concession, I push him still farther in his retreat ; and I ask him, if it be not probable, that the principle which first arranged, and still maintains, order in this universe, bears not also some remote inconceivable analogy to the other operations of nature, and among the rest to the œconomy of human mind and thought. However reluctant, he must give his assent. Where then, cry I to both these antagonists, is the subject of your dispute ? The theist allows, that the original intelligence is very different from human reason : The atheist allows, that the original principle of order bears some remote analogy to it. Will you quarrel, Gentlemen, about the degrees, and enter into a controversy, which admits not of any precise meaning, nor consequently of any determination ? If you should be so obstinate, I should not be surprised to find you insensibly change sides ; while the theist on the one hand exaggerates the dissimilarity between the supreme Being, and frail, imperfect, variable, fleeting, and mortal creatures ; and the atheist on the other magnifies the analogy among all the operations of nature, in every period, every situation, and every position. Consider then, where the real point of controversy lies, and if you cannot lay aside your disputes, endeavour, at least, to cure yourselves of your animosity.]]

And here I must also acknowledge, CLEANTHES, that, as the works of nature have a much greater analogy to the effects of *our* art and contrivance, than to those of *our* benevolence and justice ; we have reason to infer that the natural attributes of the Deity have a greater resemblance to those of man, than his moral have to human virtues. But what is the consequence ? [Nothing but this, that the moral qualities of man are more defective in their kind than his natural abilities. For, as the supreme Being is allowed to be absolutely and entirely perfect, whatever differs most from him departs the farthest from the supreme standard of rectitude and perfection.[1]

These, CLEANTHES, are my unfeigned sentiments on this subject ; and these sentiments, you know, I have ever cherished and maintained. But in proportion to my veneration for true religion, is my abhorrence of vulgar superstitions ; and I indulge a peculiar pleasure, I confess, in pushing such principles, sometimes into absurdity, sometimes into impiety. And you are sensible, that all bigots, notwithstanding their great aversion to the latter above the former, are commonly equally guilty of both.

My inclination, replied CLEANTHES, lies, I own, a contrary way. Religion, however corrupted, is still better than no religion at all. The doctrine of [2] a future state is so strong and necessary a security to morals, that we never ought to abandon or neglect it. For if finite and temporary rewards and punishments have so great an effect, as we daily find :

---

[1] [It seems evident, that the dispute between the sceptics and dogmatists is entirely verbal, or at least regards only the degrees of doubt and assurance, which we ought to indulge with regard to all reasoning : And such disputes are commonly at the bottom, verbal, and admit not of any precise determination. No philosophical dogmatist denies, that there are difficulties both with regard to the senses and to all science : and that these difficulties are in a regular, logical method, absolutely insolveable. No sceptic denies, that we lie under an absolute necessity, notwithstanding these difficulties, of thinking, and believing, and reasoning with regard to all kind of subjects, and even of frequently assenting with confidence and security. The only difference, then, between these sects, if they merit that name, is, that the sceptic, from habit, caprice, or inclination, insists most on the difficulties ; the dogmatist, for like reasons, on the necessity.]*

* [The above note, written on the concluding page of the original Part XII, below the word ' Finis,' with marks to indicate point of insertion, has been scored out, and rewritten on the concluding sheet of the manuscript. *Cf.* above, Appendix C, pp. 94–5.]

[2] [The doctrine of *added*]

How much greater must be expected from such as are infinite and eternal ?

How happens it then, said PHILO, if vulgar superstition [1] be so salutary to society, that all history abounds so much with accounts of its pernicious consequences on public affairs ? Factions, civil wars, persecutions, subversions of government, oppression, slavery ; these are the dismal consequences which always attend its prevalency over the minds of men. If the religious spirit be ever mentioned in any historical narration, we are sure to meet afterwards with a detail of the miseries which attend it. And no period of time can be happier or more prosperous, than those in which it is never regarded, or heard of.

The reason of this observation, replied CLEANTHES, is obvious. The proper office of religion is to regulate the heart of men, humanize their conduct, infuse the spirit of temperance, order, and obedience ; and as its operation is silent, and only enforces the motives of mortality and justice, it is in danger of being overlooked, and confounded with these other motives. When it distinguishes itself, and acts as a separate principle over men, it has departed from its proper sphere, and has become only a cover to faction and ambition.

And so will all religion, said PHILO, except the philosophical and rational kind. Your reasonings are more easily eluded than my facts. The inference is not just, because finite and temporary rewards and punishments have so great influence, that therefore such as are infinite and eternal must have so much greater. [2] Consider, I beseech you, the attachment, which we have to present things, and the little concern which we discover for objects so remote and uncertain. When divines are declaiming against the common behaviour and conduct of the world, they always represent this principle as the strongest imaginable (which indeed it is) and describe almost all human kind as lying under the influence of it, and sunk into the deepest

---

[1] [superstition *for* religion]

[2] [*In the manuscript the following passage is scored out :* If indeed we consider the matter merely in an abstract light : If we compare only the importance of the motives, and then reflect on the natural self-love of mankind ; we shall not only look for a great effect from religious considerations ; but we must really esteem them absolutely irresistible and infallible in their operation. For what other motive can reasonably counterbalance them even for a moment ? But this is not found to hold in reality ; and therefore, we may be certain that there is some other principle of human nature, which we have here overlooked, and which diminishes, at least, the force of these motives. This principle is the attachment, which we have, &c.]

lethargy and unconcern about their religious interests. Yet
these same divines, when they refute their speculative antagonists, suppose the motives of religion to be so powerful, that,
without them, it were impossible for civil society to subsist ;
nor are they ashamed of so palpable a contradiction. It is
certain, from experience, that the smallest grain of natural
honesty and benevolence has more effect on men's conduct,
than the most pompous views suggested by theological theories
and systems. A man's natural inclination works incessantly
upon him ; it is for ever present to the mind ; and mingles
itself with every view and consideration : Whereas religious
motives, where they act at all, operate only by starts and
bounds ; and it is scarcely possible for them to become altogether habitual to the mind. The force of the greatest gravity,
say the philosophers, is infinitely small, in comparison of that
of the least impulse ; yet it is certain that the smallest gravity
will, in the end, prevail above a great impulse ; because no
strokes or blows can be repeated with such constancy as attraction and gravitation.

Another advantage of inclination : It engages on its side
all the wit and ingenuity of the mind ; and when set in opposition to religious principles, seeks every method and art of
eluding them : In which it is almost always successful. Who
can explain the heart of man, or account for those strange
salvos and excuses, with which people satisfy themselves, when
they follow their inclinations, in opposition to their religious
duty ? This is well understood in the world ; and none but
fools ever repose less trust in a man, because they hear, that,
from study and philosophy, he has entertained some speculative
doubts with regard to theological subjects. And when we have
to do with a man, who makes a great profession of religion and
devotion ; has this any other effect upon several, who [1] pass
for prudent, than to put them on their guard, lest they be
cheated and deceived by him ?

We must farther consider, that philosophers, who cultivate
reason and reflection, stand less in need of such motives to
keep them under the restraint of morals : And that the vulgar,
who alone may need them, are utterly incapable of so pure
a religion as represents the Deity to be pleased with nothing
but virtue in human behaviour. The recommendations to

[1] [greatly *added, and then scored out*]

the Divinity are generally supposed to be either frivolous observances, or rapturous ecstasies, or a bigoted credulity. [1] We need not run back into antiquity, or wander into remote regions, to find instances of this degeneracy. Amongst ourselves, some have been guilty of that atrociousness, unknown to the EGYPTIAN and GRECIAN superstitions, of declaiming, in express terms, against morality, and representing it as a sure forfeiture of the divine favour, if the least trust or reliance be laid upon it.

But even though superstition or enthusiasm should not put itself in direct opposition to morality ; the very diverting of the attention, the raising up a new and frivolous species of merit, the preposterous distribution which it makes of praise and blame, must have the most pernicious consequences, and weaken extremely men's attachment to the natural motives of justice and humanity.

Such a principle of action likewise, not being any of the [2] familiar motives of human conduct, acts only by intervals on the temper, and must be roused by continual efforts, in order to render the pious zealot satisfied with his own conduct, and make him fulfil his devotional task. Many religious exercises are entered into with seeming fervour, where the heart, at the time, feels cold and languid : A habit of dissimulation is by degrees contracted : And fraud and falsehood become the predominant principle. Hence the reason of that vulgar observation, [3] that the highest zeal in religion and the deepest hypocrisy, so far from being inconsistent, are often or commonly united in the same individual character.

The bad effects of such habits, even in common life, are easily imagined : But where the interests of religion are concerned, no morality can be forcible enough to bind the enthusiastic zealot. The sacredness of the cause sanctifies every measure which can be made use of to promote it.

The steady attention alone to so important an interest as that of eternal salvation is apt to extinguish the benevolent affections, and beget a narrow, contracted selfishness. And when such a temper is encouraged, it easily eludes all the general precepts of charity and benevolence.

Thus the motives of <u>vulgar superstition</u> have no great [4]

---

[1] [" We need . . ." *to end of paragraph scored out, and instruction added on the margin,* " Print this passage."]   [2] [natural or *omitted*]
[3] [vulgar observation *for* common phenomenon]   [4] [no great *for* little]

influence on general conduct ; nor is their operation very favourable to morality, in the instances where they predominate.

Is there any maxim in politics more certain and infallible, than that both the number and authority of priests should be confined within very narrow limits, and that the civil magistrate ought, for ever, to keep his *fasces* and *axes* from such dangerous . hands ? But if the spirit of popular religion were so salutary to society, a contrary maxim ought to prevail. The greater number of priests, and their greater authority and riches, will always augment the religious spirit. And though the priests have the guidance of this spirit, why may we not expect a superior sanctity of life, and greater benevolence and moderation, from persons who are set apart for religion, who are continually inculcating it upon others, and who must themselves imbibe a greater share of it ? Whence comes it then, that, in fact, the utmost a wise magistrate can propose with regard to popular religions, is, as far as possible, to make a saving game of it, and to prevent their pernicious consequences with regard to society ? Every expedient which he tries for so humble a purpose is surrounded with inconveniences. If he admits only one religion among his subjects, he must sacrifice, to an uncertain prospect of tranquillity, every consideration of public liberty, science, reason, industry, and even his own independency. If he gives indulgence to several sects, which is the wiser maxim, he must preserve a very philosophical indifference to all of them, and carefully restrain the pretensions of the prevailing sect ; otherwise he can expect nothing but endless disputes, quarrels, factions, persecutions, and civil commotions.

True religion, I allow, has no such pernicious consequences : But we must treat of religion, as it has commonly [1] been found in the world ; nor have I any thing to do with that speculative tenet of [2] theism, which, as it is a species of philosophy, must partake of the beneficial influence of that principle,[3] and at the same time must lie under a like inconvenience, of being always confined to very few persons.[4]

---

[1] [commonly *for* always]   [2] [refined *omitted*]   [3] [of that principle *added*]
[4] [*Hume has added on margin, and then scored out :* Since government, reason, learning, friendship, love, and every human advantage are attended with inconveniences, as we daily find, what may be expected in all the various models of superstition ; a quality, composed of whatever is the most absurd, corrupted, and barbarous of our nature ? Were there any one exception to that universal mixture of good and ill, which is found in life, this might be pronounced throughly and entirely ill.]

Oaths are requisite in all courts of judicature ; but it is a question whether their authority arises from any popular religion. It is the solemnity and importance of the occasion, the regard to reputation, and the reflecting on the general interests of society, which are the chief restraints upon mankind. Custom-house oaths and political oaths are but little regarded even by some who pretend to principles of honesty and religion : And a Quaker's asseveration is with us justly put upon the same footing with the oath of any other person. I know, that POLYBIUS [1] ascribes the infamy of GREEK faith to the prevalency of the EPICUREAN philosophy ; but I know also, that PUNIC faith had as bad a reputation in ancient times, as IRISH evidence has in modern ; though we cannot account for these vulgar observations by the same reason. Not to mention, that GREEK faith was infamous before the rise of the EPICUREAN philosophy ; and EURIPIDES, [2] in a passage which I shall point out to you, has glanced a remarkable stroke of satire against his nation, with regard to this circumstance.

Take care, PHILO, replied CLEANTHES, take care : Push not matters too far : Allow not your zeal against false religion to undermine your veneration for the true. Forfeit not this principle, the chief, the only great comfort in life ; and our principle support amidst all the attacks of adverse fortune. The most agreeable reflection, which it is possible for human imagination to suggest, is that of genuine theism, which represents us as the workmanship of a Being perfectly good, wise, and powerful ; who created us for happiness, and who, having implanted in us immeasurable desires of good, will prolong our existence to all eternity, and will transfer us into an infinite variety of scenes, in order to satisfy those desires, and render our felicity complete and durable. Next to such a Being himself (if the comparison be allowed) the happiest lot which we can imagine, is that of being under his guardianship and protection.

These appearances, said PHILO, are most engaging and alluring ; and with regard to the true philosopher, they are more than appearances. But it happens here, as in the former case, that, with regard to the greater part of mankind, the appearances are deceitful, and that the terrors of religion commonly prevail above its comforts.

[1] Lib. 6, cap. 54   [2] *Iphigenia in Tauride*

It is allowed, that men never have recourse to devotion so readily as when dejected with grief or depressed with sickness. Is not this a proof, that the religious spirit is not so nearly allied to joy as to sorrow?

But men, when afflicted, find consolation in religion, replied CLEANTHES. Sometimes, said PHILO : But it is natural to imagine, that they will form a notion of those unknown Beings, suitably to the present gloom and melancholy of their temper, when they betake themselves to the contemplation of them. Accordingly, we find the tremendous images to predominate in all [1] religions ; and we ourselves, after having employed the most exalted expression in our descriptions of the Deity, fall into the flattest contradiction, in affirming, that the damned are infinitely superior in number to the elect.

I shall venture to affirm, that there never was a popular religion, which represented the state of departed souls in such a light, as would render it eligible for human kind, that there should be such a state. These fine models of religion are the mere product of philosophy. For as death lies between the eye and the prospect of futurity, that event is so shocking to nature, that it must throw a gloom on all the regions which lie beyond it ; and suggest to the generality of mankind the idea of CERBERUS and FURIES ; devils, and torrents of fire and brimstone.

It is true ; both fear and hope enter into religion ; because both these passions, at different times, agitate the human mind, and each of them forms a species of divinity, suitable to itself. But when a man is in a cheerful disposition, he is fit for business or company or entertainment of any kind ; and he naturally applies himself to these, and thinks not of religion. When melancholy, and dejected, he has nothing to do but brood upon the terrors of the invisible world, and to plunge himself still deeper in affliction. It may, indeed, happen, that after he has, in this manner, engraved the religious opinions deep into his thought and imagination, there may arrive a change of health or circumstances, which may restore his good humour, and raising cheerful prospects of futurity, make him run into the other extreme of joy and triumph. But still it must be acknowledged, that, as terror is the primary principle of

[1] [all *for* most]

religion, it is the passion which always predominates in it, and admits but of short intervals of pleasure.

Not to mention, that these fits of excessive, enthusiastic joy, by exhausting the spirits, always prepare the way for equal fits of superstitious terror and dejection ; nor is there any state of mind so happy as the calm and equable. But this state it is impossible to support, where a man thinks, that he lies, in such profound darkness and uncertainty, between an eternity of happiness and an eternity of misery. No wonder, that such an opinion disjoints the ordinary frame of the mind, and throws it into the utmost confusion. And though that opinion is seldom so steady in its operation as to influence all the actions ; yet it is apt to make a considerable breach in the temper, and to produce that gloom and melancholy, so remarkable in all devout people.

It is contrary to common sense to entertain apprehensions or terrors, upon account of any opinion whatsoever, or to imagine that we run any risk hereafter, by the freest use of our reason. Such a sentiment implies both an *absurdity* and an *inconsistency*. It is an absurdity to believe that the Deity has human passions, and one of the lowest of human passions, a restless appetite for applause. It is an inconsistency to believe, that, since the Deity has this human passion, he has not others also ; and, in particular, a disregard to the opinions of creatures so much inferior.

[¹ *To know God*, says Seneca, *is to worship him.* All other worship is indeed absurd, superstitious, and even impious. It degrades him to the low condition of mankind, who are delighted with entreaty, solicitation, presents, and flattery. Yet is this impiety the smallest of which superstition is guilty. Commonly, it depresses the Deity far below the condition of mankind ; and represents him as a capricious Dæmon, who exercises his power without reason and without humanity ! And were that divine Being disposed to be offended at the vices and follies of silly mortals, who are his own workmanship ; ill would it surely fare with the votaries of most popular superstitions. Nor would any of human race merit his *favour*, but a very few, the philosophical theists, who entertain, or

---

¹ [This passage in brackets, an addition made in an early revision, is written on the margin, then scored out, and rewritten, together with the next paragraph, on the second last sheet of the manuscript.]

rather indeed endeavour to entertain, suitable notions of his divine perfections : As the only persons entitled to his *compassion* and *indulgence* would be the philosophical sceptics, a sect almost equally rare, who, from a natural diffidence of their own capacity, suspend, or endeavour to suspend all judgment with regard to such sublime and such extraordinary subjects.]

[[¹ If the whole of natural theology, as some people seem to maintain, resolves itself into one simple, though somewhat ambiguous, at least undefined proposition, *that the cause or causes of order in the universe probably bear some remote analogy to human intelligence* : If this proposition be not capable of extension, variation, or more particular explication : If it afford no inference that affects human life, or can be the source of any action ² or forbearance : And if the analogy, imperfect as it is, can be carried no farther than to the human intelligence ; and cannot be transferred,³ with any appearance of probability, to the other qualities of the mind : If this really be the case, what can the most inquisitive, contemplative, and religious man do more than give a plain, philosophical assent to the proposition, as often as it occurs ; and believe that the arguments, on which it is established, exceed the objections which lie against it ? Some astonishment indeed will naturally arise from the greatness of the object : Some melancholy from its obscurity : Some contempt of human reason, that it can give no solution more satisfactory with regard to so extraordinary and magnificent a question. But believe me, CLEANTHES, the most natural sentiment, which a well-disposed mind will feel on this occasion, is a longing desire and expectation, that Heaven would be pleased to dissipate, at least alleviate, this profound ignorance, by affording some more particular revelation to mankind, and making discoveries of the nature, attributes, and operations of the divine object of our Faith. A person, seasoned with a just sense of the imperfections of natural reason, will fly to revealed truth with the greatest avidity : While the haughty dogmatist, persuaded that he can erect a complete system of theology by the mere help of philosophy,

---

¹ [This paragraph in double brackets, written on the second last sheet of the manuscript, after the above paragraph, is an addition made in the final revision, in 1776. *Cf.* above, Appendix C, pp. 94–5.]

² [steady sentiment *omitted*]   ³ [transferred *for* extended]

disdains any farther aid, and rejects this adventitious instructor. To be a philosophical sceptic is, in a man of letters, the first and most essential step towards being a sound, believing Christian ; a proposition which I would willingly recommend to the attention of PAMPHILUS :   And I hope CLEANTHES will forgive me for interposing so far in the education and instruction of his pupil.]]

CLEANTHES and PHILO pursued not this conversation much farther ; and as nothing ever made greater impression on me, than all the reasonings of that day ; so I confess, that, upon a serious review of the whole, I cannot but think, that PHILO's principles are more probable than DEMEA's ; but that those of CLEANTHES approach still nearer to the truth.

SUPPLEMENT

THE

L I F E

O F

DAVID HUME, Esq.

WRITTEN BY HIMSELF.

L O N D O N:

PRINTED FOR W. STRAHAN; AND
T. CADELL, IN THE STRAND.

MDCCLXXVII.

Mr. Hume, a few months before his death, wrote the following short account of his own life ; and, in a codicil to his will, desired that it might be prefixed to the next edition of his Works. That edition cannot be published for a considerable time. The Editor, in the mean while, in order to serve the purchasers of the former editions ; and, at the same time, to gratify the impatience of the public curiosity ; has thought proper to publish it separately, without altering even the title or superscription, which was written in Mr. Hume's own hand on the cover of the manuscript.

MY OWN LIFE

IT is difficult for a man to speak long of himself without vanity; therefore, I shall be short. It may be thought an instance of vanity that I pretend at all to write my life; but this Narrative shall contain little more than the History of my Writings; as, indeed, almost all my life has been spent in literary pursuits and occupations. The first success of most of my writings was not such as to be an object of vanity.

I was born the 26th of April 1711, old style, at Edinburgh. I was of a good family, both by father and mother: my father's family is a branch of the Earl of Home's, or Hume's; and my ancestors had been proprietors of the estate, which my brother possesses, for several generations. My mother was daughter of Sir David Falconer, President of the College of Justice: the title of Lord Halkerton came by succession to her brother.

My family, however, was not rich, and being myself a younger brother, my patrimony, according to the mode of my country, was of course very slender. My father, who passed for a man of parts, died when I was an infant, leaving me, with an elder brother and a sister, under the care of our mother, a woman of singular merit, who, though young and handsome, devoted herself entirely to the rearing and educating of her children. I passed through the ordinary course of education with success, and was seized very early with a passion for literature, which has been the ruling passion of my life, and the great source of my enjoyments. My studious disposition, my sobriety, and my industry, gave my family a notion that the law was a proper profession for me; but I found an unsurmountable aversion to everything but the pursuits of philosophy and general learning; and while they fancied I was poring upon Voet and Vinnius, Cicero and Virgil were the authors which I was secretly devouring.

My very slender fortune, however, being unsuitable to this plan of life, and my health being a little broken by my ardent application, I was tempted, or rather forced, to make a very feeble trial for entering into a more active scene of life. In 1734, I went to Bristol, with some recommendations to eminent merchants, but in a few months found that scene totally un-suitable to me. I went over to France, with a view of prosecuting my studies in a country retreat ; and I there laid that plan of life, which I have steadily and successfully pursued. I resolved to make a very rigid frugality supply my deficiency of fortune, to maintain unimpaired my independency, and to regard every object as contemptible, except the improvement of my talents in literature.

During my retreat in France, first at Reims, but chiefly at La Fleche, in Anjou, I composed my *Treatise of Human Nature*. After passing three years very agreeably in that country, I came over to London in 1737. In the end of 1738, I published my Treatise, and immediately went down to my mother and my brother, who lived at his country-house, and was employing himself very judiciously and successfully in the improvement of his fortune.

Never literary attempt was more unfortunate than my Treatise of Human Nature. It fell *dead-born from the press*, without reaching such distinction, as even to excite a murmur among the zealots. But being naturally of a cheerful and sanguine temper, I very soon recovered the blow, and prose-cuted with great ardour my studies in the country. In 1742, I printed at Edinburgh the first part of my Essays : the work was favourably received, and soon made me entirely forget my former disappointment. I continued with my mother and brother in the country, and in that time recovered the knowledge of the Greek language, which I had too much neglected in my early youth.

In 1745, I received a letter from the Marquis of Annan-dale, inviting me to come and live with him in England ; I found also, that the friends and family of that young noble-man were desirous of putting him under my care and direction, for the state of his mind and health required it. I lived with him a twelvemonth. My appointments during that time made a considerable accession to my small fortune. I then received an invitation from General St. Clair to attend him as a secretary to his expedition, which was at first meant against Canada, but ended in an incursion on the coast of France. Next year, to wit, 1747, I received an invitation from the General to attend him in the same station in his military embassy to the courts of Vienna and Turin. I then wore the uniform of an officer, and was introduced at these courts as aid-de-camp to the general, along with Sir Harry Erskine and Captain Grant, now General Grant. These two years were almost the only interruptions which my studies have received during the course of my life : I passed them agreeably, and in good company ; and my appointments, with my frugality, had made me reach a fortune, which I called independent, though most of my friends were inclined to smile when I said so ; in short, I was now master of near a thousand pounds.

I had always entertained a notion, that my want of success in publishing the Treatise of Human Nature, had proceeded more from the manner than the matter, and that I had been guilty of a very usual indiscretion, in going to the press too early. I, therefore, cast the first part of that work anew in the Enquiry concerning Human Understanding, which was published while I was at Turin. But this piece was at first little more successful than the Treatise of Human Nature. On my return from Italy, I had the mortification to find all England in a ferment, on account of Dr. Middleton's Free Enquiry, while my performance was entirely overlooked and neglected. A new edition, which had been published at London of my Essays, moral and political, met not with a much better reception.

Such is the force of natural temper, that these disappointments made little or no impression on me. I went down in 1749, and lived two years with my brother at his country-house, for my mother was now dead. I there composed the second part of my Essays, which I called Political Discourses, and also my Enquiry concerning the Principles of Morals, which is another part of my treatise that I cast anew. Meanwhile, my bookseller, A. Millar, informed me, that my former publications (all but the unfortunate Treatise) were beginning to be the subject of conversation ; that the sale of them was gradually increasing, and that new editions were demanded. Answers by Reverends, and Right Reverends, came out two or three in a year ; and I found, by Dr. Warburton's railing, that the books were beginning to be esteemed in good company. However, I had fixed a resolution, which I inflexibly maintained, never to reply to any body ; and not being very irascible in my temper, I have easily kept myself clear of all literary squabbles. These symptoms of a rising reputation gave me

encouragement, as I was ever more disposed to see the favourable than unfavourable side of things ; a turn of mind which
it is more happy to possess, than to be born to an estate of ten
thousand a year.

In 1751, I removed from the country to the town, the
true scene for a man of letters. In 1752, were published at
Edinburgh, where I then lived, my Political Discourses, the
only work of mine that was successful on the first publication.
It was well received abroad and at home. In the same year
was published at London, my Enquiry concerning the Principles
of Morals ; which, in my own opinion (who ought not to judge
on that subject), is of all my writings, historical, philosophical,
or literary, incomparably the best. It came unnoticed and
unobserved into the world.

In 1752, the Faculty of Advocates chose me their Librarian,
an office from which I received little or no emolument, but
which gave me the command of a large library. I then formed
the plan of writing the History of England ; but being frightened
with the notion of continuing a narrative through a period of
1700 years, I commenced with the accession of the House of
Stuart, an epoch when, I thought, the misrepresentations of
faction began chiefly to take place. I was, I own, sanguine
in my expectations of the success of this work. I thought that
I was the only historian, that had at once neglected present
power, interest, and authority, and the cry of popular prejudices ; and as the subject was suited to every capacity, I
expected proportional applause. But miserable was my disappointment : I was assailed by one cry of reproach, disapprobation, and even detestation ; English, Scotch, and Irish,
Whig and Tory, churchman and sectary, freethinker and
religionist, patriot and courtier, united in their rage against
the man, who had presumed to shed a generous tear for the
fate of Charles I. and the Earl of Strafford ; and after the first
ebullitions of their [1] fury were over, what was still more mortifying,
the book seemed to sink into oblivion. Mr. Millar told me,
that in a twelve-month he sold only forty-five copies of it.
I scarcely, indeed, heard of one man in the three kingdoms,
considerable for rank or letters, that could endure the book.
I must only except the primate of England, Dr. Herring, and
the primate of Ireland, Dr. Stone, which seem two odd excep-

---

[1] [Hume's MS., R.S.E., has ' this ' not ' their ']

tions. These dignified prelates separately sent me messages not to be discouraged.

I was, however, I confess, discouraged ; and had not the war been at that time breaking out between France and England, I had certainly retired to some provincial town of the former kingdom, have changed my name, and never more have returned to my native country. But as this scheme was not now practicable, and the subsequent volume was considerably advanced, I resolved to pick up courage and to persevere.

In this interval, I published at London my Natural History of Religion, along with some other small pieces : its public entry was rather obscure, except only that Dr. Hurd wrote a pamphlet against it, with all the illiberal petulance, arrogance, and scurrility, which distinguish the Warburtonian school. This pamphlet gave me some consolation for the otherwise indifferent reception of my performance.

In 1756, two years after the fall of the first volume, was published the second volume of my History, containing the period from the death of Charles I. till the Revolution. This performance happened to give less displeasure to the Whigs, and was better received. It not only rose itself, but helped to buoy up its unfortunate brother.

But though I had been taught by experience, that the Whig party were in possession of bestowing all places, both in the state and in literature, I was so little inclined to yield to their senseless clamour, that in above a hundred alterations, which farther study, reading, or reflection engaged me to make in the reigns of the two first Stuarts, I have made all of them invariably to the Tory side. It is ridiculous to consider the English constitution before that period as a regular plan of liberty.

In 1759, I published my History of the House of Tudor. The clamour against this performance was almost equal to that against the History of the two first Stuarts. The reign of Elizabeth was particularly obnoxious. But I was now callous against the impressions of public folly, and continued very peaceably and contentedly in my retreat at Edinburgh, to finish, in two volumes, the more early part of the English History, which I gave to the public in 1761, with tolerable, and but tolerable success.

But, notwithstanding this variety of winds and seasons, to which my writings had been exposed, they had still been making such advances, that the copy-money given me by the booksellers, much exceeded anything formerly known in England ; I was become not only independent, but opulent. I retired to my native country of Scotland, determined never more to set my foot out of it ; and retaining the satisfaction of never having preferred a request to one great man, or even making advances of friendship to any of them. As I was now turned of fifty, I thought of passing all the rest of my life in this philosophical manner, when I received, in 1763, an invitation from the Earl of Hertford, with whom I was not in the least acquainted, to attend him on his embassy to Paris, with a near prospect of being appointed secretary to the embassy ; and, in the meanwhile, of performing the functions of that office. This offer, however inviting, I at first declined, both because I was reluctant to begin connexions with the great, and because I was afraid that the civilities and gay company of Paris would prove disagreeable to a person of my age and humour : but on his lordship's repeating the invitation, I accepted of it. I have every reason, both of pleasure and interest, to think myself happy in my connexion with that nobleman, as well as afterwards with his brother, General Conway.

Those who have not seen the strange effects of modes, will never imagine the reception I met with at Paris, from men and women of all ranks and stations. The more I resiled[1] from their excessive civilities, the more I was loaded with them.[2] There is, however, a real satisfaction in living at Paris, from the great number of sensible, knowing, and polite company with which that city abounds above all places in the universe. I thought once of settling there for life.

I was appointed secretary to the embassy ; and, in summer 1765, Lord Hertford left me, being appointed Lord Lieutenant of Ireland. I was *chargé d'affaires* till the arrival of the Duke of Richmond, towards the end of the year. In the beginning of 1766, I left Paris, and next summer went to Edinburgh, with the same view as formerly, of burying myself in a philosophical

---

[1] [Hume's MS. has ' recoiled,' not ' resiled ']

[2] [Hume has written and then struck out : ' Dr. Sterne told me, that he saw I was [wording too heavily scored to be legible] torn in the same manner that he himself had been in London ; but he added, that his vogue lasted only one winter.]

retreat. I returned to that place, not richer, but with much more money, and a much larger income, by means of Lord Hertford's friendship, than I left it ; and I was desirous of trying what superfluity could produce, as I had formerly made an experiment of a competency. But, in 1767, I received from Mr. Conway an invitation to be under-secretary ; and this invitation, both the character of the person, and my connexions with Lord Hertford, prevented me from declining. I returned to Edinburgh in 1768, very opulent (for I possessed a revenue of 1000 l. a year), healthy, and though somewhat stricken in years, with the prospect of enjoying long my ease, and of seeing the increase of my reputation.

In spring 1775, I was struck with a disorder in my bowels, which at first gave me no alarm, but has since, as I apprehend it, become mortal and incurable. I now reckon upon a speedy dissolution. I have suffered very little pain from my disorder ; and what is more strange, have, notwithstanding the great decline of my person, never suffered a moment's abatement of my spirits ; insomuch, that were I to name the period of my life, which I should most choose to pass over again, I might be tempted to point to this later period. I possess the same ardour as ever in study, and the same gaiety in company. I consider, besides, that a man of sixty-five, by dying, cuts off only a few years of infirmities ; and though I see many symptoms of my literary reputation's breaking out at last with additional lustre, I knew [1] that I could have but few years to enjoy it. It is difficult to be more detached from life than I am at present.

To conclude historically with my own character. I am, or rather was (for that is the style I must now use in speaking of myself, which emboldens me the more to speak my sentiments) ; I was, I say, a man of mild dispositions, of command of temper, of an open, social, and cheerful humour, capable of attachment, but little susceptible of enmity, and of great moderation in all my passions. Even my love of literary fame, my ruling passion, never soured my temper,[2] notwithstanding my frequent disappointments. My company was not unacceptable to the young and careless, as well as to the studious and literary ; and as I took a particular pleasure in the company

---

[1] [Hume's MS. has ' I know that I had but few years to enjoy it ']
[2] [Hume's MS. has ' humour,' not ' temper ']

of modest women, I had no reason to be displeased with the reception I met with from them. In a word, though most men any wise eminent, have found reason to complain of calumny, I never was touched, or even attacked by her baleful tooth : and though I wantonly exposed myself to the rage of both civil and religious factions, they seemed to be disarmed in my behalf of their wonted fury. My friends never had occasion to vindicate any one circumstance of my character and conduct : not but that the zealots, we may well suppose, would have been glad to invent and propagate any story to my disadvantage, but they could never find any which they thought would wear the face of probability. I cannot say there is no vanity in making this funeral oration of myself, but I hope it is not a misplaced one ; and this is a matter of fact which is easily cleared and ascertained.

April 18, 1776.

LETTER

FROM

ADAM SMITH, LL.D.

TO

WILLIAM STRAHAN, Esq.

LETTER FROM ADAM SMITH, LL.D.
TO WILLIAM STRAHAN, ESQ.[1]

Kirkaldy, Fifeshire, Nov. 9, 1776.

Dear Sir,

It is with a real, though a very melancholy pleasure, that I sit down to give you some account of the behaviour of our late excellent friend, Mr. Hume, during his last illness.

Though, in his own judgment, his disease was mortal and incurable, yet he allowed himself to be prevailed upon, by the entreaty of his friends, to try what might be the effects of a long journey. A few days before he set out, he wrote that account of his own life, which, together with his other papers, he has left to your care. My account, therefore, shall begin where his ends.

He set out for London towards the end of April, and at Morpeth met with Mr. John Home and myself, who had both come down from London on purpose to see him, expecting to have found him at Edinburgh. Mr. Home returned with him, and attended him during the whole of his stay in England, with that care and attention which might be expected from a temper so perfectly friendly and affectionate. As I had written to my mother that she might expect me in Scotland, I was under the necessity of continuing my journey. His disease seemed to yield to exercise and change of air, and when he arrived in London, he was apparently in much better health than when he left Edinburgh. He was advised to go to Bath to drink the waters, which appeared for some time to have so good an effect upon him, that even he himself began to entertain, what he was not apt to do, a better opinion of his own health. His symptoms, however, soon returned with their usual violence, and from that moment he gave up all thoughts of recovery, but submitted with the utmost cheerfulness, and the most perfect complacency and resignation. Upon his return to Edinburgh, though he found himself much weaker, yet his cheerfulness never abated, and he continued to divert himself, as usual, with correcting his own works for a new edition, with reading books of amusement, with the conversation of his friends ; and, sometimes in the evening, with a

---

[1] [*Cf.* above, p. 91]

party at his favourite game of whist. His cheerfulness was so great, and his conversation and amusements run so much in their usual strain, that, notwithstanding all bad symptoms, many people could not believe he was dying. "I shall tell your friend, Colonel Edmondstone," said Doctor Dundas to him one day, "that I left you much better, and in a fair way of recovery." "Doctor," said he, "as I believe you would not chuse to tell any thing but the truth, you had better tell him, that I am dying as fast as my enemies, if I have any, could wish, and as easily and cheerfully as my best friends could desire." Colonel Edmondstone soon afterwards came to see him, and take leave of him ; and on his way home, he could not forbear writing him a letter bidding him once more an eternal adieu, and applying to him, as to a dying man, the beautiful French verses in which the Abbé Chaulieu, in expectation of his own death, laments his approaching separation from his friend, the Marquis de la Fare. Mr. Hume's magnanimity and firmness were such, that his most affectionate friends knew, that they hazarded nothing in talking or writing to him as to a dying man, and that so far from being hurt by this frankness, he was rather pleased and flattered by it. I happened to come into his room while he was reading this letter, which he had just received, and which he immediately showed me. I told him, that though I was sensible how very much he was weakened, and that appearances were in many respects very bad, yet his cheerfulness was still so great, the spirit of life seemed still to be so very strong in him, that I could not help entertaining some faint hopes. He answered, "Your hopes are groundless. An habitual diarrhœa of more than a year's standing, would be a very bad disease at any age : at my age it is a mortal one. When I lie down in the evening, I feel myself weaker than when I rose in the morning ; and when I rise in the morning, weaker than when I lay down in the evening. I am sensible, besides, that some of my vital parts are affected, so that I must soon die." "Well," said I, "if it must be so, you have at least the satisfaction of leaving all your friends, your brother's family in particular, in great prosperity." He said that he felt that satisfaction so sensibly, that when he was reading a few days before, Lucian's Dialogues of the Dead, among all the excuses which are alleged to Charon for not entering readily into his boat, he could not find one that fitted him ; he had no house to finish, he had no daughter to provide for, he had no enemies upon whom he wished to revenge himself. " I could not well imagine," said he, " what excuse I could make to Charon in order to obtain a little delay. I have done every thing of consequence which I ever meant to do, and I could at no time expect to leave my relations and friends in a better situation than that in which I am now likely to leave them ; I, therefore, have all reason to die contented." He then diverted himself with inventing several jocular excuses, which he supposed he might make to Charon, and with imagining the very surly answers which it might suit the character of Charon to return to them. " Upon further consideration," said he, " I thought I might say to him, ' Good Charon, I have been correcting my works for a new edition. Allow me a little time, that I may see how the Public receives the alterations.' But Charon would answer, ' When you have seen the effect of these, you will be for making other alterations. There will be no end of such excuses ; so, honest friend, please step into the boat.' But I might still urge, ' Have a little patience, good Charon, I have been endeavouring to open the eyes of the Public. If I live a few years longer, I may have the satisfaction of seeing the downfal of some of the prevailing systems of superstition.' But Charon would then lose all temper and decency. ' You loitering rogue, that will not happen these many hundred years. Do you fancy I will grant you a lease for so long a term ? Get into the boat this instant, you lazy loitering rogue.' "

But, though Mr. Hume always talked of his approaching dissolution with great cheerfulness, he never affected to make any parade of his magnanimity. He never mentioned the subject but when the conversation naturally led to it, and never dwelt longer upon it than the course of the conversation happened to require : it was a subject indeed which occurred pretty frequently, in consequence of the inquiries which his friends, who came to see him, naturally made concerning the state of his health. The conversation which I mentioned above, and which passed on Thursday the 8th of August, was the last, except one, that I ever had with him. He had now become so very weak, that the company of his most intimate friends fatigued him ; for his cheerfulness was still so great, his complaisance and social disposition were still so entire, that when any friend was with him, he could not help talking more, and with greater exertion, than suited the weakness of his body. At his own desire, therefore, I agreed to leave Edinburgh, where I was staying partly upon his account, and returned to my mother's house here, at Kirkaldy, upon condition that he would send for me whenever he wished to see me ; the physician who saw him most frequently, Doctor Black, undertaking, in the mean time, to write me occasionally an account of the state of his health.

On the 22nd of August, the Doctor wrote me the following letter :

" Since my last, Mr. Hume has passed his time pretty easily, but is much weaker. He sits up, goes down stairs once a day, and amuses himself with reading, but seldom sees any body. He finds that even the conversation of his most intimate friends fatigues and oppresses him ; and it is happy that he does not need it, for he is quite free from anxiety, impatience, or low spirits, and passes his time very well with the assistance of amusing books."

I received the day after a letter from Mr. Hume himself, of which the following is an extract. [1]

Edinburgh, 23rd August, 1776.

" My Dearest Friend,

" I am obliged to make use of my nephew's hand in writing to you, as I do not rise to-day. . . .

" I go very fast to decline, and last night had a small fever, which I hoped might put a quicker period to this tedious illness, but unluckily it has, in a great measure, gone off. I cannot submit to your coming over here on my account, as it is possible for me to see you so small a part of the day, but Doctor Black can better inform you concerning the degree of strength which may from time to time remain with me.

Adieu, &c."

Three days after I received the following letter from Doctor Black.

Edinburgh, Monday, 26th August, 1776.

" Dear Sir,

" Yesterday about four o'clock afternoon, Mr. Hume expired. The near approach of his death became evident in the night between Thursday and Friday, when his disease

---

[1] [The complete letter is given above, p. 92]

became excessive, and soon weakened him so much, that he could no longer rise out of his bed. He continued to the last perfectly sensible, and free from much pain or feelings of distress. He never dropped the smallest expression of impatience ; but when he had occasion to speak to the people about him, always did it with affection and tenderness. I thought it improper to write to bring you over, especially as I heard that he had dictated a letter to you desiring you not to come. When he became very weak, it cost him an effort to speak, and he died in such a happy composure of mind, that nothing could exceed it."

Thus died our most excellent, and never to be forgotten friend ; concerning whose philosophical opinions men will, no doubt, judge variously, every one approving, or condemning them, according as they happen to coincide or disagree with his own ; but concerning whose character and conduct there can scarce be a difference of opinion. His temper, indeed, seemed to be more happily balanced, if I may be allowed such an expression, than that perhaps of any other man I have ever known. Even in the lowest state of his fortune, his great and necessary frugality never hindered him from exercising, upon proper occasions, acts both of charity and generosity. It was a frugality founded, not upon avarice, but upon the love of independency. The extreme gentleness of his nature never weakened either the firmness of his mind, or the steadiness of his resolutions. His constant pleasantry was the genuine effusion of good-nature and good-humour, tempered with delicacy and modesty, and without even the slightest tincture of malignity, so frequently the disagreeable source of what is called wit in other men. It never was the meaning of his raillery to mortify ; and therefore, far from offending, it seldom failed to please and delight, even those who were the objects of it. To his friends, who were frequently the objects of it, there was not perhaps any one of all his great and amiable qualities, which contributed more to endear his conversation. And that gaiety of temper, so agreeable in society, but which is so often accompanied with frivolous and superficial qualities, was in him certainly attended with the most severe application, the most extensive learning, the greatest depth of thought, and a capacity in every respect the most comprehensive. Upon the whole, I have always considered him, both in his lifetime and since his death, as approaching as nearly to the idea of a perfectly wise and virtuous man, as perhaps the nature of human frailty will permit. ←

I ever am, dear Sir,

Most affectionately your's,

ADAM SMITH.

INDEX OF PROPER NAMES